CW01151338

Food Security for Rural Africa

At least fifty years of projects aimed at the rural poor in Africa have had very little impact. Up to half of the children of these countries are still suffering from stunting and malnutrition. Soil degradation and poor crop yields are ubiquitous. Projects are almost always aimed at helping local people to solve their problems by growing for the market. In some countries, projects link poor villagers into cooperatives to produce a commercial output. In other countries, projects target more competent entrepreneurial villagers. Almost all these projects fail after several years. Even those that are successful make few inroads into the problems.

While the slogan 'feeding the farmers first' comes from the Philippines, it is particularly applicable to much of Africa, where household food security can come from household production. This book explains how projects can be designed that increase food security through subsistence production. Focusing on particular people and projects, it gives a sociological analysis of why this is so difficult to manage. This book challenges the models promoted by academics in the field of development studies and argues against the strategies adopted by most donor organizations and government bodies. It explains why commercial projects have been so ubiquitous even though they rarely work. It gives practical tips on how to set up villages and farms to achieve sustainable solutions that also provide plenty of nutritious food. The book is written to be accessible and engaging. For anyone planning to work in the rural areas of Africa, this book is required reading.

Terry Leahy is Conjoint Senior Lecturer in the School of Humanities and Social Science at Newcastle University, Australia.

Routledge Contemporary Africa Series

The Development of African Capital Markets
A Legal and Institutional Approach
Boniface Chimpango

China, Africa and Responsible International Engagement
Yanzhuo Xu

Joke-Performance in Africa
Mode, Media and Meaning
Edited by Ignatius Chukwumah

The Media and Aid in Sub-Saharan Africa
Whose News?
Lena von Naso

Political Culture, Change, and Security Policy in Nigeria
Kalu N. Kalu

African Science Education
Gendering Indigenous Knowledge in Nigeria
Jamaine Abidogun

Power in Contemporary Zimbabwe
Edited by Erasmus Masitera and Fortune Sibanda

Unfolding Narratives of Ubuntu in Southern Africa
Edited by Julian Müller, John Eliastam and Sheila Trahar

Reimagining Science and Statecraft in Postcolonial Kenya
Stories from an African Scientist
Denielle Elliott with Davy Kiprotich Koech

Food Security for Rural Africa
Feeding the Farmers First
Terry Leahy

Food Security for Rural Africa
Feeding the Farmers First

Terry Leahy

Routledge
Taylor & Francis Group
LONDON AND NEW YORK

First published 2019
by Routledge
2 Park Square, Milton Park, Abingdon, Oxon OX14 4RN

and by Routledge
711 Third Avenue, New York, NY 10017

Routledge is an imprint of the Taylor & Francis Group, an informa business

© 2019 Terry Leahy

The right of Terry Leahy to be identified as author of this work has been asserted by him in accordance with sections 77 and 78 of the Copyright, Designs and Patents Act 1988.

All rights reserved. No part of this book may be reprinted or reproduced or utilised in any form or by any electronic, mechanical, or other means, now known or hereafter invented, including photocopying and recording, or in any information storage or retrieval system, without permission in writing from the publishers.

Trademark notice: Product or corporate names may be trademarks or registered trademarks, and are used only for identification and explanation without intent to infringe.

British Library Cataloguing-in-Publication Data
A catalogue record for this book is available from the British Library

Library of Congress Cataloging-in-Publication Data
Names: Leahy, Terry (Sociologist), author.
Title: Food security for rural Africa : feeding the farmers first / Terry Leahy.
Other titles: Routledge contemporary Africa series ; 10.
Description: Feeding the farmers first | Series: Routledge contemporary Africa series ; 10
Identifiers: LCCN 2018020317 | ISBN 9780815354062 (hardback) | ISBN 9781351134156 (ebook) | ISBN 9781351134125 (mobipocket)
Subjects: LCSH: Food security–Africa, Sub-Saharan. | Food supply–Africa, Sub-Saharan. | Agriculture–Economic aspects–Africa, Sub-Saharan. | Africa, Sub-Saharan–Rural conditions.
Classification: LCC HD9017.A3572 L43 2018 | DDC 338.1967–dc23
LC record available at https://lccn.loc.gov/2018020317

ISBN: 978-0-8153-5406-2 (hbk)
ISBN: 978-1-351-13415-6 (ebk)

Typeset in Times New Roman
by Wearset Ltd, Boldon, Tyne and Wear

Contents

List of illustrations vii
Preface and acknowledgements viii

1 Food security as a global and African problem 1
   Vignette A: low input technologies 21

2 The UK paradigm and an alternative strategy 33
   Vignette B: how much land do you need? 54

3 Hunger as a fatal strategy – a Zambian case study 57
   Vignette C: smoothing out the bumps in food security 75

4 Why do projects fail? What could work? 80
   Vignette D: working for food – working for money 102

5 Teaching them to fish – entrepreneurial ideology and rural projects 105
   Vignette E: what is a farmer? 124

6 Leading farmer projects and rural food security, Uganda 129
   TERRY LEAHY AND FRANCIS ALINYO

   Vignette F: a permaculture design for a Ugandan household 146
   TERRY LEAHY AND KAREN STEWART

7	**An embedded project – Chikukwa**	157
	Vignette G: what to eat to avoid diabetes and heart trouble	179
8	**A winning formula – projects that work**	182
	TERRY LEAHY AND MONIKA GOFORTH	
	Vignette H: composting toilets in Africa	201
9	**The political economy of food security strategies**	209
	References	214
	Index	226

Illustrations

Figures

F.1	Residential area – map	153
F.2	Residential area – three dimensional diagram	154
F.3	The whole farm – map	155
F.4	The whole farm – three dimensional diagram	156
H.1	The Jenkins 'Humanure' system – part one	204
H.2	The Jenkins 'Humanure' system – part two, compost bins	204
H.3	The Malawi school toilet system – side view	205
H.4	The Malawi school toilet system – from above	206
H.5	The arborloo	207
H.6	The tippy tap	208

Tables

1.1	Rates of stunting for children under five	3
7.1	Enough food by ward	159

Preface and acknowledgements

Over the last fifteen years, my academic work and my field trips to Africa have focused on food security projects. In 2003 I was convenor of the Masters of Social Change and Development degree at Newcastle University in Australia. We had a particularly active international officer, David Wise, who was keen to recruit students from many countries in Africa. He shared with our dean Terry Lovat the view that the rich countries had a responsibility to give assistance to the developing world, through projects that were practical and could build capacity at the local level. At that time the Australian government was running a programme of liaison with South Africa to help that country to establish 'LandCare' in South Africa. 'Landcare' in Australia had been started by farmers. They had set up local associations to deal with land degradation and to promote sustainable agriculture. The Australian government had initiated a programme to help South Africa to set up a similar network through its agriculture departments. As part of that liaison, the Australian government was offering scholarships for agricultural officers from South Africa to come to Australia for postgraduate study. David Wise managed to recruit ten of these students to undertake the Masters of Social Change and Development at the University of Newcastle, as a first intake. In subsequent years, our programme recruited hundreds of international students from different parts of the world. African students were always a key part of that mix. Initially, the rural development projects of particular interest to the African agricultural officers were covered in a variety of ways. First through courses in project design, evaluation and research methodology. Along with these were courses that were open to student initiative, such as special projects and research projects. In these I started to teach the material on food security and rural development that was later to become a subject in our degree.

My students taught me a lot. As they developed their special projects we would meet to plan their research. I suggested reading and talked through the situations they had faced as agricultural officers. We worked out what they could do for their research and they went back in our summer break to do interviews and conduct participant observation. Their research was conducted in the rural areas where they had been working as agricultural officers. For the most part, the work they had been doing did not concern large commercial farms, usually owned by white people. Instead they had been attending to the farming enterprises of rural smallholders, black people who had been relocated into 'native reserves' in the colonial period. Poverty in these rural villages was extreme. Cropping for household food supply was common, both in South Africa and the other African countries from which our students came. However, it was unfortunately very typical that this cropping did not provide an adequate diet. There were hungry periods and diets were short of many essential nutrients. Our research uncovered the statistics on all this – stunting of children under 5 years old, nutrient deficiencies and unemployment.

The research of my students showed me that most of the projects being run in the villages were not really working to relieve food insecurity. They were mostly oriented to attempts to turn very poor rural smallholders into successful entrepreneurs of small businesses. In many cases they were intended to set up money making cooperatives for local people to join together to make an income from their joint production. Mostly, these projects failed in the longer term. The businesses did not make money or fell apart. Food insecurity remained.

In 2006 I visited South Africa to investigate the situation on the ground. I decided to spend part of my time with agricultural officers driving out to visit various projects that the departments had initiated. The other part of my time was spent staying in the villages. On this first trip, I spent more than two months in two rural villages hosted by local people. My previous students, who had now returned to their jobs, helped me immensely with all this. In particular Linah Mokoena arranged my stay in Lilydale, Limpopo province, with a local primary teacher, Margaret Themba. Abram Shabangu arranged my stay with the chief's wife, Thoko Zibi in Khayakhulu in North West province. I went on visits to projects with these two ex-students and also with other students from our degree – Caroline Makgopa, Philetus Nyandane, Lehman Lindeque and Charles Mojela. On some occasions I went with other officers from their departments to visit village projects.

There were subsequent visits (2009, 2010, 2014) and in these I extended my research to include neighbouring countries which had a similar history of colonization by Britain: Malawi, Zambia, Zimbabwe, Uganda, Kenya, Namibia. In Uganda I was given assistance by my previous student, Francis Alinyo, who was working in a remote area next to a national park. I also developed contacts with people involved in NGO work in Africa. These partly came out of the permaculture movement. I attended an international permaculture conference in Malawi in 2009 where I met Elijah Kyamuwendo from the Kulika project in Uganda and the team from the CELUCT project in Zimbabwe, Chester Chituwu, Eli and Ulli Westermann, Phineas Chikoshana, Sam Chimbarara, Julious Piti and Patience Sithole. In 2009, I also developed contacts in African universities that were interested in my research on rural projects: Namibia Polytechnic; Makerere University in Uganda; University of Fort Hare in South Africa; Walter Sisulu University in South Africa.

In 2010, I went to visit these universities. I started off in Namibia, presenting lectures and discussing the situation with staff there. In Eastern Cape I was hosted by Francois Lategan, a lecturer in agricultural extension from Fort Hare.

I stayed in Alice for a month, talking with people from the university and visiting the villages. Later I stayed in Mthatha, hosted by Professor Peggy Luswazi from Walter Sisulu University. There, I attended a conference on rural development, as well as a national anthropology conference on the coast. I followed that up with visits to talk to agricultural officers and visit sites in Limpopo and North Western province. After my time in South Africa, I moved to Uganda, visiting the highlands, talking to academics and students at Makerere University and interviewing people from the Kulika project. In 2009, I had been invited to prepare a documentary on the CELUCT project in the Chimanimani district of Zimbabwe. In 2010, following my time in Uganda, I went there with my sister, Gillian Leahy, to do the filming. On the way, I stayed with a local permaculture activist, Anna Brazier, who introduced me to Zimbabwe. After we arrived in the villages, Gillian and I did long days, filming interviews and people's farm projects. We took in both the Chikukwa clan villages where CELUCT was working and the wider district of Chimanimani, where the TSURO project was operating. After this I stayed a month in Zambia at the Tiko project near Katete. I had been contacted by the founder, Elke Kroeger-Radcliffe, and invited. This was a great opportunity to interview local people and to observe agricultural strategies in rural Zambian villages, which surrounded the project on all sides.

In 2014 I secured another six months of study leave from my university and returned to further investigate projects that were working well. I first stayed in Port St John in the Eastern Cape to work with the Is'Baya project. Most of the time I spent with the chief field officer, Paul Oliphant, who took me to meetings that he was having with the village representatives and beneficiaries from the project. At the office I spoke with founders and executive officers, Peter Jones and Rose Du Preez. I stayed in two different villages with project monitors from the project, local people appointed to connect the beneficiaries of the project with the project office. These monitors took me to interview local households that were part of the project and to look at their agricultural strategies. Andile Sontlaba was the monitor at Khluleka village, which was in one of the drier parts of Eastern Cape. My next stay was at Noqhekwana village, which is on the coast and receives a lot more rainfall. The monitor there was Thembi and I stayed in her sister's house.

The second half of my visit in 2014 was spent at the CELUCT (Chikukwa) project in Chimanimani. I was assigned a guide who was a young man from the chief's clan, Zeddy Chikukwa. I also visited households with Sam Chimbarara, one of the project officers. I attended meetings of the project, both with beneficiaries and with the executive. I also made visits to the sites of the TSURO project, which covers the whole of the Chimanimani district, with a number of different project officers. I was hosted by Ulli Westermann. As part of this I visited the dryland site of the PORET project run by Julious Piti.

Beyond all this, my research has been informed by the investigations conducted by my postgraduate students from Africa. Some of these have been Blessings Susuwele, Ezra Mbendera, Unathi Sihlahla, Rita Makwakwa, Mooko

Motheo and Thembekile Madondo. These people have participated enthusiastically in our courses and spoken up about their experiences as we discussed the situation on the ground.

To all these people and the numerous others who I have not been able to mention I offer my heartfelt thanks.

The co-authors in this book are all people who have been encountered in this process of investigation. Debbie Jean Brown was a fellow researcher I met in Zambia. Francis Alinyo was one of my postgraduate students from Uganda. Monika Goforth and Karen Stewart were our students as well. They are two young people from the rich countries who aim to make a difference through their development work. They have subsequently gone on to do just that, Monika in Guatemala and Karen in Bougainville and Queensland.

This book would not have been possible without the support of my family and friends in Australia. My partner Pamela Nilan has always been a great role model for how to deal with academia and maintain one's enthusiasm for research and writing. Her work in Indonesia has shown me what it means to conduct ethnographic research in a developing country. She is a skilled author and has helped me to work out how to write in a way that is accessible and authoritative at the same time. She is also one of the founders of our Masters of Social Change and Development Programme and was the convenor before I took up that role. My friend Lena Rodriguez has supported me as a colleague, teaching our degree with the amazing international students that we have been lucky enough to encounter. More recently she has helped me with editing and corrections for this book. My children, Viv and Lily, are a constant delight and have always been interested in what I have been working on. My sister Gillian has spared no effort to turn her film making skills to helping me document one of the most successful and innovative food security projects ever established in Africa. In the end, as people always say, the mistakes in this book are all mine.

I will not use up space in the rest of this preface to explain the book in detail. Clearly I have been concerned to work out what is going wrong with food security projects in Africa. Why do they so often fail and why have they had such a small impact on rural poverty and malnutrition? What kinds of projects could work better to deal with these problems?

The chapters in this book are written with postgraduate students and fellow academics in mind. I am especially hoping that the book will be used in African universities in courses in development studies, agricultural extension, social work and education. Professionals in all these fields have a vital role to play in improving the situation in the villages. Likewise, international NGOs working in Africa can make a big difference if they know what can work. Students from the rich countries study international development because they want to join organizations that can assist the developing world. This book is designed to help them to see what is going on at the local level in Africa; to understand what kinds of projects could work and what kind of projects are likely to fail.

The vignettes in this book are written in a less academic tone and are much shorter than the chapters. The aim of these vignettes is to provide some more of the nuts and bolts that agricultural officers, social workers, teachers and NGO staff will need in the field. Ideally I would like to see these vignettes printed out for discussion in a lunch break, or for a seminar, to get these on the ground professional staff thinking about what might work well in the projects to which they are connected.

Many of the observations and suggestions in this book challenge the models promoted both by academics in the field of development studies and by large donor organizations. What is evident is that with a very few exceptions the poorest of the poor are not going to become successful commercial farmers. Projects designed with that aim in mind have made little impact on food insecurity. This book therefore makes the case that alternatives that embed the notion of 'feeding the farmers first' will be more successful.

1 Food security as a global and African problem

Terry Leahy

The subtitle for this book, *Feeding the Farmers First*, refers to a particular type of strategy for food insecurity problems in rural sub-Saharan Africa. The book will concentrate on areas of Southern and Eastern Africa where the authors have conducted field research. These are countries where a history of British colonialism has created similar patterns of land use and employment. Development strategies must be adapted to the cultural, political and economic realities of a particular region, rather than assuming that one size fits all. Yet there is no doubt that many other countries of Africa, and indeed the world, could benefit from the perspective elaborated here.

Feeding the farmers first

'Feeding the farmers first' is a slogan devised by MASIPAG in the Philippines. MASIPAG is an organization of 30,000 smallholder farms (Wright 2008). The members are reacting to extreme poverty and food insecurity, despite decades of promises and quite drastic land reform. Land reform in the Philippines has been compromised by a cycle of debt. Smallholder farmers get into debt to engage in 'modern' agriculture (MASIPAG 2013). Far too often, they end up selling their land to discharge the debt. Even when this disaster has not happened, the small income they are deriving from selling their agricultural products, after paying off their debts, has been insufficient for food security. MASIPAG wants a long term solution that can ensure food security and remove the cycle of debt. A central part of their approach is 'feeding the farmers first'. As Gabriel Diaz, a farmer and trainer from Mindanao, explains:

> There is a big difference between the MASIPAG and non-MASIPAG farmers. In MASIPAG, the farmer holds the decisions. For farmer-led agriculture the farmer is not dependent on the inputs or seeds from other people. He has control over the inputs and can reduce them. The inputs we use come from the farm. The focus is the security of the family. We don't get hungry. The first thing we think of in our farm is our family having enough to eat. This is before going to market.
>
> (Bachmann *et al.* 2009: 22)

This strategy flies in the face of decades of development advice. Most rural development projects attempt to move farmers out of 'traditional subsistence' farming and into commercial farming. Instead, MASIPAG proposes that these smallholders make family 'subsistence' their *first* priority.

When I talk about 'subsistence' farming I am using the term to talk about the way what is being produced enters the economy. Farming is 'for subsistence' if the food being produced is distributed *without money changing hands*. What often gets assumed is that 'subsistence' farming *has to be* inefficient, small scale, traditional and incapable of producing a good yield. While all these negative descriptions may make sense for particular instances of subsistence agriculture, there is nothing about the concept of 'subsistence' that makes any of this inevitable. 'Subsistence' farming can make use of the latest science, as well as much traditional knowledge, and can produce a good yield and not just a 'bare subsistence'. The bad odour of 'subsistence' farming is very hard to shift. The de facto solution has been to promote 'subsistence' without using that term. The phrase 'household food security' is often used. In reality, *household food security* could come about in any number of ways. People could buy food from a supermarket! The MASIPAG slogan, 'feeding the farmers first', is more honest. It also achieves another useful goal. The aim of this strategy is *not* to prevent farmers from growing a crop to get some cash. In today's economy everyone needs money. After what is 'first' has been sorted out – feeding the farmers and their families – then it would clearly make sense 'second' to go on to grow a cash crop.

The MASIPAG strategy is to move farmers towards 'sustainable agriculture' and organic farming. Environmentalists argue that high input farming is destroying soils (Pretty 1999). There is also an economic argument. MASIPAG aims to remove the cycles of debt that can end up with farmers losing their land. Because they are using inputs produced on the farm, MASIPAG farmers do not have to take out a loan to buy inputs.

> [F]armer empowerment means increasing the control of farmers over their economic circumstances by 'breaking the chains of economic dependence'. Dependence here refers to the cycle of indebtedness that many farmers face as they borrow money to buy farm inputs and then need to sell rice to recoup costs, effectively tying them to a capitalist, corporatized agriculture.
>
> (Wright 2008: 226)

This introduction may give the reader a sense of where the argument of this book is going. Before getting into this in detail, this chapter will consider three topics: current issues of food security in the world in general and in Africa in particular; the typical remedies being proposed by mainstream economists; the contrasting approaches typically proposed by leftist critics of this economics mainstream.

Hunger as a global and African problem

The *Global Nutrition Report* of 2016 was prepared by an independent expert group associated with the International Food Policy Research Institute (IFPRI 2016). Out of a world population of seven billion, two billion people are suffering from an inadequate diet, leading to a deficiency of micronutrients such as vitamin A, calcium, iron and the like. Nearly 800 million people are suffering from a deficiency of calories. These broad patterns of malnutrition are reflected in specific and enduring consequences for children. Of 667 million children world wide, 159 million are stunted, too short for their age, and 50 million do not weigh enough for their height – defined as 'wasted' (IFPRI 2016: 2). These problems of malnutrition are declining in every region except Africa. For Asia the number of children who are suffering from stunting declined from 190 million in 1990 to 91 million in 2014. The number suffering from stunting increased in Africa over the same period from 47 million to 58 million (IFPRI 2016: 17). For the countries with which this book is most concerned, the rates of stunting for children under five are detailed in Table 1.1.

Of particular concern, more than 20 per cent of reproductive women suffer from anaemia, going up to 40 per cent in Kenya and Tanzania (IFPRI 2016).

Reductions in malnutrition have varied between different Asian countries, with the greatest improvements taking place in China. For example, the percentage of stunted children has declined overall in Asia from 38 per cent in 2000 to 23 per cent in 2015 (UNICEF 2017). Yet in South Asia, there are still 40 per cent of children under five stunted (IFPRI 2016: 3; UNICEF 2017). The success of Asian countries in reducing malnutrition and the failure of Africa to do likewise is often a key point of discussion.

The 2015 *Regional Overview of Food Security Africa* (FAO) considers these problems in more detail, giving a more optimistic picture of trends in sub-Saharan Africa. It is estimated that about a quarter of the population are suffering from malnutrition currently, compared to about a third in 1990 (FAO 2015: 1). At the

Table 1.1 Rates of stunting for children under five

Country	Percentage stunting children under five
Namibia	23.1
South Africa	23.9
Kenya	26.0
Zimbabwe	27.6
Botswana	31.4
Lesotho	33.2
Uganda	34.2
Tanzania	34.7
Zambia	40.0
Malawi	42.4

Source: IFPRI (2016: 120).

same time, the *absolute* numbers have increased. There are now 218 million undernourished people in sub-Saharan Africa compared to 176 million in 1990 (FAO 2015: 1). The decline in the percentage prevalence of malnutrition in Africa comes in part from economic expansion and the corresponding increase in employment, wages and purchased household food provision. Yet this economic expansion is mostly in the extractive production of mineral resources, with a constantly diminishing contribution from the agricultural sector – in which most of the poor are located (FAO 2015: 17).

Forty years or more of international projects and government interventions to commercialize agriculture have not actually improved the lot of the rural African underclass. Problems revealed in the 1950s, such as vitamin deficiencies and stunting, are still endemic (Barkworth and Harland 2009; Department of Agriculture 2002; Japan Association 2008). South Africa is the wealthiest country in this region. Yet in 2000 about 35 per cent of the total population were suffering from food insecurity and up to 27 per cent of young children were suffering from stunting (Department of Agriculture 2002: 22–23). Estimates of stunting for preschool children remain unacceptably high. In 2010, 33 per cent for Southern Africa and 45 per cent for Eastern Africa, including such countries as Zambia and Malawi (de Onis *et al.* 2011: 144). In sub-Saharan Africa there were 204 million chronically undernourished people in 2002, of which 80 per cent were from rural households (Haile 2005: 2169). In Malawi, 60 per cent of children under five and 57 per cent of women are suffering from vitamin A deficiencies. Eighty per cent of children under five and 27 per cent of women are suffering from anaemia due to iron deficiency (Japan Association 2008: 39).

Throughout this region, woodlands are deforested, fuel wood is in short supply, soils are packed down hard and crop yields are low (Japan Association 2008; Marenya and Barrett 2007). Farmers are not using fertilizers or other inputs because they cannot afford them. For example in Tanzania, only 15 per cent of farmers are using fertilizer and crop productivity is 1.7 tonnes per hectare, compared with yields of 3.5 to 4 tonnes that are possible (Wolter 2008: 14). The environmental and productivity effects of poor agricultural techniques are compounded by high rates of population growth and smaller plot sizes (Marenya and Barrett 2007).

Definitions of malnutrition and food security

International definitions of malnutrition are based on medical science. For example calories consumed per day; micronutrients, assessed through a blood test; wasting and stunting, assessed through age in relation to body measurements (Leathers and Foster 2009). A minimum estimated average daily energy requirement is 2,200 kcal. The average intake in sub-Saharan Africa was estimated at 2,150 kcal/day in 2003, an improvement from 2,050 per day thirty years earlier (FAO 2003b: 4).

In 1983 and again in 1986, 'food security' was defined by the FAO as secure access to foods necessary for an active and healthy life – a definition based on medical science. By 1996, the definition took into account people's cultural understandings of food. There is no point in policies that supply medically sufficient nutrients if people do not find them acceptable *as food*.

> Food security [is] a situation that exists when all people, at all times, have physical, social and economic access to sufficient, safe and nutritious food that meets their dietary needs and food preferences for an active and healthy life.
>
> (FAO 2003b: 28)

This is the definition that will be used in this book. What will become apparent is that nutritional adequacy, workable project design and culturally acquired food preferences do not necessarily line up.

Mainstream economists on food security

Dominant thinking on hunger and food security comes from mainstream economics writers. I will take *The World Food Problem: Toward Ending Undernutrition in the Third World* (Leathers and Foster 2009), as a representative authoritative textbook from the point of view of mainstream economics. The book falls into two main sections. One outlines the problems and the other looks at solutions. The basic perspective of mainstream economists is that food security can be alleviated by economic development, increasing the incomes of the poor so that they can buy food. They see this development as a transition away from traditional subsistence agriculture into a globalized commercial agriculture. They oppose most forms of government intervention in the economy, seeing these as hindering the economic growth that will ultimately solve all problems. At most, governments should build roads and facilitate marketing. As we shall see, Leathers and Foster develop this approach through a discussion of a variety of particular issues.

Explaining the problems

Leathers and Foster describe the 2008 food crisis as an example of the global problems of food security. Food prices on the international market rose steadily from 2000 to 2006 and then escalated dramatically between 2006 and 2008. The price of basic staple foods soared. For example maize went from $164 to $287 per metric tonne between 2007 and 2008. Overall grain prices were 3.34 times what they had been in 2000 (Leathers and Foster 2009: 85). The implication that I draw from this is that on a small plot of land, you can be caught out by a sudden spike in the cost of basic foods – unable to sell your cash crop for sufficient income to pay for your food. By contrast if your small plot produces enough for your own needs and you are not depending on cash income to pay for inputs, you can ride out an economic crisis.

Leathers and Foster acknowledge the food security problems of sub-Saharan Africa as unique. Whereas in other part of the world the food produced per capita has continually increased, that has not been the situation in sub-Saharan Africa – 'in 2005, food production per capita was about 12 per cent lower than it was in 1961' (Leathers and Foster 2009: 132). To add to this, the 'poverty level' which is always measured in dollars of cash income, actually went up between 1970 and 1998 – from 53 per cent poor to 64 per cent (Leathers and Foster 2009: 157). Notwithstanding these grim statistics, the economic situation has recently improved, with a doubling of GDP in Africa (FAO 2015: 17). Yet the problems of under-nutrition have remained. Africa is clearly a continent in which the usual prescriptions of economists have not applied. Africa did not work its way out of food insecurity through modernization and enterprise. In more recent periods, economic improvement has taken place but has not ended hunger for the poor.

Turning to Asian success stories, Leathers and Foster cite evidence intended to show the futility of subsistence agriculture. A Vietnamese survey of subsistence versus market oriented farmers shows that the latter 'have higher incomes, lower poverty rates and larger farms; that they are more likely to live in an area that has a market or a commercial enterprise; and that they produce more 'high-value and industrial crops' (Leathers and Foster 2009: 210). Let us begin with two factors from this report and take these as the causal roots of the phenomenon being described. One is that the farmers with larger landholdings are the ones most likely to produce for the market. Clearly, these farmers can readily add a commercial enterprise to their subsistence farming and make money from that. Farmers with smaller plots may be better advised to concentrate on subsistence. Even farmers with larger landholdings may do better by maintaining their subsistence agriculture to supply family food needs, while they use their extra land for commercial production. The second factor is that farmers are more likely to make an income from commercial farming if they live in an area with good markets, usually an area serviced by good roads and close to a town or city, an area in which other farmers are also engaged in commercial enterprises. So these commercial options are not available to farmers in less well favoured sites. Such farmers may do better to improve their subsistence rather than taking off into risky commercial ventures.

If we take these two factors as the primary drivers behind the successes of those participating in market agriculture we can make sense of the other elements of the findings. 'Poverty rates' are always defined in terms of cash income, usually in US dollars per day. It is a truism that those who engage in commercial farming will have less poverty and higher incomes than those who are purely subsistence farmers. That does not mean that it is necessarily a viable strategy for subsistence farmers to sell part of their crop to get income, as I will explain. Farmers who are growing at least some produce for the market are more likely than subsistence farmers to be growing high value crops. On at least some of their farm they may grow flowers, coffee, tobacco and the like. The subsistence farmer would be better off growing crops that provide good nutrition and do not require purchased inputs to flourish.

Let me suggest another interpretation of the correlation between higher income and market oriented farming. We know that these commercial farmers are more likely to live close to a major centre. Let us assume they are people who have spent years working in these local centres, saving some of their earnings. They have put some of this money into improving their farms – by buying land, irrigation, farming tools, livestock, synthetic fertilizers and pesticides, hybrid seeds, fencing materials. This becomes a virtuous circle. Saved off-farm income goes into building the farm, which also turns a profit. None of this logic applies to subsistence farmers who do not happen to have this backing in extra-farm income. They cannot jump-start a process towards higher income by concentrating on high value cash crops instead of subsistence crops. That is most likely to be a route to further hunger, increased poverty and debt.

Adjoining this discussion is some evidence of the relevance and efficacy of subsistence strategies. A study from India shows that small family farms gain better yields per hectare than large farm businesses. The explanation is that family members will work to produce, even if the value of what they are producing is less than the going wage for rural employment. The reason for this behaviour is not explained by Leathers and Foster. The wages these family workers could earn off the farm may be higher than the cash value *at the farm gate* of what they are producing on their family farm. But the food they are producing on their family farm would cost more to buy (*at retail prices*) than the value of the wages they are giving up. Linked to this is the fact that on these small family farms, family members may 'have no higher-valued use for their time' (Leathers and Foster 2009: 207). This means either (a) these farmers are doing subsistence because they cannot get paid off-farm employment that will earn them sufficient income to pay for family food needs or (b) they are doing subsistence because producing higher value cash crops to sell will not actually enable the family to buy enough food. I will come back to this.

The authors point to the continued relevance of subsistence farming. For example in Nigeria 85 per cent of rural families sell *less than half* of their produce on the market; the rest is consumed by the family, which counts as subsistence. In the 1990s, 60 per cent of India's farmers had less than a hectare of land and produced no marketable surplus (Leathers and Foster 2009: 210). The argument of *Feeding the Farmers First* will be that such farmers are not showing a blind allegiance to an outdated economic model but are making a rational choice.

Leathers and Foster present an explanation of the failure of these small subsistence farmers to satisfy food needs. The intention of the examples is to show that subsistence farming *never could* produce enough food. They cite a study from Ghana, arguing that yields are insufficient and that family labour is insufficient. Average yields of maize were between 0.6 and 2.7 tonnes per hectare. If a Ghanaian required all their calories from maize (say 2,400 per day) they would need a cropping area of 0.1 to 0.4 hectares – because the annual food needs per person are 0.24 tonnes of maize:

> We can see how a farm of 1–2 hectares might be barely enough to provide a subsistence diet for a family, and we can see how precariously the family's

8 *Food security: a global/African problem*

food security might rest on the hope of good weather and freedom from pests and diseases.

(Leathers and Foster 2009: 210)

Let me examine this argument. At 0.6 tonnes per hectare, you would need a cropping field of 2.4 hectares to feed a family of six (with 0.24 tonnes of maize each). It is certainly true that many African rural households do not have 2.4 hectares of cropping land. For the poor, one hectare is more typical. Yet using organic methods you could readily improve yield to at least 2 tonnes per hectare (Pretty 1999). So, on 0.72 hectare you could grow enough maize to feed six people. To have a year's supply in reserve, you would need 1.44 hectares. While one hectare of cropping land is pretty typical for the rural poor of Africa, there is usually more village land available that is at present being used to graze cattle – owned by the richer households. Distributing even some of this would ensure adequate cropping fields for subsistence in most of Africa.

Leathers and Foster back up this discussion with an assessment of the amount of labour required to produce maize in this Ghana site:

The farmers in this study worked between 1,900 and 4,050 days per hectare. One farmer in the study worked 40.5 hours on a 0.01-hectare experimental plot, and produced 10 kilograms of maize … In order to generate 2,400 calories per capita per day, he would need 27 such plots (0.27 hectares), requiring 1,094 days of labor per year … This gives us a clear indication of how undernutrition can coexist with subsistence agriculture.

(Leathers and Foster 2009: 210)

Taking the first sentence of this, a family of six could manage one hectare by doing an amount of days per hectare falling between these extremes ($6 \times 365 = 2{,}190$ days). With a yield of two tonnes per hectare they would produce enough food on 0.7 hectares. Yet this time study research is quite implausible. When I have lived in villages and gone to visit the cropping fields, I have usually found that only a few of the households with cropping plots were working the land at any one time. At certain times of the year families do work very long hours, planting, weeding or harvesting. Yet in much of the year the fields look after themselves.

The authors go on to cite a participant of this study who owned two bullocks and a cow. He was able to work fewer hours (doing more with his animal traction) and to get a higher yield (using manure). This farmer is calculated to need only 200 hours to grow sufficient food for his own consumption (Leathers and Foster 2009: 210). This example is of a piece with most suggestions about how the rural poor may improve their situation – by adopting the practices of their rich fellow villagers. While Leathers and Fosters note the prevalence of subsistence agriculture, they cite research which suggests it could never be viable. These two claims cannot both be true.

Policy suggestions from mainstream economists

Raising the incomes of the poor

Leathers and Foster begin their analysis by looking at policies which raise the incomes of the poor and enable them to buy more food. The route they favour is economic growth in the private sector – secured through the removal of government intervention, the 'Washington consensus'. Deregulating trade; privatizing government assets; cutting taxes and cutting spending. Property should be privately owned and available on the market, enabling farmers to take on loans, with their farms as collateral (Leathers and Foster 2009: 275). The authors cite the success of globalization. Comparing Africa to South-East Asia, incomes per capita were similar in the 1970s. But by 1997, they were three times higher in South-East Asia. This difference is associated with the greater participation of the South-East Asian countries in international trade – between 1985 and 1995, their exports grew at a rate of 12 per cent per year, compared to only 3 per cent per year in Africa. Under-nutrition fell in Asia from 41 per cent in 1970 to 12 per cent in 2002. By comparison, under-nutrition in Africa only dropped from 36 per cent to 32 per cent (Leathers and Foster 2009: 278–279).

There are a few problems with this argument. Asian countries did not make these achievements by following the Washington consensus – there were very significant government interventions in all these countries (Chang 2002). To take South Korea as a key example, from 1949 to 1955, the government appropriated large holdings from landlords and ensured that ownership was limited to three hectares, that those who farmed the land had to own it and that farming land could not be leased out (Kwon and Yi 2009: 774). Despite policies for liberalizing trade and cutting government spending in African countries, under-nutrition is still at alarming levels. While economic growth may reduce hunger, it clearly does not eliminate it, with 12 per cent in Asia remaining hungry. What is the best policy for that 12 per cent? Big increases in the income and nutrition of the poor in Asia are far from universal. They are most marked for China, where the removal of statist inefficiency has reshaped the economy. Other parts of Asia have not done so well – South Asia has enormous problems with malnutrition despite economic policies remarkably similar to the Asian Tiger economies. Where lessons for Africa are concerned, the most interesting refutation is that given by Hoogvelt (2001; see also Mather and Adelzadeh 1998; Timmer 2005). There is a limit to the amount of exports from developing countries that can be absorbed by the rich countries. By getting in first, these Asian countries have cornered that market. This note of caution is particularly relevant to agricultural commodities – there is a limit to how much coffee can be consumed. Competition between developing countries has seen the prices of luxury agricultural exports plummet as new producers enter the market. Whole villages of coffee, palm oil, sugar, cotton, cacao and the like have been rooted up (Mortimore 1998).

Timmer (2005) explains various features of the African situation that prevent the rural poor from taking up this export led route out of poverty. On smallholdings without huge capital investment it is difficult to meet the quality requirements and quantitative predictability required by international food buying companies. These requirements are way beyond the capacities of farmers without much education and without the money to buy inputs. The rural poor in Africa are mostly in villages a long distance from coastal ports, without suitable roads to transport produce where it might be assembled, packed and sent overseas. Governments in Africa do not have the funds to make these investments, and international bodies are intent on cutting their spending.

A succinct refutation of the argument for economic growth as a solution is the following. Given improvements in labour productivity (with new machinery) and given increasing population, the economy needs to constantly grow – just to soak up the extra employment required to absorb these changes. In South Africa, the economic growth rate required to prevent unemployment from *growing* is actually 6 per cent of GDP per annum (Reilly 2006). It is very rare for the South African economy to meet this growth rate and it is one of the most successful economies in Africa. The failure of the African countries to reduce rural poverty relates to these parameters. The economy is not growing at a sufficient rate to reduce rural unemployment. In South Africa the rate of joblessness (those who are unemployed and those who have stopped looking for work) was 36 per cent in 2017 (Gumede and Mbatha 2017). The formal rate of unemployment (the narrow definition) was 28 per cent in the country as a whole and 52 per cent in rural areas (Davies 2012; Gumede and Mbatha 2017) – meaning that the real rate of unemployment in rural areas must be close to 70 per cent.

Leathers and Foster go on to look at typical welfare state measures to raise the incomes of the poor.

They oppose income redistribution. Taxing the rich and giving money to the poor will just raise the price of basic foods – as the poor demand more the price will go up. This is a strange argument coming from two economists. Surely an increase in the price of basic foodstuffs would lead new players to enter the farming industry. In South Africa, where pensions have funded old people and mothers of young children, there has been no escalation of cereal prices coming out of that extra demand. The real story is quite complicated. Cereal prices are in fact set by US producers – at such a low price that without government protection, South African farmers cannot compete. While commercial farmers have abandoned cereal production, the pension system has saved many from starvation, using their welfare payments to purchase cheap US imports!

The second welfare state policy they discuss is minimum wages. According to Leathers and Foster the problem with this is that owners of capital will substitute machinery for labour, employing fewer workers. Whether this is necessarily a problem is another matter. Keynesian economists do not believe that governments should rely on the whims of investors to supply adequate employment. Instead, governments need to step in to fund projects to ensure full employment (Connors and Mitchell 2013).

The third welfare state policy they consider is land reform. They argue that land reform is likely to take land away from successful commercial farmers and give it to less efficient producers of food – a welfare benefit to the rural poor but a problem for the poor who are buying food. This argument must be a joke for the region of Africa considered in this book. Most commercial producers are not producing food for the poor, but instead run game farms for tourists or produce luxury goods (tea, coffee, sugar, beef, chocolate, tobacco, cotton) for wealthy consumers in the rich countries. Targeted land redistribution could take place without any impact on food production for national consumption. The aim would be to maintain profitable large farms producing food for national consumption and to redistribute some of the less profitable privately owned land to smallholders – who want to grow food for their families and add to their income with some surplus production.

While the arguments of Leathers and Foster may not add up, they are a very good guide to the thinking of mainstream economists and the government bodies which take their advice. Given that these neo-liberal economic ideas are likely to *continue* to dominate state policy, what are the options for non-state actors?

Government subsidies to lower food prices

Leathers and Fosters condemn policies which artificially depress prices so the poor can afford food. They maintain that such policies can damage the profitability of farming, reducing the incentives for local farmers. One example is Egypt where retail prices for cereals were set by the government at 37 per cent of the world retail price. Wheat was sold in subsidized government stores. Average calorie consumption exceeded nutritional requirements even for the poorest 12 per cent of the population (Leathers and Foster 2009: 309). Despite these encouraging outcomes, Leathers and Foster are largely critical. The government was spending 17 per cent of its budget on food subsidies. They were using scarce foreign exchange to feed the poor, when they could have been investing in industrial start-ups. Egyptians were getting wheat so cheaply that they were over-consuming it. This argument is backed by an argument to show that the policy was damaging to society.

> Because of the depressed price of wheat, Egyptians eat more wheat than they would if they were paying the world price. A loss to Egyptian society associated with this overconsumption results because government pays more for wheat bought at world market prices than Egyptians are willing to pay for that wheat.
>
> (Leathers and Foster 2009: 310)

This is a tautology of economics. It says nothing about whether this policy worked or not. It clearly did work. Poor Egyptians were eating more wheat than they could have afforded at world prices. There was a loss to the Egyptian government because they had to pay money for this imported wheat. Egyptians would not have bought the wheat at world prices. The scenario in which *they* paid for the wheat and the government avoided the expense is null and void. Was this policy really 'a loss to Egyptian society'?

Overall, Leathers and Foster argue that such programmes cost money that could be better spent. Subsidy and price controls in Africa have led countries into debt. As they sought loans to pay off these debts, the IMF made ending the subsidies a condition of their loans. Results were mixed. In three of four African countries where this took place, the number of people who were undernourished declined, while in the other one (Zambia) it increased. Leathers and Foster see the failures of these programmes as rooted in corruption, mismanagement, the cost of state marketing monopolies and so on (2009: 310–311).

My reservations about these arguments are as follows. While this expenditure was certainly part of what led governments into debt, it was only one aspect of the total situation, for example 10 per cent of the budget in Zambia. In the Zambian case, the debts were incurred as the international price of copper fell. The government had relied on taxes on copper and were caught short with projects they could no longer afford. Whether this level of debt was truly a 'problem' depends on your economic theory. From the point of view of many economists, such debt is quite viable, so long as government funded programmes use up extra capacity in the economy (Connors and Mitchell 2013). It may well be that corruption and mismanagement hampered these policies, so that money was spent without relieving food insecurity. Yet better managed projects might have worked well enough.

From the point of view that will be taken in this book, the important issue is not whether these welfare state measures could have worked and made sense at the time. The significant issue is that international economic organizations (the IMF and the World Bank) were able to dictate conditions to developing country governments and end these programmes. They are unlikely to be revived. The poor need an alternative that is politically viable. Since at least 1980, the World Bank and IMF have imposed these neo-liberal conditions on governments in Africa with the aim of stimulating economic growth. There certainly has been some economic growth. However, where the rural poor are concerned, this economic progress has not made a huge dent in food security problems. They are still very much in evidence.

Redistribution of food – the inefficiency of subsistence

Leathers and Foster consider an argument posted on the *Hearts and Minds* website. If people in the United States were to eat 10 per cent less meat, it would free up 12 million tonnes of grain, enough to feed 60 million people (2009: 324). As economists, they point to a number of flaws. If a section of the US population reduced meat consumption, the price of meat would fall. Half of the meat the altruists did not buy would be purchased by those who could now afford meat. The world price of grain would fall with less demand from the meat industry. Farmers would grow less grain. With cheaper prices the rich world and the rich of the developing countries would eat more grain. In other words, the normal processes of the market would undermine an attempt to free up grain for the poor by eating less meat. Maybe a proposal like this should be implemented by government – how could they do this? The government could tax US consumers so they spent less on food. Leathers and Foster estimate an increase in taxes by 50 per cent would be required to get a 10 per cent reduction in food spending! Then the government would have to buy the grain that was no longer purchased in the US and distribute it in the developing world, with consequent costs in transport and corruption. It could cost the US economy $50 billion (Leathers and Foster 2009: 326). Ultimately, they maintain, such a proposal is not realistic politically.

These arguments constitute a *reductio ad absurdum* based on market economics. It would make more sense for middle class consumers in the United States to spend 10 per cent of their current food budget on well targeted projects. These projects would be designed to help the poor of developing countries grow food for their own families. This might have a minor effect on the US economy by diverting spending from local consumption. The strategy of NGO gifting could move money from the rich countries into developing country economies to help increase the amount of food grown for subsistence, rather than sale. For example paying for the training of agricultural project staff, for cheap materials such as fencing wire, cement, hand tools and the like. This spending would generally have a beneficial effect on the local economies, creating demand. A successful programme might reduce the market demand for cereals, free up commercial holdings for other cash crops and reduce cereal prices to African consumers. Not exactly an economic disaster. It would be an economically efficient way for first world consumers to redistribute income and assist the poor. Much smaller donations from the middle class of rich countries are more likely than what is recommended by *Hearts and Minds*. Yet even small changes can have a catalytic effect if projects work well, inspire imitation and gain local government support.

This discussion leads Leathers and Foster to acknowledge that they are looking at this from the point of view of a market economy. They argue that two other possible systems have been tried, 'neither with notable success in eliminating undernutrition' (Leathers and Foster 2009: 329). One such system is state owned centrally planned production. The other is subsistence agriculture. Leathers and Foster begin their argument against subsistence by citing a study of Kenyan smallholders who were reducing their dependence on subsistence and growing sugar as a commercial crop: 'the return to labor for sugar was three times the daily agricultural wage rate and significantly higher than the return to maize' (Leathers and Foster 2009: 340). The farmers who had started growing sugarcane had higher incomes and the calorie consumption of their households was higher.

The study referred to by Leathers and Foster (Kennedy 1994) was undertaken to investigate the impact of cash cropping on income and nutrition. Some farmers in the area being studied had enrolled in a government owned sugar cooperative that organized production and distributed inputs. The government also bought the crop. The study compared incomes in 1984 before the project started and in 1985–7 after the first crop of sugar had been sold. The new entrants to the sugar cooperative were producing an average of 1,761 Kenya shillings worth of crops for their own family consumption and marketing 791 shillings worth of crops. The non-sugar farmers were growing 1,302 shillings worth of crops for home consumption and marketing 365 shillings worth of crops. The new entrants were getting an annual average of 1,285 shillings from non-agricultural earnings compared to 1,041 shillings for the non-sugar farmers. The non-sugar farmers had considerably less land. For the new entrants, farms were on average 5 hectares – for the non-sugar farmers 3.4 hectares. For the non-sugar farmers, 40.3 per cent of their land was devoted to food crops for home consumption and 4.1 per cent to non-food crops. For the new entrants, 36.4 per cent of their farms were devoted to food crops and 15.3 per cent to non-food crops. In terms of area per person devoted to food crops for home consumption, the new entrants were devoting an average of 0.17 hectares and the non-sugar farmers 0.14 hectares.

This study does not confirm the view of Leathers and Foster that subsistence 'does not work'. Instead, both the cash crop sugar producers and those not growing sugar were continuing to grow a large part of their effective income as subsistence food production. In fact the ones who were also growing sugar were growing a greater quantity of subsistence crops, and using more hectares per person to grow subsistence crops. The farmers who were growing sugar cane were the ones who had more land. They could afford to grow a surplus crop, because they had extra land to do it. The research suggests that those involved in the sugar project were the wealthier farmers, with more land, more cattle, more manure, and more money to buy fertilizer. Consequently they invested more heavily in family food production. They were also the ones with an edge in non-farm income, which provided them with cash for inputs for their subsistence production. It would have been difficult for the non-sugar producers to move into growing a commercial crop and copying the affluence of their neighbours. They did not have the land, did not have the manure, did not have the animal traction and did not have the cash income to pay for inputs.

This study is misleading as a comparison of subsistence cropping with commercial cropping. The supposed commercial cropping represented in this study was heavily subsidized by the Kenyan government. As the authors of the study point out, 'had the government used the world price of sugar to set the producer price for sugarcane, incomes of farmers would have been negative' (Kennedy 1994: 255). So the study cannot be held up to show that *commercial agriculture* is the way for the poor to improve their nutrition. The sugar programme was a kind of welfare state intervention. It is more aptly compared with income support schemes which may well be a lot more efficient in the use of government funds! The impact of this project on calorie consumption was less than jaw dropping. In the 1985–6 survey, 30 per cent of households in the new entrants sample were getting less than 80 per cent of the recommended calories per day, while 33 per cent of the non-sugar farmers were getting less than 80 per cent of recommended calories (Kennedy 1994: 256). Clearly this difference relates to all aspects of the wealth of the new entrants group – greater farm size; more subsistence production per person; more income from cash crops; more non-farm income. What is truly remarkable is how *little* difference there was between these cohorts. The difference could have all been due to the greater amount of land per hectare devoted to subsistence cropping in the new entrants group. These figures hardly give one any grounds for thinking that commercial projects have been proved to 'eliminate malnutrition'. Much better results could readily have been obtained by improving subsistence production.

Leathers and Foster draw their second example from Guatemala and a survey of 400 rural households. About half had started growing snow peas and vegetables for the export market. The value (per hectare) was about fifteen times that of the value of maize (per hectare). However, snow peas take a lot of work to grow. So the value (in hours of work) of snow peas was in fact only double the value of maize (Leathers and Foster 2009: 341). Accordingly it would not have made sense to abandon subsistence agriculture and just grow a commercial crop. They would have had to pay more than double the farm gate value of maize to get maize at retail prices. And so it proves when we look at the detail (von Braun *et al.* 1989)! The export crop growers were using less of their total land area to grow subsistence crops (52 per cent compared to 78 per cent) but were growing *more* maize for home consumption than the farmers who had not taken up this commercial option. On the same farm size, the export agriculture farmers were getting 30 per cent more yield – because they were using more fertilizers, doing more weeding and were better educated (von Braun *et al.* 1989). So this research does not in fact back up the view that 'subsistence does not work'. Instead it shows that poor farmers in Guatemala who can maintain their subsistence cropping *and also* grow some cash crops are doing better than those who only maintain their subsistence. The households which had benefited from this strategy used *some* of their extra income to buy food – but less than expected.

The research also shows why this commercial option is not being taken up by *all* the farmers. The households most likely to grow cash crops are those with larger land holdings, better education, better road access and the capability to finance inputs upfront. There are some serious disincentives. Inputs are financed through loans. If they cannot be paid off, farmers may lose their land. These inputs cost thirteen times more than inputs typically used on the maize crops. The uncertainty and risk is exacerbated by fluctuating prices – in one year the value of snow peas went from 0.1 to 2.0 quetzals per pound (von Braun *et al.* 1989: 11). All this risk means that poor families would be well advised to maintain their subsistence and strengthen it – so that their food needs do not depend on market crops. The context also shows why a commercial option like this is not likely to be viable across the developing world. A freezing plant for snow peas had to be established. After freezing, the crop had to be transported by refrigerated trucks to an airport. All of this depends on good transport and local infrastructure, uncommon in the developing world.

Finally, Leathers and Foster broaden their argument by referring to a survey of seventy-eight developing countries that grow some cash crops and some staple crops. Growth in cash crops positively correlated to growth in staple food production (2009: 341). What is going on here? These are countries where export industries have been very successful in triggering economic growth – what are called the 'Tiger economies' of Asia. These low wage economies have been successful in entering the international market for consumer goods. Former subsistence smallholders have got factory jobs. Their new wages have spurred a growth in commercial agriculture for local staples. The money and infrastructure coming out of this has enabled richer farmers to buy the necessary machinery and inputs to enter the global agricultural market. While this is very significant for the previously undernourished smallholders of these countries, it does not justify the usual conclusions about subsistence agriculture. These Tiger economies, despite their progress, still have a significant number of undernourished rural smallholders. South Asia is the standout example. What can be done for these people? In addition, these Tiger economies have captured and saturated a lot of this global market (Timmer 2005). In other developing countries, smallholders on minuscule farm plots are unable to enter this global competition. Subsistence is not a relic of traditional values, but a response to a current economic situation that is not easily swept away with a magic wand.

Policies to increase the supply of food

Farmers will be likely to produce more food if the cost of production goes down. What can be done to make this happen? Reduce input prices, maintain or improve the quality of resources, encourage investment and develop new technologies to increase productivity. Much of *Food Security for Rural Africa* will absolutely endorse these suggestions. Leathers and Foster reject welfare state versions of these policies. Where subsidies on fertilizer are concerned, they say that most of the subsidy money went to big producers rather than the poor. Yet the poor *also* benefited from these subsidies. As Leathers and Foster note, when governments in Africa responded to World Bank pressure by removing these subsidies in the 1990s, fertilizer use was reduced. Yields and calorie intake fell (2009: 348). However they do not draw the obvious conclusion – restore the subsidies. Instead the problem is inefficient fertilizer markets with: 'risk, seasonal demand, high transport costs, underdeveloped financial service markets, and cash constrained farmers' (Leather and Foster 2009: 348).

It seems unlikely that these problems will vanish, particularly for farmers who must rely on subsistence to feed their families. They cannot afford to buy fertilizers and they cannot get a loan because the chances of paying it back are slight. These problems lead Leathers and Foster to another solution typical of mainstream economists. It is communal title which makes it hard for African farmers to get credit. They cannot enter a contract for a loan, with the promise to sell their land if they are unable to pay back the debt. In fact, freehold title in other countries of the developing world has led many small farmers into unpayable debt. The eventual outcome has been that they have lost their land. Customary title in Africa prevents this outcome and secures the poor at least some possibility of feeding their families by growing food (Potts 2000; Wright 2008).

Food security: a global/African problem 17

At the end of this chapter, the authors are considering technologies which may increase productivity. They cite the use of *Mucuna pruriens* as an intercrop. This is a legume vine which can be grown interspersed among the maize plants. As they point out, yields of maize double or triple (2009: 365). This is almost posted as an aside here. Yet the implications are very significant. While the rest of the book keeps telling us that increased income and economic activity is the only way for the poor to solve their hunger problems, this short addendum suggests otherwise.

Mainstream economics fails the poor

The two authors summarize their approach with recommendations that are endlessly multiplied in the literature on these topics. One is that governments should invest more in agricultural research and provide the poor with better access to credit and markets. Rather than providing welfare, governments should encourage the poor to enter the market, produce high value agricultural crops and use the income to buy food. This strategy has proved to be a pipe dream. After forty years, it is time to try something else. The second suggestion is to improve economic growth, by appropriate 'macroeconomic policies' (Leathers and Foster 2009: 375) – in other words, free trade, de-regulation of labour markets and low taxes. Such measures are supposed to reduce the price of food. Yet such a reduction would be of little use to those whose wages are too low to buy food at any conceivable price. These largely unemployed poor are an intractable problem in this policy framework.

There is no doubt that *world* hunger and poverty have been reduced during the neo-liberal period. One factor is the curtailment of state ownership and interference in China. Between 1970 and 1990, the number of hungry people in China dropped from 406 million to 189 million. If you remove China from the equation, the number of hungry people in the world actually increased by 11 per cent between 1970 and 1990 (Lappé *et al.* 1998: 61). The second is the boom in export production in the 'Tiger' economies, with a consequent stagnation of wages in the rich countries. Neither of these developments have had an enormous impact on hunger and poverty for certain sections of the global population. Nor is it likely that these changes can take place in the other countries of the developing world – the market for global middle class consumers is already saturated. It has been thoroughly tied up by the Tiger economies that entered this game first.

Critique of leftist approaches

To consider an approach that is often supported by the left, I am looking at a popular book on food security issues, written by Frances Moore Lappé *et al.*, *World Hunger: 12 Myths* (1998). While there is much in this that makes sense, the intention to cover the global problems of hunger through the one interpretive scheme is a concern. For me, hunger in developing countries occurs in a number of different economic contexts. Remedies have to take these different contexts into account. In one situation, rural smallholders have sufficient land on which to grow their family food needs but are still hungry. In a second, the poor do not have access to land and their problem is that they have insufficient money to buy food. In a third, they may be tenant farmers. The money they are getting for their produce is insufficient to pay rent to the landholder *and also* buy food. These differing contexts may be joined together in various ways, but they need to be considered separately.

For Lappé *et al.*, the central problem causing hunger is that poor people in developing countries are growing 'cash crops' for export to the rich countries. Instead they should be growing 'food crops' for people in their own countries. Let us look at two sentences which exemplify this approach. Explaining why these problems are particularly severe in Africa, the authors write: 'Public resources, including research and agricultural credit, have been channelled to export crops to the virtual exclusion of peasant produced food crops such as millet, sorghum and root crops' (Lappé *et al.* 1998: 11). Colonial policy and foreign aid have: 'placed decisions over land use and credit in the domain of men. In many cases that has meant preferential treatment for cash crops over food crops' (Lappé *et al.* 1998: 11).

Both of these sentences refer to the failure to prioritize credit for *women*, who are more likely to favour 'food crops', rather than 'cash crops'. The reference to the problem of credit implies that women would be producing these 'food crops' for a cash income – borrowing money to pay for inputs, selling the crop and paying back the loan. By implication the term 'food crop' here must refer to *commercial crops* grown for national consumption. Yet the reality is that crops like millet, sorghum and root crops are almost always grown by African women *for home consumption*. While it may make perfect sense for women to give priority to basic cereal crops when they are farming *for home consumption*, they are unlikely to follow this system of priorities if they are farming commercially. For example, if they have a subsistence field growing a cereal crop and another field growing a surplus for sale, they will make the rational decision to grow a surplus crop that will fetch the highest price, whether a food crop for national consumption or an export crop. The supposed problem of credit does not apply to the food crops which women will grow for their *home consumption*. They would not take out a loan because would not be selling their crop – and would be unable to pay the loan back.

So Lappé and Collins are employing the dichotomy food crop/cash crop to cover a multitude of options with very different implications. By trying to amalgamate all the different developing country problems into one schema, the authors end up confusing quite different contexts. What could make a lot more sense is to start off with the distinction subsistence crops versus commercial crops. Then, within the category 'commercial crops' we could distinguish crops grown for the national market and crops grown for the export market.

Lappé *et al.* see wholescale food imports as a sign that local production has failed to meet national needs. The poor have been cut out of access to food,

Food security: a global/African problem 19

while the products of their national agriculture are being bought up by the rich countries and by rich consumers. For example in Africa by 1995, eleven African countries were net exporters of food. Over one-third of the grain being consumed was imported. Lappé *et al.* believe that insufficient food was being produced and retained for local consumption – 213 million Africans were undernourished (Lappé *et al.* 1998: 10). The (insufficient) quantities of grain that came into Africa were being sold at low prices – undercutting local peasant producers. With grain prices so low, poor farmers had to sell their harvests at rock bottom prices. Later in each year, grain merchants would put the prices up and these same farmers would be unable to buy food (Lappé *et al.* 1998: 18).

According to Lappé *et al.*, a likely consequence of this kind of situation is that the rural poor go into debt and lose their land. This means they lose the means to grow food for home consumption and the capacity to make a living by selling agricultural products: 'more than half a billion rural people in the third world are either landless or have too little land to feed their households' (Lappé *et al.*, 1998). When small farmers lose their land in this manner, the land is bought up and amalgamated into large farms. The owners are likely to install high tech agricultural machinery – producing more with less need for manual labour. As small farmers lose their land, employment in agriculture declines.

This narrative suggests the poor of the world speak with one voice and have the same interests. This may not always be the case. For farmers who are *selling* crops, rather than growing them for the family, the most sensible strategy is crops that fetch a high price. If these turn out to be *export* crops, so be it. Farmers growing *food* crops for sale in their own country want high prices for food. However, the urban poor prefer cheap food. If imported food is cheaper they will buy it – even though the competition may deprive local smallholders of an income. Poor employees on farms would like high wages, backed up by profitable crops and low food prices – even if the food is imported and the crops are exported. Farmers who are growing for subsistence may be neutral on these issues – *market prices* for food are irrelevant to their home consumption.

Let us *imagine* a context in which all these various interests would line up like ducks in a row. In this scenario, fifty years ago a developing country, which we will call Gardenia, had a booming rural sector. A large part of the population were farmers on small plots, protected from overseas competition by strong tariffs. Farm gate prices for the local market were high and most farmers did not bother with export crops. The urban poor would buy local food at the prices set by local smallholder farmers. There was some modest employment of the rural landless poor (only a small fraction of the population). What happened next was that the government of Gardenia took the advice of the World Bank, tariffs were abandoned and the food market flooded with cheap imports. For the first few years after this change, the urban poor improved their lives with cheaper food. However, the poor smallholder families in Gardenia lost the income they had been getting from crops grown for the national market. They took out loans to finance their farming. But with low prices, they were unable to pay back their debts. Eventually large numbers lost their farms. This land was taken over by big conglomerates, producing exports for the international market – using a lot of machinery and inputs. They employed only a small fraction of the people who had lost their farms. With so many unemployed, the wages of urban workers and of the rural poor fell, making it hard to feed a family on the money – even for those with a job. So the urban poor were not finding the cheaper prices of food a great boon.

While the above scenario does not really apply to Africa (for reasons that will become clear), it has certainly played out in many regions of the world. The recommendations favoured by Lappé et al. make sense for this scenario. The first item on their agenda is land reform – taking land back from the big conglomerates and giving it to poor rural workers. They want land reform engineered so that the small farms established in this way cannot be sold on the market to pay off debts. Smallholder farmers would be growing food to provide for their nation. Tariffs in the developing country would protect these smallholders from competition with cheap food imports. High prices in national markets would discourage export farming. Tariff barriers in the rich countries would help to stop agricultural products being drained out of the developing countries. The developing country government would make sure that 'anyone who wants a job can get one', so that those who were not farmers could buy food (Lappé et al. 1998: 106). The government would control food prices, so the poor could buy food.

We could call this proposal a 'strong welfare state' strategy. It reconciles the different interests I have been describing. While high prices for food benefit in-country producers, they increase food prices for wage earners. However, the government steps in to rescue the disadvantaged, with systems of price control or rationing. As has been pointed out by mainstream economists, this is a considerable expense to government – a kind of social welfare. It could be better to pay income support directly, rather than tampering with the price of food. While Lappé et al. may be wrong about the detail, it seems likely that *some* kind of welfare state solution could indeed be effective. However, my view is that an effective and thorough welfare state solution is very unlikely politically. People are starving while we are waiting for the political will to develop this leftist solution. The aim of this book is to take a long look at what might be more politically practicable right now. In the next chapter we will consider approaches to these problems that are more firmly rooted in the particularities of the African situation.

Vignette A
Low input technologies

Terry Leahy

A strange controversy

It seems odd that the usefulness of low input technologies is so controversial. Every study of the African situation notes the limited uptake of synthetic fertilizers, pesticides and herbicides, along with limited use of tractors and animal traction. This is always part of the explanation of low yields – with household food shortages the result. What studies also note is that poor rural households do not buy these inputs because they cannot afford them. You might think that would be the end of the story. Clearly yields are not going to be increased by anything that costs serious money. If you are farming for subsistence you are not going to get a cash income from your crop to pay for inputs for your next crop. Accordingly, those who are giving advice might as well start looking at low input technologies to see if they might help. This conclusion becomes controversial in a number of ways. One is to question whether these technologies *work* in Africa. If the answer is in the negative, there are a variety of suggestions. Often, the authors simply assert that these low input technologies are not much help unless villagers also apply synthetic fertilizers according to the recommended dosages. Not a particularly useful suggestion. Alternatively, the argument is that better marketing, credit provisions and infrastructure will be supplied by government. The idea behind this is that smallholders will be able to *purchase* inputs more cheaply and use cheap credit to *buy* inputs. Governments are not likely to implement these policies in any coherent and effective manner. In any case they could never work for the poor. By and large the poor are not marketing their crop and consequently cannot *buy* inputs with the proceeds from a previous crop. If they took out credit, no matter how cheaply, they would not be able to pay it back.

This book argues that some of the problems that critics identify for low input agriculture can be overcome through a process of cultural and local change, assisted by well designed projects. The science suggests it is not unrealistic to hope for a *doubling* of maize yields, with similar increases for other crops. This would be achieved by changes which would also provide fodder, leafy vegetables, wood, manure and protein. This vignette acknowledges and considers the widespread view that low input agriculture is too labour intensive to be feasible.

I will argue that the labour intensity of low input agriculture has been overplayed. In any case, the extra time required is paid back through the increase in yields that can be achieved. This vignette considers three basic technologies.

- legumes and mulching;
- reduced tillage and conservation agriculture;
- water harvesting.

Legumes and mulching

If nothing is done to stall this process, soils lose fertility in the years after a field has been cleared for crops. Partly this is the result of soil erosion. It also is an effect of the exposure of soils with ploughing, destroying soil life. It also derives from the export of nutrients in cropping. The nutrients from the soil get taken up into the crop. As the crop is harvested, the nutrients leave the field. This is called 'nutrient mining'. For Kenya, average annual net nutrient mining is estimated to be 42 kg nitrogen per hectare, 3 kg phosphorous per hectare and 29 kg potassium per hectare (Marenya and Barrett 2006: 516). A 3.5 tonne per hectare crop of maize removes the equivalent of 275 kg of fertilizer from the soil (World Agroforestry Centre 2010: 9). The impact of this is constantly declining yields. Florentin et al. (2011: 7) look at the situation in Paraguay in South America. In the first year after clearing the land, the maize yield is 2.678 tonnes per hectare but after twenty years it drops to 1.169 tonnes per hectare.

One solution to these problems is to use synthetic fertilizers, which supply nutrients such as nitrogen, phosphorus and potassium. Soil scientists have determined the amount necessary for particular crops. African smallholder farmers do not use synthetic fertilizers to the extent recommended. The average fertilizer use for thirty-five crops, including cash crops, in western Kenya is less than 17 kg nitrogen per hectare per year and 12 kg phosphorus per hectare per year – compared to the official extension recommendations of 75 kg nitrogen and 25 kg phosphorus (Marenya and Barrett 2006: 519). In Zambia, 69 per cent of smallholder farmers are not using synthetic fertilizer at all (World Agroforestry Centre 2010). More intensive land use in Africa has not been accompanied by an increase in fertilizer use. In East Asia, nitrogen input per hectare jumped from 23 kilos per hectare to 94.3 kilos per hectare between 1977 and 2007. In Africa nitrogen inputs increased from 2.0 kilos per hectare to only 6.3 kilos per hectare (Headley and Jayne 2014: 24).

Low input solutions to the export of nutrients are various. Avoid export of nutrients where feasible. Do not burn the straw after harvest and do not feed it to cattle. Concentrate nutrient resources on the farm. Manure derives nutrients from pasture which are then applied to cropping fields. Bringing in leafy mulch also concentrates nutrients. Composting improves the availability of nutrients. Intercrops can bring up nutrients from deep in the soil, making them available to crops. For example Mucuna 'mobilizes phosphorus from the soil' (Buckles and Triomphe 1999: 81).

Low input agriculture uses leguminous plants to 'fix' nitrogen in the soil, bringing that key nutrient in from the air. Legume plants have a symbiotic relationship with particular types of soil bacteria (rhizobium). These bacteria draw nitrogen from the air and fix it in their bodies. In turn, as the bacteria infect the roots of the legume, the nitrogen becomes available to the legume plant through its roots. This nitrogen can also be used by cereal crops growing together with the legumes, their roots drawing on the nitrogen the legume provides. Legumes come in a variety of shapes and sizes. They often have pods (beans) in which the seeds are contained. They may have leaflets on opposite sides of the stem (like acacias). The flowers are usually either a fluffy ball (as in acacias) or a pea flower (as in peas and beans). Different legumes have different capacities to fix nitrogen. For example, experiments in Malawi determined that pigeon pea in a maize/pigeon pea intercrop might fix 60 kg of nitrogen per hectare and cow peas in a maize/cow pea combination might fix between 10 and 20 kg of nitrogen per hectare (Njira *et al.* 2017: 1348). The quantities of nitrogen made available by legumes are comparable to amounts recommended from synthetic fertilizers (60 kg per hectare).

In agriculture there are a number of ways to use legumes.

As a source of mulch or dug in

Grow groves of tree legumes (for example *Leucaena leucocephala* or *Calliandra calothyrsus*) and cut the leafy branches to make a nitrogen rich mulch to apply to the cropping field. This will break down to provide soil carbon and food for soil biota, allow water to infiltrate, soften the soil, hold rainfall and block soil erosion. The branches can also supply fodder.

A study in the Central Highlands of Kenya (Mugwe *et al.* 2009: 53–55) incorporated mulch sourced from legume tree branches. Using Calliandra, the yields of maize on the experimental station were up to 13 tonnes per hectare, compared with typical local yields of 1.4 tonnes. On the farmers' own fields, the yield of maize was 4.4 tonnes per hectare. Soils on the experimental station performed better because they already had a high content of organic matter, something which this practice will provide to farmers over time. With synthetic fertilizer, farmers' own fields could get 3.9 tonnes per hectare and with cattle manure 4.2 tonnes per hectare (Fischler and Wortmann 1999; Tarawali *et al.* 1999).

As 'improved fallows'

Grow legumes in rotation with cereals. For example grow *Sesbania sesban* trees for two years. Cut, keep the branches for firewood and leave the twigs and the leaves on the ground. Then plant the crop. Sesbania sesban is an indigenous legume that grows fast and escapes free ranging livestock. It is resistant to fire and can survive a drought. World Agroforestry cites research in Zambia. Growing maize without fertilizer the yield was typically 1 tonne per hectare. With fertilizer it was 5 tonnes. Fallowing for two years with Sesbania sesban, yields were more than 4 tonnes per hectare (2010: 16). Research in Eastern Zambia near Katete found that a two to three years Sesbania fallow enabled a maize yield in the following year of 5 to 6 tonnes per hectare. By comparison, the yield with synthetic fertilizer was 4.9 tonnes per hectare and with a traditional weedy fallow it was 1.5 tonnes per hectare. The harvest of firewood was 15 to 20 tonnes per hectare (Kwesiga et al. 1999: 52). A study in Kenya tried out mixed species fallows, Sesbania with either Crotalaria, Siratro, Groundnut or Tephrosia. After a fallow of twelve to fifteen months, yields of maize in the following year were two to five tonnes higher than with natural weed fallows or continuous maize cropping (Kamiri et al. n.d.; see also Fischler and Wortmann 1999; Lahmar et al. 2012).

As alley cropping

Grow bands of legume bushes alternating with bands of cereal crops – for example *Calliandra calothyrsus*, *Leucaena leucocephala* or *Gliricidia sepium*. Just before planting the cereal, prune the bushes quite short so that they do not compete with the cereal crop. Mulch the leafy matter. The roots will assist the cereal to grow. World Agroforestry cites a Malawi study using Gliricidia alternating with rows of maize. Yields were 5 tonnes per hectare in good years and averaged out at 3.7 tonnes compared to control plots getting 0.5 to 1 tonne per hectare (2010: 16).

As a legume parkland

The indigenous tree *Faidherbia albida* can be planted at up to 150 trees per hectare (World Agroforestry Centre 2010) with the cereal crop underneath. In the wet season, when the cereal crop is growing, the Faidherbia loses its leaves. It does not compete with the crop for light. The leafy mulch provides a soil cover and the roots of the Faidherbia fix nitrogen. This technology was traditional in parts of the Sahel region and is ideal for dryer situations. For example, in Zambia, maize grown without fertilizer in the vicinity of Faidherbia trees yields 4.1 tonnes per hectare compared to 1.3 tonnes for maize nearby – but outside of the tree canopy (World Agroforestry Centre 2010: 12).

As an intercrop

A herbaceous legume is grown interspersed with the cereal crop. The legume provides mulch, fixes nitrogen and suppresses weeds. Over time, the intercrop improves the soil quality by supplying organic material for soil organisms. It improves the softness of the soil so it is easier to plant seeds and the roots can go further into the soil. It harvests water, by preventing rainwater runoff, improving the infiltration of water and conserving soil moisture.

Intercrops may be planted at the same time as the cereal crop. More usually the intercrop is delayed so that the cereal is well established before the intercrop gets going. A well known combination is the 'velvet bean' vine, *Mucuna pruriens* with maize. It is planted two to four weeks after the maize plants have been sown. It may be pruned while the maize is maturing. After harvest the tendrils of the Mucuna grow up around the dead maize stalks and take over the field. In the late dry season, the maize stalks and Mucuna vines are slashed so that the field is ready for maize to be planted again. This technology was first reported after research on the Kekchi of Guatemala and Honduras (in 1969). Yields there are between 2.5 and 4.5 tonnes per hectare and these systems have been in place for more than twenty-five years (Buckles and Triomphe 1999: 76).

The Legume Research Network reports similar results from trials in Kenya. The first issue of its newsletter (Njarui and Mureithi 1999) gives figures for trials where velvet bean was intercropped with maize and cut as a mulch. In Machakos the yield was 4 tonnes per hectare, in Kabete 3.62 tonnes per hectare (with a control plot getting 1.76 tonnes). In Kitale maize stover was also used along with the velvet bean mulch; yields were 5.7 tonnes per hectare. In Kisii the maize yield was 6.4 tonnes per hectare, with control plots getting 3.2 tonnes. In Embu the maize yield was 6.48 tonnes per hectare. In these trials the velvet bean intercrop left 4 tonnes of dry matter as a mulch. These fields taken as a whole were getting 27 per cent more yield than when manure was used as a fertilizer and 37 per cent more yield than when synthetic fertilizer was used. They were getting at least double the control plots where no fertilizers had been used.

In the second issue of the LRNP newsletter, Kirungu *et al.* report on Kitale in Kenya (2004: 4). In this region farmers have stopped using fertilizers because of the cost. Yields are now averaging 0.8 tonnes per hectare. By using 12 tonnes per hectare of compost or cattle manure, this can be boosted to 3.3 tonnes. The field trials relayed velvet bean – planting the legume after the maize has been established, allowing it to grow on the stover after the maize harvest and slashing and digging in the velvet bean mulch before the next maize planting. Yields at different sites using this technology were between 4.4 and 6.7 tonnes per hectare (see also Mugwe *et al.* 2009: 55).

Other legume intercrops are cow peas, sunhemp and *Dolichos lablab*. Lablab is sometimes preferred to Mucuna because the pods are edible. Yields of maize in Madagascar using maize and lablab were 3.9 tonnes per hectare (Kassam *et al.* 2009: 6).

Mulching

A mulch cover is ideally quite thick, for example four tonnes per hectare. One source of the leafy matter for a mulch is legume plants, grown in the combinations considered above. But mulch can also come from grasses or indeed any leafy matter. Mulch can simply be the straw left after a harvest. Collecting and distributing mulch to this extent is clearly a time consuming operation. But as the research cited below makes clear, this initial work is justified by the extent of the increase in yield.

The organic matter in a mulch gradually breaks down and feeds soil organisms. An indicator of this organic matter is the amount of carbon in the soil. Organic matter provides nutrients for plants and holds moisture. USA Department of Agriculture studies indicate moisture holding capacity can be increased by 40 per cent (Kassam et al. 2009: 3). Organic matter softens soils, making them easier to work. The roots of crop plants can go deep and access more nutrients. The mulch prevents a hard crust forming on the top of the soil, repelling water. Instead water infiltrates through the mulch. The mulch protects soil moisture from evaporation on hot days. Heavy rainfall events can lead to soil erosion on exposed soils. Soil with a good mulch cover will absorb rain.

Studies that isolate the effects of mulch show its efficacy. For example at a site in Southern Zimbabwe (465 mm rainfall), all fields were treated with 3 tonnes per hectare of manure and 20 kg of nitrogen as synthetic fertilizer. Using conventional ploughing practice, the yields were 676 kg per hectare *without* mulch and 2,018 kg *with 8 tonnes of mulch* per hectare (Mupangwa et al. 2012: 142).

It has been argued that mulching is not a useful technology for maize: where average rainfall goes above 1,000 mm – seedlings can become waterlogged (Rusinamhodzi et al. 2011: 663). Yet in the high rainfall sites of Honduras and Guatemala, maize is intercropped with Mucuna, slashed to leave a thick mulch cover – with excellent results. If waterlogging is a problem, the cover crop could be dug in, rather than slashing it to form a mulch. Another solution could be a more moisture tolerant crop, for example potatoes, cassava, sweet potatoes, plantains, enset. Current practice, eroding soils and destroying humus, is *not* the answer!

Reduced tillage and conservation agriculture

'Tillage' is the use of ploughs or hoes to break up the soil. Tillage softens the soil so it is ready to take seeds. It uproots weeds so that they do not compete with the crop plants. Mouldboard and disc ploughs are used to turn the soil over completely. Soil scientists argue that tillage like this reduces soil fertility. The exposed soil is easily eroded by rain. Exposure to air 'oxidizes' the living soil humus and kills it. The heat of the sun fries soil organisms. The level immediately below the ploughing is gradually compacted – the plough never reaches that level and the weight of plough, tractors or oxen pushes the soil down hard. Roots cannot penetrate beyond this 'hardpan'. On the surface of an exposed soil, dirt forms a crust, repelling rainwater which drains away rather than sinking into the ground (Hobbs 2007).

A technology that is gradually being adopted is low till cultivation. In industrial farming, a long narrow blade (a chisel plough) is used to create a deep thin furrow (ripping), cutting the hardpan left by previous cultivation. Fertilizer and seed are placed along those ripped lines. A tractor seeding punch can be used to drill a small hole and drop the seed in. In manual cultivation, small basins are dug. For example in the late dry season dig a four litre basin for each maize plant. Add a cup of manure (or compost) and a spoonful of lime. Refill the basin, mixing in the soil you have dug up. When the first rains arrive, plant three maize seeds in the basin. Later, select the strongest seedling and pull up the other two. These technologies are called variously 'zero', 'conservation' or 'reduced' tillage.

Reduced tillage is combined with intercropping with legumes and mulching. These techniques gradually soften the soil and make it easier to plant seeds without first ploughing. In 2006 the FAO decided to create a new term, 'conservation agriculture' (CA) to refer to this package. On its current website it defines CA as:

1 Continuous minimum mechanical soil disturbance.
2 Permanent organic soil cover.
3 Diversification of species grown in sequences and/or associations (FAO 2018; see also World Agroforestry Centre 2010).

Some version of CA has been taken up quite widely. Large commercial operations save on soil preparation. Ripping the field costs less than turning the soil over. Herbicides control weeds, saving on labour. Rotations reduce pest attacks as the pests of a particular crop find it harder to get established. Intercropping with legumes supplements synthetic fertilizers, also reducing costs. More organic matter improves soil quality. Mulch protects the soil from erosion, storing water and reducing irrigation costs. Accordingly, farmers in industrial settings have leapt upon CA. In Latin America, no-till agriculture has been adopted on 60 per cent of the cropland area. Crops and the range of climatic situations are similar to those of Africa – for example soybean, maize, wheat, sunflower, canola, cassava and potato, with cover crops such as lupins, vetch, Mucuna, Dolichos and Cajanus. The USA, Canada and Australia are also enthusiastic, with between 15 and 27 per cent of agricultural land under CA (Kassam et al. 2009: 312). Other parts of the world have been slower to take this up. African farming has not been hugely impacted by CA – for example only 0.4 per cent of agricultural land in Zimbabwe and 2.4 per cent in South Africa (Kassam et al. 2009: 312).

There clearly is a low income/low input version of CA. To prepare the seed bed, comparatively richer farmers will use animal traction and a ripper. The poorer farmers will dig planting basins with hoes. The rural poor will not be using herbicides to kill weeds but will be slashing weeds with a machete or digging them up with hoes. A flat hoe with a sharp blade, an *ashasha*, can be pushed into the soil and cut weed roots, an effective tool from Nigeria (Mortimore 1998). Intercropping with nitrogen fixing legumes can diversify planting and provide organic soil cover. Farm households with small plots will not *rotate* non-food crops and cereals. Yet they may rotate staple crops such as maize, sorghum, cassava. Along with these they will plant food intercrops such as beans, cow peas, pumpkins, peanuts, bambara nuts.

Studies of reduced tillage agriculture in comparison with conventional ploughing are rare. Most such studies complicate the issue by including the other aspects of the CA package (mulching and diversity). An exception is a study of the Babati area of Tanzania, where rainfall is usually below 600mm per year. One set of plots was treated with ripping with a chisel plough, the other set with conventional ploughing. The following results were in a year with adequate rainfall. With no fertilizing method being used at all, the ripped plots were getting 3.6 tonnes yield and the conventional plots 1.3 tonnes. With the use of 5 tonnes per hectare of cattle manure, the ripped plots were getting 4.8 tonnes and the conventional plots 1.8 tonnes (Rockström 2000: 10).

Supposed problems with CA in Africa

All this sounds good in theory, but the slow uptake of CA in Africa does not inspire confidence. Corbeels *et al.* (2014) note that only 1 per cent of the total cropland area in Zambia, Kenya and Zimbabwe is using CA. Projects instructing farmers in CA have few lasting impacts. After the project and its incentives leaves, the technologies lapse – 'a 95% dis-adoption rate' (Ngoma *et al.* 2014: 2). In Zambia the government has vigorously promoted 'conservation farming' since the 1980s. Despite this, by 2012 only 4 per cent of small and medium sized farm households practised key CA techniques of minimal soil disturbance and planting basins (Arslan *et al.* 2013; Corbeels *et al.* 2014). Similar problems have been encountered in promoting mixed cropping with nitrogen fixing green manures and 'improved fallows' (Giller *et al.* 2009). Marenya and Barrett cite a project in Western Kenya that persuaded 50 per cent of smallholder participants to implement agroforestry. After two years only 10 per cent were using it. By contrast the proportion of those using manure at the beginning of the study was 48 per cent and after two years it had not declined. The figures for fertilizer use were also stable – 30 per cent (2006: 523). So farmers who could *afford* cattle (manure) and fertilizer had maintained those technologies.

In response to this situation, Giller *et al.* (2009) promote the 'heretic's view' that CA is an unsuitable technology for smallholders in Africa. This articulation of the problems has been widely cited and is close to becoming a new orthodoxy, especially in academic circles. I will outline each of the problems that Giller and his colleagues identify and systematically respond to their arguments.

- **Herbicides and weeding. Herbicides are too expensive. Yet the manual weeding necessary for CA is too time consuming.**

Giller and colleagues are correct in arguing that subsistence farmers will not *buy* herbicides. However, the extra time spent in *manual* weeding is unlikely to be a barrier to CA adoption. They cite a study of two sites in Zambia. Where there was a time penalty for CA, it was an additional sixty hours of work *per year* per hectare, hardly a reason to eschew a technology that adds between 60 and 200 per cent to yields (Goeb 2013; Ngoma *et al.* 2015)!

Giller and colleagues argue that this technology ends up foisting more work on women who generally do the manual weeding (see also Valbuena *et al.*

2012: 182). This comment must apply to approximately 40 per cent of farmers, those who own cattle. In such families, men take care of the cattle, and the ploughing. The women do planting and weeding. Ploughing functions as the first weeding. The second and third weeding are done by women. With CA, men use a ripping chisel plough and weeds are not disturbed. So women have to *manually* weed the field prior to sowing the crop – three weeding episodes in total. Making sense of Giller's comment. However, in *poorer* households (the other 60 per cent) *all* agriculture is manual. This manual work may actually drop with CA. In the first instance the field is dug with little basins where each maize plant is to be grown. It is not hoed from one edge to the other, saving what is often women's work. The weeds would be slashed and left on the ground as mulch, a lot less work than hoeing a whole field. The second and third weeding for the crop would be exactly the same as in conventional tillage. However, there would be a lot fewer weeds. A thick layer of mulch and a cover crop *suppresses* weeds (World Agroforestry 2010). Research in Paraguay compared the percentage of weed plants growing in fields with a green manure cover crop to fields without such a crop – with 100 per cent representing the weed plants present *without* such a cover crop. For a cover crop of Mucuna, only 5 per cent of the typical number of weeds came up, for sunhemp 7 per cent, jackbean 14 per cent and pigeon pea 19 per cent (Florentin *et al.* 2011: 16).

Farmers are by no means universal in condemning the CA package for the extra work required. For example Kirungu et al. describe the reactions of participants to a trial in Kenya, where the use of a legume achieved yields between four and six tonnes per hectare.

> Although the legumes require labour to establish (land preparation plus two weedings), farmers feel that growing the green manure in situ is less labour intensive than making, managing and applying compost or FYM [Farmyard Manure]. Farmers have also commented on the legume's ability to reduce the incidence of annual weeds in the subsequent maize crop and the improvement in soil physical properties especially soil tilth.
>
> (2000: 4)

Why are green manure crops regarded by Giller *et al.* as too labour intensive when *spreading manure* (for those who can afford it) is so well established (Marenya and Barrett 2006: 523)?

- **Inability to buy seeds for cover crops.**

One or more of the favoured cover crops are already established in pockets in every locality in Africa. The seeds are available to be multiplied up.

- **The need to save crop residues for mulch would deprive cattle (see also Lahmar *et al.* 2012). The typical expectation is that cattle will graze on the stover after harvest. Stover is a key food for cattle.**

The expectation that cattle will graze stover reflects the power of village cattle owning elites. Farmers could grow hedges and keep the cattle out of their fields if there was the political will to move to CA. What is absolutely necessary is to exploit every niche for the production of leafy matter. Quick growing legume trees can provide mulch for cropping fields and fodder for livestock. As Serraj and Siddique (2012: 4) remark: 'In sites with relatively high feed and fuel pressure, the introduction of CA would probably require increasing biomass production and/or developing alternative sources to alleviate the opportunity costs of leaving some crop residues as mulch.'

- **The shortage of mulch in dry climates with sandy soils. Even if the stover is *not* eaten by cattle, it is insufficient, and quickly breaks down.**

As above, legume trees must be planted for mulch and fodder. In dry climates the technique of parkland planting with *Faidherbia albida* works extremely well to provide nitrogen in soils, shade in the dry season and mulch in the growing season. Conventional cultivation is removing organic matter, nutrients and carbon from these soils. This is unsustainable. One wonders what alternative Giller and his colleagues propose.

- **Mulch left on fields harbours pests.**

There are a variety of organic solutions to these problems (see later chapters). In any case, the capacity of CA to deliver greater yields, despite such supposed problems, is well established. One concern is that mulch encourages termites. Scientific opinion is that termite activity actually improves soil productivity (Lahmar *et al.* 2012). Intercrops of sunhemp, desmodium or marigolds can prevent infestation with root knot nematodes (Otipal *et al.* 2003). Sunhemp deters the weed species Striga – a pest in maize crops.

- **The need to purchase lime.**

African soils are often deficient in lime, an issue whatever technology is being used. Using planting basins means that manure and lime can be targeted to a particular cereal plant, rather than spread across the whole field. A teaspoon for each maize plant could be sourced at a fraction of the cost of fertilizers and hybrid seed packages.

Despite the dis-adoptions and the low uptake, there *are* smallholders who are enthusiastic about CA. The World Agroforestry Centre (2010) cites two. Mr Mwinga in Zambia uses early planting, minimum tillage and crop rotation. He used to use eight bags of fertilizer per hectare and get 1.25 tonnes of maize per hectare. He now uses four bags and gets 8 tonnes. The family grow all their own maize and have some left over to sell. They have bought oxen, a new iron roof and a kitchen unit (2010: 2). Mr Majoni in Malawi was using fertilizers and getting 1.5 to 2 tonnes of maize yield per hectare. Now he is planting rows of Gliricidia between his maize rows and getting 3.5 tonnes (2010: 2).

It seems truly odd that well educated commercial farmers are adopting CA in such numbers in many countries of the world – and yet it supposedly cannot work in African conditions. The failures are presented as technical limitations of African geography. This is a ludicrous assertion. At the end of the day the reasons for failure to adopt must be cultural and political. Other chapters in this book will consider what these reasons might be.

Water harvesting

Water can be harvested using earth works. For wetter conditions large bunds (mounds) run at the same height in the landscape (on the contour) and have the effect of terracing, trapping water running down the slope. There is also a ditch (swale) running either above or below the bund. You dig the ditch and pile the dirt up to form the bund. Bunds can be strengthened with grasses, such as vetiver or Napier grass which help the bund to resist rainfall erosion. If farms are small, the contour bunds will run across different holdings and can be constructed by voluntary working bees. For dryer conditions, particular crop plants may be given a mini catchment, for example one metre across and fifty centimetres deep. These little crescent dams trap water and direct it to the crop plant. Water harvesting is an element of traditional agriculture in many African countries (Rockström 2000; Lahmar et al. 2012).

During the colonial period, governments conscripted work parties of local people to construct contour bunds. In the long term, these constructions were not very useful. The bunds I have seen from this period were very minimal in size (about 30 centimetres) and in a heavy rainfall event, the bund would be breached and eroded, ceasing to function. A useful bund is at least 70 centimetres high and 150 centimetres across, with the corresponding ditch just as big. Making matters worse, coercive labour recruitment invited resistance and these colonial structures were never properly maintained.

Contour lines for a bund can be measured and marked out using an 'A frame', a wooden triangle with a cross bar, say two metres high and two metres at the bottom. The cross bar is measured and the halfway point marked. A string drops from the apex and is attached to a stone that hangs below the cross bar. If the two feet of the A are exactly on the level the string swings at the halfway mark. If one leg is higher the string hangs away from that side. To mark out a contour you begin by finding a level and mark the two points. Then, swing one leg sideways and find the next level point for that leg. And so on, marking out a flat line across the landscape.

Heavy rainfall in the wet seasons sees water racing down slopes, causing erosion. Running across the surface, water leaves the fields. A bund prevents this. The water ponds on the upper side of the bund and gradually sinks into the ground, moving slowly down the slope. This moisture supports crop growth in the wet season. It keeps the soil moist during the dry season, aiding companion crops and maintaining soil biota. Gradual release of water maintains year round water flow. Without this, streams and springs dry up, the rainwater has left the catchment.

Conclusions

This vignette shows that low cost/low input solutions can at least double yields. Where maize is concerned, typical yields now hover around one tonne per hectare. They could go from two tonnes to six tonnes, depending on rainfall. These solutions require work and may take some time to show results. Some attempts to implement these strategies will fail. As Bunch (1997) suggested long ago, experiments on farmers' fields should start small and be given time to show results. Given persistence and farmer participation, the efficacy of these technologies would become obvious. What could be established is a new culture of smallholder farming – solving food security problems to a very large extent. Economically, these technologies are the only long term solutions for farmers doing subsistence agriculture.

2 The UK paradigm and an alternative strategy

Terry Leahy

The UK academic paradigm

A key strand of thinking about African food security problems comes from research conducted by development economists and geographers working in the UK. In this chapter, this perspective will be called 'the UK academic paradigm'. Very detailed and thorough research has been conducted, for example in Mali, Nigeria, Kenya, Ghana, Zimbabwe and South Africa. There is much overlap between the findings of this research and the analysis developed in this book, but there are some key differences. The authors of this paradigm are critical of the disasters of neo-liberal economics and the 'Washington consensus'. Yet they do not favour global welfare state solutions of the kind recommended by Lappé *et al*. Their aim instead is to encourage projects that work through the participation of the poor, constructing piecemeal tactics adapted to particular situations. While all of this makes good sense, there are other aspects of their recommendations that *Food Security for Rural Africa* will question. The government interventions they advocate are unlikely. The projects they favour, based on boosting commercial production, cannot establish food security.

Participation

The keystone of the UK paradigm is participation: 'A dictatorial "transformation approach" to development initiatives must be replaced with a more democratic form of development which has Africans, both rural and urban, as its main focus and genuinely seeks to fulfil their needs and aspirations' (Binns *et al*. 2012: Kindle 629). The emphasis on participatory strategies relates to the work done by Robert Chambers and the 1959 book, *Rural Development: Putting the Last First* (Chambers 1983). In this and later writings, Chambers castigated development researchers for failing to make contact with the rural poor. He was critical of governments and NGOs for projects which had little impact on their lives. His solution was to devise a set of project strategies to ensure genuine participation. For example, a meeting of the local people would be called and the facilitator would encourage people from the community to get up and speak, to draw maps, write lists of problems and work out solutions. The name given to this method was *Participatory Rural Appraisal – PRA* (Chambers 2005; see also Defoer and Scoones 2001: 170).

These ideas were taken up by governments and world bodies. Yet writers from the UK paradigm are aware that projects still have difficulty meeting the needs of the poor. For example, Binns *et al.* (2012) consider a project in Durban, South Africa, that helped local stallholders to improve their marketplace. As they note, the project tended to help people who were more 'wealthy' to begin with: 'Unfortunately, for the underprivileged majority in the city, there is minimal evidence that a significant reduction in poverty has been achieved' (Binns *et al.* 2012: Kindle 7855).

Authors of the UK paradigm conclude that projects need to be *more* conscientious about being participatory and more carefully adjusted to *local* situations after thorough consultation and research with local people. So, for Durban, the failure was due to: 'a lack of resources, a failure to involve the beneficiaries in decision-making' (Binns *et al.* 2012: Kindle 7835).

Like the paradigm writers, I believe that without local participation and enthusiasm, projects will never work. Like them, I believe that projects must be constantly adjusted in consultation with beneficiaries. Yet there are several 'buts' here. To begin with, local people are not naïve. They know very well what kinds of projects are being funded by NGOs and governments. If they are asked to explain what it is that might help them, they will choose something that is likely to get funded. The mindset of donors amounts to an *idée fixe* so overwhelming that almost all projects take the following form – a project designed to help a poor person to become a petit entrepreneur of their agricultural or craft production. Given this, participation can only have one outcome, however local and bottom up the method of investigating needs.

To add to this bias, local people themselves share this orientation. They are committed to a particular path to modernity, a path promised by the leaders of the liberation struggles. 'Development' implies a well paid job, or a successful enterprise, sufficient income to live in a 'modern' manner – a house with an iron roof rather than thatching, children sent to school in a proper uniform. They will *participate* by asking for a project to assist them in this modernization, a project promising a cash income. Gender divisions in Africa cement this bias. Men look to projects that they hope will assist them into profitable work. There is an unfortunate legacy stemming from colonial conscriptions into agricultural remediation. It is perceived as stigmatizing to work without the expectation of an income. Women have a different orientation. Their responsibility is the household food supply; often achieved through subsistence production. They are fully engaged in this work, and may not come to the meetings where projects are set up.

The problem is that projects with a commercial orientation rarely work and rarely last. When they do work, they help the richer members of the community and pass over the poor. I pose the question of participation quite differently, starting off by asking what kind of project could actually achieve food security. The next question is how to get the necessary participation to give this solution a thorough trial – so that local people can *see* that it works. Projects can only work if they are feasible in the cultural and economic context of the villages. Without that, participatory enthusiasm cannot be maintained.

Diverse livelihoods

A second plank of the UK paradigm is the concept of 'diverse livelihoods'. There is a 'diversity in agro-ecological conditions and socio-economic circumstances' which makes it unwise to reach for 'tailor-made recommendations' (Defoer and Scoones 2001: 164). The poor of rural Africa cobble together a range of strategies for livelihood and do not rely on any one economic pathway. For example, they may do some subsistence agriculture, they may do some paid work on other people's farms, they may migrate into town for a job, they may have some small business making and selling a local product, they may sell some agricultural produce (Binns *et al*. 2012). Any given household will variously rely on all these strategies at different times, adjusting the mix depending on the circumstances. For example a bad drought that wipes out crops will mean that some members of the family migrate into town to get a job (Mortimore 1998).

The UK paradigm identifies a typical problem of the grand projects of the 1970s and 1980s as attempts to promote *just one* of these paths exclusively – for example persuading farmers to use *all* their land to grow just *one* profitable cash crop. Given the uncertainty of the African context, such one eyed projects cannot work. For example, it is quite common for regions in Africa not to have a regular annual rate of rainfall but perhaps to have two good years and five bad years, or some other unpredictable combination (Mortimore 1998). So any agricultural enterprise is tentative, risking the use of expensive inputs. Market fluctuations are another issue. A whole area may be planted out to cotton, with disastrous consequences for livelihoods if the market collapses (Mortimore 1998). A diverse livelihood strategy is the most rational way to proceed. Projects should help the rural poor with particular aspects of their diverse strategy rather than trying to find the one cure-all solution.

The emphasis of the UK paradigm is that given the diverse circumstances of different smallholder farmers in Africa a one-size-fits-all strategy can never work (Scoones *et al*. 2005). Yet surprisingly, we shall find that the recommendations of these authors are almost always the same, regardless of the circumstances:

- small entrepreneurial projects with individual farmer families;
- better roads;
- credit facilities for smallholder farmers;
- better marketing systems for inputs and produce;
- bottom up participation.

This chapter will begin to explain why these recommendations are unlikely to be implemented successfully and why the recommended strategy cannot deal with the food security problems of the rural poor.

Subsistence versus commercial – a tired antithesis

The emphasis on diverse livelihoods relates to another aspect of the UK paradigm. Projects in Africa since the 1980s have been almost exclusively targeted to commercialization. This is the orientation of mainstream economics, an approach that has also been the central focus of the development policy of IMF and the World Bank. The solution for the developing world is to abandon low tech subsistence agriculture and develop a fully commercial agricultural sector, like the rich countries. The UK paradigm resists this approach. As their detailed studies show, subsistence production must be part of any package of diverse livelihoods for the rural poor of Africa (Binns et al. 2012; Mortimore 1998). It can provide effective income when cash income is low; it can help families to ride out declines in the price for cash crops; it can even help them to withstand droughts – as subsistence crops of sorghum, millet and cassava do better than most cash crops in a drought. At the same time, a strategy that attempted to rely on subsistence completely would also be problematic. Families need cash and welcome the additional income from cash crops. If a drought is sufficiently severe, households may depend on cash income from relatives working in town or depend on income from minor enterprises. Cash income can buy inputs for household subsistence crops. Consequently, the authors of the UK paradigm see the antithesis between cash cropping and subsistence farming as a tired opposition that has passed its use by date.

Yet the UK paradigm's endorsement of subsistence is somewhat partial. Authors in the UK paradigm see subsistence as unable *to reliably feed* African smallholder families and imply that a commitment to subsistence is driving families into poverty. For example, Binns et al. (2012: Kindle 3349) make the following comment: 'a major determinant of rural poverty is an over-dependence of the majority of the population on subsistence farming as a result of persistent food insecurity'. This statement *blames* subsistence farming for the impoverishment of African farmers. Africans cannot get employment in the market economy – they are too busy growing food for their own table. They are doing this because they do not have food security. The remedy cannot be subsistence because that is causing the problem – the remedy must be more money coming in from the market so they can buy all the food they need. Against this interpretation, let me suggest that there is a scarcity of paid employment or feasible opportunities for entrepreneurial profit. Consequently, the rural poor lack the means to *buy* food. It is this that is driving African farmers to subsistence agriculture.

Supposed constraints of subsistence

A number of constraints to food security through subsistence agriculture are often mentioned by writers from the UK paradigm.

1 Families do not have enough land to grow all their food supplies

This is implied in findings which compare the farm sizes of rich, poor and medium households. For example, Chibudu et al. (2001) look at two different regions in Zimbabwe, Mangwende and Chivi. In both cases the richer farmers have more land and more cattle. In Mangwende the richer households have an average of 4.1 hectares of cropping fields and ten cattle, and the poorer

The UK paradigm and alternatives 37

households have an average of 1.8 hectares of fields and no cattle at all. In Chivi, the discrepancies are similar.

Mortimore suggests land shortage as a constraint on subsistence production in a region of Northern Nigeria. With a 'satisfactory' rainfall, the average cropping land *per person* (about one hectare) might produce close to a tonne of grain (feeding three people). Yet, rainfall is often unsatisfactory. In only two years of a thirteen year period did families in fact grow enough to feed their family for the whole year. 'Given the unavoidable fluctuations in the rainfall, and the risk from pests or disease, achieving this notional level of productive capacity is an erratic struggle. Is land shortage, then, a cause of production failure in the drylands?' (Mortimore 1998: 103).

2 Subsistence strategies require so much labour that they cannot produce adequate food for a household

> Labour supply is the main limiting factor on Kano farms ... Households with a high proportion of very young or old members are often constrained in their farming unless they have access to voluntary help from outside the household or can afford to hire labour.
>
> (Binns *et al.* 2012: Kindle 2583)

In a detailed account of two regions of Africa, Mortimore talks about the restraints created by labour insufficiency when growing cereals: 'The labour required for effective bird-scaring in the season of grain formation is always beyond the resources of farming households; and children of school age are needed on the farm for this task' (Mortimore 1998: 87). Labour constraints also restrict necessary weeding. In summarizing his findings, Mortimore suggests these labour constraints could only be alleviated by *hiring* labour. Labour constraints mean low yields and insufficient food (Mortimore 1998: 104).

3 Sufficient yield to feed a family is impossible without some method of fertilizing the fields, and without cattle for draught power

Using cattle manure depends on the cash income used to buy the cattle in the first place. Synthetic fertilizers and hybrid high yield seeds also depend on cash income. As Binns *et al.* put it:

> the most important food production system in eastern and southern Africa, is [one] in which maize is grown as a staple subsistence crop ... This system is extremely labour intensive, relies heavily on cattle for draught power, and has relatively poor crop yields due to shortages of fertilizers and pesticides (both of which are costly).
>
> (2012: Kindle 2888 – see also English *et al.* 1994; Konde *et al.* 2001; Toulmin and Scoones 2001)

Those without access to large livestock cannot get adequate fertility by composting leafy matter without manure (Konde *et al.* 2001: 62). The success of the Machakos agricultural economy in Kenya is based on cash sales, allowing the purchase of cattle and synthetic fertilizers (English *et al.* 1994). In Zimbabwe, Mangwende, with ready access to commercial outlets in Harare, did better at soil fertility than Chivi, a more remote site (Chibudu *et al.* 2001). 'Access to both fertilizer and manure (through the purchase of livestock) is then critically dependent on getting access to cash' (Chibudu *et al.* 2001: 158).

4 Subsistence farmers cannot grow sufficient grain to last a whole year, they cannot store enough to last between harvests or cover bad seasons

Mortimore explains this. In dryland farming regions, grains store very well, with only 4 per cent losses per annum. So annual household food shortages are a puzzle. The reason is that households end up by selling some of the grain they have stored for their food supply. In Dagaceri, Nigeria, 73 per cent of households both sold and bought grain in a given year; selling to acquire cash and then buying in food later.

> [P]oor households have difficulty in producing a grain reserve. Their poverty also prevents them from maintaining it, as their urgent need for income (not to mention gifts, religious obligations like zakkat (tithes), taxation, or bribes) constantly makes demands on it.
> (Mortimore 1998: 106)

Why these constraints are not real

The chapters of this book will argue that these constraints do not explain the failure of African families to produce sufficient food. The real problems are not the ineluctable constraints of subsistence agriculture but the very malleable constraints of culture and technological information. The following points begin to explain why *Food Security for Rural Africa* does not endorse the critique of subsistence agriculture outlined above:

1. It is true that some African families lack sufficient *cropping* land. However there are many more who are suffering from under-nutrition who have a perfectly adequate amount of land. A doubling of cereal yields would secure sufficient calories for almost all households. This is a perfectly feasible target, using organic technologies. Many poor Africans are living in villages where a large part of the land is grazed by cattle owned by an elite. The cropping fields of the poor could be doubled by attending to this *political* barrier.
2. African families have quite enough labour for adequate subsistence production. Different technologies could help. For example *Mucuna pruriens* (a leguminous vine) as a living mulch, intercropped with maize to suppress

weeds, rather than daily weeding with a hoe. The supposed insufficiency of labour also comes from socially constructed cultural and institutional constraints that could be otherwise. In the past, children would scare birds on cereal crops, allowing a good harvest of drought hardy sorghum and millet. Now parents and the state alike insist that children must attend school. These crops have been abandoned because there is no one to protect the ripening harvest. Yet schools could close for a few months when the crop is ripening. These same children, whose welfare supposedly requires them to attend school, are stunted from malnutrition. It is not uncommon to find even 20 year olds in the villages *still attending high school*, while their family crops languish for lack of attention.

3   Manure from cattle and synthetic fertilizers are not the only paths to soil fertility. Even poor farmers, without cash savings, could multiply small livestock (poultry, guinea pigs, pigeons, rabbits) to provide manure and protein. These authors never mention human manure and composting toilets. When they are arguing the necessity for capital intensive cattle ownership they fail to mention intercropping with legumes. In other passages in their writings these authors know these alternative solutions work and have been promoted – with minimal uptake (Chibudu *et al*. 2001: 146). Yet they do not regard this lack of interest as any kind of a puzzle to be explored! Their conclusion is that the only farmers who *could* deal with soil fertility effectively are the ones who are doing so now, with the benefits of a cash income.

4   It is argued that the rural poor cannot store sufficient grain from their harvest to last a whole year. Daily exigencies will tempt the poor to dispose of their assets and end up short later in the year. This problem applies to cash income as well as to subsistence crops. Project design can be tailored to alleviate this problem.

Commercial farming as the foundation of agricultural productivity

There is another way in which these authors do not overcome the 'tired antithesis' of subsistence and commercial agriculture. While they recognize the necessary role of subsistence in a diverse sustainable livelihood, they think that adequate subsistence can only be attained in cases where commercial farming has taken off (Scoones *et al*. 2005). 'Access to livestock, labour, credit and markets are of particular importance in explaining which farmers are best able to maintain and improve the fertility of their soils' (Toulmin and Scoones 2001: 171).

Studies from a variety of regions of Africa, in countries such as Ethiopia, Nigeria, Kenya, Zimbabwe back up the claim that the farmers who are looking after their soil fertility and getting good yields are the farmers selling a surplus of cash crops. The pursuit of a cash income drives the farming reforms necessary to maximize yield. These farmers begin by trying to increase their yield on their surplus cash crops. 'Overall, cash-crop land receives the major share of both mineral and organic fertilizers applied' (Toulmin and Scoones 2001: 177).

Over time, these technologies spread to the household subsistence crops. Food security is also improved by the income from cash crops. Surplus commercial crops bring in cash. Cash can buy cattle, manure or inorganic fertilizer. This improves production. Some of this is sold, producing even more cash. Farmers may also purchase more cropping land. As Mortimore summarizes this argument: 'Only an increase in the profitability of primary production can justify the investments that are necessary to improve productivity and arrest degradation' (1998: 195; see also English et al. 1994).

Problems with the cash crop solution to rural poverty

There is much to be admired in the detailed comparisons of farming systems that have led to these conclusions. Nevertheless I will suggest two qualifications to this analysis.

The first is that the correlation between cash income and food security is weak. In the UK paradigm literature this issue is rarely addressed; there is a lot more on nutrient balances in soils. Machakos in Kenya is praised for having arrested a process of land degradation by embracing commercial agriculture. Production of basic staples has stabilized at 200 kg per person of maize equivalent – 'the level required for basic subsistence' (English et al. 1994: x). Accordingly, a CBS study 'found district children to be average for Kenya in terms of height for age and weight for height' (1994: 38). In other words, there must be 26 per cent of children under five who are stunted. Not exactly an impressive outcome. The second qualification is this. The cash used to purchase inputs and intensify farming does not *initially* come from the cash crops which these inputs fertilize. This process usually gets started because the successful farmer comes back to the village with savings from a period of well paid employment. It has been typical for men to invest in cattle while they are working, and retire early to manage their farms (Ferguson 1990). They may also have some savings in cash, which can be used to purchase inputs.

Konde et al. (2001) compare farmer households in Southern Ethiopia. TC is 36 years old and a comparatively richer farmer from the Ethiopian Highlands. He only inherited 0.2 hectares but has been able to buy more land and now has 3.5 hectares. He has eleven cattle, four of which are used for ploughing. Five of his cattle live at home on the farm and the others are loaned out for fattening. He sells these cattle and also makes money as a trader in consumer goods. This income has enabled him to increase his holdings and he is also able to buy 150 kg of synthetic fertilizer every year. He is also able to pay workers to help him in peak periods on the farm. Using this assistance, he has constructed contour bunds and spread manure and compost. All his fields are doing well in terms of nutrient balance – either neutral or positive (Konde et al. 2001: 68). TC is a farmer who has been able to purchase the capital requirements – land and cattle – to enable a productive and profitable production, to maintain soil fertility and increase yield. The cash required to start this process came from his trading activities off the farm.

By comparison, HS is 60 years old and also lives in the Ethiopian highlands. His cropping field is only a quarter of a hectare but rainfall is good. He used to own some cattle that he inherited from his father, but he has had to sell them all. Some were sold to pay for funerals and others at times when food was short. He now has a loan arrangement for a few cows. He fattens them for the owners and keeps the manure for his fields. He can only buy 2 kg of synthetic fertilizer in a year. The area he has planted out to enset (a root crop related to bananas) has been shrinking in recent years. He has had to harvest the plants prematurely due to crises of food shortage. He has also had to reduce the area planted to other root crops because he cannot manage to fertilize them adequately. Half his fields are in nutrient balance but half are losing nitrogen every year(Konde *et al*. 2001: 68). This is a farmer who is unable to produce sufficient food for his family to live. He is running down his farming assets to try to maintain sufficient food supplies. The fact that he does not own cattle is creating a barrier which prevents him from maintaining the fertility of his soils.

Well, maybe this is what diverse livelihoods is all about. Profitable involvement in the cash economy is required to boost subsistence production and food security. However, opportunities for off-farm income are *not available* to large numbers of the poor. Averages for unemployment start at 20 per cent (in the most wealthy countries of the region) and go up from there, reaching up to 80 per cent in rural areas (Binns *et al*. 2012: Kindle 999). This underclass are the ones facing most hunger. The problem is not the research itself but the *interpretation*. Authors in the UK paradigm take these findings to mean that facilitating commercial projects is the only way to improve food security (and agricultural productivity) in rural Africa. Yet what they are describing as a solution can only work for the *richer* villagers.

Let us consider which villagers in Africa could embrace the UK paradigm. For example Konde *et al*. (2001) presents a table of rich and poor farmers in an Ethiopian district – the 'poor' are two-thirds of all households. The poor hold an average of one head of cattle and 0.2 head of sheep; the rich, 6 to 9 cattle and 1.4 sheep. The external income of the poor is 61 shillings per annum, the rich get 385 to 700 shillings. The poor do not have sufficient livestock to maintain soil fertility using manure and they do not have sufficient income to buy synthetic fertilizers. Mortimore reports that in the Machakos district of Kenya, 62 per cent of farmers were able to own an ox drawn plough, and 38 per cent were too poor to manage this expense (1998: 168). Chibudu *et al*. (2001) compare two districts of Zimbabwe. Mangwende is close to the capital Harare and serviced by good roads. There is also good rainfall. 'The growth of the Harare market and the good and relatively cheap transport access has meant that the trade in vegetables has become exceptionally lucrative' (Chibudu *et al*. 2001: 145).

By contrast, the district of Chivi is more remote and has less rainfall. These differences are reflected in variations in the use of manure and bought fertilizer. In Mangwende, 96 per cent of farmers apply bought fertilizer to their home cropping field. Only 20 per cent do so in Chivi (Chibudu *et al*. 2001: 144). The Mangwende farmers are working according to the UK paradigm, strengthening their subsistence production with cash brought in through their commercial farming. The Chivi farmers are unable to do this, locked into soil degradation, with underproduction of subsistence the outcome. In Mangwende the richer farmers have a positive nutrient balance in nitrogen of 51 kg per hectare, and the poor are getting a negative balance of minus 6 kg per hectare. In Chivi, the richer farmers are getting a negative balance of minus 13 kg per hectare! The poorer farmers are doing even worse with minus 28 kg per hectare. We can see in the comparison of districts that the UK paradigm solution is working particularly well where there are good roads and good markets. In both districts, those doing better are the richer farmers, leaving a majority without the resources to grow adequate food.

The unhappy truth is that the UK paradigm does not really have any answers for African farmers who do not start into their farming with some capital earned in the broader market economy. Yet given underemployment, this is a sizeable portion of the population. In rare moments of candour, authors from the UK paradigm acknowledge that given their analysis, rural food sufficiency is an impossible target for most. Agricultural readjustment will mean that many of the rural poor will move to urban centres.

> Rather than trying to stem the flow, policies need to support those leaving the land, and refocus on agriculture in different ways for those who remain as rural producers ... a selective regeneration of agriculture by entrepreneurial smallholders might be feasible, but only if these farmers are given the opportunity to [accumulate] the land and productive inputs they need to become surplus producers.
> (Scoones *et al.* 2005: 9–10; see also Binns *et al.* 2012; English *et al.* 1994: Konde *et al.* 2001)

In other words, the poor, who are unable to feed themselves, should be urged to move to town, where there are no jobs and no unemployment benefits. The land that they farm should be bought up by more successful farmers, aided by the state. It is not surprising that many rural Africans see this as a bad bargain. As Potts remarks: 'Throughout Africa, rights to rural land have been, and remain, absolutely vital as a security net for urban people' (Potts 2000: 828).

Given the unlikelihood of jobs growth sufficient to absorb this rural under class in permanent urban employment and the equal unlikelihood of generous welfare payments, *Food Security for Rural Africa* is written to consider how this underclass might actually feed themselves. The research coming out of the UK paradigm shows some successes for a few – while for the most part, food insecurity is still a way of life. Where well funded projects have almost all been devoted to turning smallholders into successful petit entrepreneurs, it would be a surprise if none had been successful. Yet it is by now high time that projects which aim to improve household food provision *without cash income being necessary*, were tried out.

As leftist critique

Authors from the UK paradigm see their work as a leftist critique of the dominant neo-liberal Washington consensus. After all, their founding text is called *Putting the Last First* and they emphasize the necessity for the genuine participation of the poor. They see the neo-liberal departure of the state as a mistake where the poor are concerned. While there may have been some positive consequences from liberalization for those who have been able to get into a profitable export market, even these success stories are not without flaw, with low wages paid to workers and price collapses on the world market. For poorer farmers, the withdrawal of state support through parastatals, subsidies and extension systems has 'increased impoverishment for many' (Scoones, Devereux and Haddad 2005: 4; see also Binns *et al.* 2012). The removal of fertilizer subsidies has drastically reduced yields (e.g. Konde *et al.* 2001: 74).

UK paradigm policy recommendations seek to remedy these errors of neo-liberalism. Binns *et al.* (2012) provide a typical list. Governments in Africa should help farmers to increase production by 'paying them good prices for their crops' (Kindle 867), suggesting price control or subsidies. Food subsidies in the European Union and North America should be wound back so that developing country farmers have better access to these export markets. It is necessary to 'improve the transport systems' and 'marketing' (Kindle 878). While 'African governments cannot afford the financial outlay', rich country governments should come to the party and fund this (Kindle 878). Permanent rural markets are required to give African farmers the incentive to produce a surplus for sale (Kindle 3259). Investment in agricultural intensification should include support for GM technology (Kindle 3373). Government will conduct research and promote high tech options through extension services. These recommendations are repeated constantly by authors in the UK paradigm. Scoones summarizes the conditions necessary to improve agricultural production as 'access to markets, good quality infrastructure, knowledge and technology and secure tenure' (2001: 35). Konde *et al.* have a similar recipe to deal with soil fertility issues in Ethiopia: 'Increasing fertilizer inputs to crop production in the shoka fields remains a major practical and policy challenge, requiring attention to credit institutions, infrastructure development and input supply market reform' (2001: 76).

The implication is not that governments should restore the fertilizer subsidies of a previous era. Instead, they should facilitate the purchase of fertilizer (for commercial production) via loans. The government will drive down the price of fertilizer by improving roads and engineering a more competitive market environment for agricultural inputs. Access to credit and markets will drive production increases. Public-private partnerships will undercut uncompetitive traders. Small packages of fertilizer will be made available, through micro credit, to those with smallholdings (Toulmin and Scoones 2001: 203).

Writers in the UK paradigm occasionally endorse state intervention with price controls and subsidies. This is a marked departure from the position of mainstream economics. For example Scoones *et al.* maintain: 'Addressing coordination and market failures ... requires support for regulated monopolies, franchises, trader and farmer associations, combined with price guarantees, price support and/or input/output/credit subsidies' (2005: 4).

While these various settings for government intervention are a crucial aspect of the UK paradigm, the emphasis is also on bottom up local projects which might fit with their analysis of the problems and solutions. The aim is to fund projects to kick-start commercial production. The intention is not the 'commercialization' of agriculture that mainstream economists promote. Instead it is the strengthening of commercial agriculture *as but one aspect* of a 'diverse livelihoods' strategy. Yet strangely, there is no faith in projects to strengthen *subsistence* as part of a diverse livelihood strategy. As Binns *et al.* state unequivocally: 'approaches must be grounded in effective entrepreneurship if tangible progress is to be made on the ground' (2012: Kindle 8145).

In fact, *successful* projects designed to kick-start entrepreneurial development are quite rare. At the end of *Africa: Diversity and Development*, Binns *et al.* cite two projects in the Durban region of South Africa that meet their criteria. One of these is to facilitate a trader's market at a transport hub. While this project is relatively successful, the authors acknowledge that it helps the privileged and does not touch the poor. A project that is claimed to have been better targeted is located in Zimbabwe, near the town of Masvingo – with a population of 10,000. Traditionally honey is collected to make beer. With the high price of honey, it made sense to expand this practice and commercialize it more fully. Seventy members of the community joined together to create a collective, making the hives and processing the honey. The local mission has provided training and 'critically, a market outlet, as it transports the honey to local retailers in Masvingo' (2012: Kindle 7907). Income from honey sales can be 150 per cent higher than that from traditional crop farming. This is a part time activity so the members continue to grow food on their subsistence fields.

This sounds like an excellent project. Nevertheless, consider the following. The project is successful as a 'managed business' project. The continued managerial input of the mission forms a crucial element; not something that can be readily replicated. The project is premised on the proximity of the community to a major town, something which is by no means common. It has improved the lives of a mere *seventy* households in a community of 10,000 persons. It would be unlikely that this number could be increased – as the local market for honey will have been saturated. As we shall attempt to establish in the following chapters, a project which had aimed to increase subsistence production might have made a lot more difference to food security for a lot more members of the community. Lately, villagers all over Zimbabwe have decided that producing and selling honey is the way to boost household income. Honey is marketed by the side of the road and by many local cooperatives. I have visited a cooperative that has the latest equipment for large scale processing and for quality control. It has not done well. Competition from other countries and other regions of Zimbabwe has wound back sales after an initial flurry.

Overall, my response to the UK paradigm is as follows. It is unlikely that African governments or international donors will provide the money to make these state based policy interventions work – for example road funding, market building, credit subsidies, price controls. The strategy of kick-starting commercial agriculture in rural areas has a long history and it is very rare for any of these projects to work. The success stories described in these accounts are of whole districts that for various reasons have been unusually well favoured for commercial development – such as Machakos in Kenya. Even in such cases, the favoured strategy of the UK paradigm is only available to those who have developed their capital through well paid work away from their farms. There is no solution for the vast majority of the poor in any of this. Hoping that they will leave farming and get a job in town is not a solution. Writers in this paradigm display a disturbing lack of interest in the many low cost technologies that are available for subsistence producers.

Subsistence agriculture – the African context

In the next section I will begin to outline some of the key ideas of *Food Security for Rural Africa*.

Worker-peasants and farmer housewives

In much of Southern and Eastern Africa the colonial dispensation has created a very different pattern of land ownership from that which obtains in other parts of the developing world; tipping the scales in favour of subsistence. White commercial farmers took up a large part of the best land in these countries (Potts 2000). At the same time, colonial governments allocated some land for 'native reserves'. Employment for black men meant travelling from these native reserves to take up jobs in mining, industry or agriculture. In this 'circular migration' young men left home to get work, coming back to their villages for holidays and returning permanently on retirement, often by the age of forty (Ferguson 1990; Potts 2000). Women and children stayed in the villages, farming the land, along with men who were unable to get a job.

Subsistence agriculture has been a key part of this arrangement. Low wages have meant that it was not possible for African men to earn enough to pay for their families to eat. Subsistence production has been an economic necessity. The rural tenure arrangements set up by colonial governments were designed to facilitate household food provision. In theory, chiefs hold the land in trust for their communities. In practice, families hold the land as cropping plots, residential land and community grazing areas, with land passing down from parents to their children. This land cannot be sold. The community is meant to make sure that all families have a plot for subsistence cropping. This has been an economic symbiosis, with paid work away from home providing for cash needs, while household food provision has allowed for the 'reproduction' of the working class – feeding the next generation of workers. A system of 'worker-peasants and farmer housewives' as Potts calls it (2000).

46 *The UK paradigm and alternatives*

There have been a number of reasons why this arrangement is much resented. One is that black families have been forced into subsistence agriculture because the wages paid to black workers have been insufficient to support an African family. The solution most black Africans would like to see is employment and an adequate wage. These rural/urban divisions were originally set up to prevent the formation of a strong black working class, to force Africans to live half of their lives in the villages, breaking their industrial muscle (Potts 2000). To achieve true citizenship, it is believed, Africans must live in just the one place with sufficient income to pay for their food needs. These political considerations have made African post-colonial governments ready to listen to international economic advisers who have promoted commercialization. The system of low wages, subsistence agriculture and circular migration is seen as a holdover from the most oppressive days of colonialism (Potts 2000). The arguments of international experts have been all about the great leap forward from pre-industrial subsistence economies, dogged by poverty, to the affluence of modern capitalist market economies.

The argument for commercialization as the solution to problems of rural poverty has been monumentally effective (Department of Agriculture 2002; FARA 2006; MAAIF 2000; Magadzi 2008; Parliamentarians 2006). In the 1970s the World Bank argued that 'African farmers needed to be modernized and monetized' (Williams 1996: 141). In 1987, the South African Development Bank provided loans to subsistence farmers who aspired to become commercial smallholders. In 1993 the World Bank advised the incoming majority government in South Africa with the same formula. This orientation to rural development is fostered by New Partnership for Africa's Development (NEPAD) through the development of the Framework for African Agricultural Productivity (FAAP) and the Comprehensive African Agricultural Development Programme (CAADP).

> Increasing agricultural productivity implies a transformation from traditional to modern agriculture, which involves both technical change and the presence of input, seasonal finance and marketing systems to increase farm production and deliver it to consumers at a competitive price.
>
> (FARA 2006: 8)

National governments in Africa have brought their agricultural policy in line with this dictum. For example the Ugandan Plan for Modernisation of Agriculture states its mission to be: 'eradicating poverty by transforming subsistence agriculture to commercial agriculture' (MAIFF 2000: vi). This faith in commercialization is shared by the new black middle class and endorsed in academic commentary: 'With policies to improve access to inputs, such as fertilizers or fuel, and the support of governments, Africa can move from subsistence agriculture to commercial farming' (Webersik and Wilson 2008: 406). 'To retain viable livelihoods, small producers ... need to move from a focus on production for home consumption and occasional marketing of surpluses to production for the market' (Chipeta *et al.* 2008: 8; see also FAO 2003a; Leavy and Poulton 2007; Maxwell and Fernando 1989; Wolter 2008).

Growth in the agricultural economy is expected to provide the poor with employment. Increased food production will drive down urban food prices. The rural economy will pick up as farmers invest locally (FAO 2003a; FARA 2006; Magadzi 2008). The South African government aims to 'foster the participation of all in the mainstream economy' (Department of Agriculture 2002: 25). The inadequacy of subsistence provision is blamed on the 'narrow production base' rather than on the absence of interventions to support subsistence farming (Department of Agriculture 2002: 26). Household food security is to be improved by 'commercialising agriculture to increase income and employment generation' (Department of Agriculture 2002: 30).

At the level of the provincial departments of agriculture, this approach is reflected in funding priorities. The 2008 Budget speech from the Limpopo Minister of Agriculture shows how this works out (Magadzi 2008). The funding going to interventions to improve household food provision (subsistence) is minuscule compared to funding investments for commercial strategies. The total budget for agriculture was approximately one billion rand and only R5 million went to household food production initiatives, delivering support packages to only 1,800 households. Meanwhile, to take just one example, a tea plantation was restored at a cost of R75 million – to the benefit of 2,450 workers. For the funding nominated for household food security, the priority was still to commercialize production. For example, layer projects which provided good quality layers and a start up package of layer mash so that the poor could *sell* eggs to earn money.

The persistence of subsistence agriculture

Despite a half century in which subsistence agriculture has been vilified and neglected, it is still a huge part of agricultural production in all these African countries. It contributes much to the wellbeing of rural African families, whether or not it is the option they would choose if they had a better alternative (Potts 2000). Let us look at the situation in South Africa, the country where the departure from subsistence agriculture has been most marked. Even here subsistence production in rural areas is still persistent (Cousins 2007; Perrett 2001; Shackleton *et al.* 2001). Non-market food provision has been estimated at between a quarter and half of food provision in studies of the villages (Shackleton *et al.* 2001: 592). More than 600,000 South African households engage in farming to produce most of their food and another million add to their diet by farming – 15 per cent of households in total (Watkinson and Makgetla 2002: 2). Poorer households are more likely to be involved in growing some of their own food – 39 per cent of the ultra poor; 22 per cent of the poor and less for higher income groups (Watkinson and Makgetla 2002: 3). In summary: 'Farming for own consumption is widespread in South Africa and can be understood as a strategy by poor rural households to save income' (Watkinson and Makgetla 2002: 3).

There is a reason why subsistence agriculture has been abandoned in some parts of South Africa. The post-apartheid government committed itself to old age pensions and child support. So villagers can now get by without growing their own food. Yet abandonment of subsistence agriculture is by no means universal. For example in Limpopo province most villagers still grow crops. Even in provinces where this change has proceeded furthest, people are still using their communal lands to collect wood and graze their cattle. About a third of the villagers in these provinces are also using their large residential blocks to grow food.

It may seem that subsistence agriculture has been abandoned in parts of South Africa because the welfare alternative is feeding villagers adequately, without the necessity for subsistence household production. However, as the following detailed example will explain, this is very far from the case. As noted above, 27 per cent of children in South Africa are stunted from malnutrition (Department of Agriculture 2002: 22–23). They are using the pensions to buy enough basic carbohydrate, but they are not getting everything else they need – it is too expensive. Let us consider the following example from the field work.

In 2014, I stayed in Noqhekwana village in Eastern Cape with two unmarried sisters. Thembi and Pamela were mainly living on the child support grants, with some assistance from a sister working in town. Between them they look after five children. They do not grow any of their own food. They have six goats, kept to be sold if there is a family emergency. Once a year they will attend a ceremony where they get some goat to eat. They go shopping once a month – after they get their child support payment. They buy five tins of fish, and chicken pieces to eat three times a month. They do not buy any beef or mutton. They do not buy dried beans or peanuts but get five cans of baked beans. So there is not much protein for two adults and five children. In their monthly shop they buy a 12.5 kg bag of maize meal, a 25 kg bag of white rice, 12.5 kg of white flour, a 10 kg bag of potatoes and 10 kg of white sugar. They do not buy any milk. They get two litres of sunflower oil for cooking. The vegetables they buy are drumhead white cabbages, onions and tomatoes. They also buy some peppers grown in the village. This inadequate nutrition is typical for those who are living on welfare. The diet is short on protein (and iron). There are few raw fruits (vitamin C) and even cooked leafy vegetables are uncommon (vitamin A). When Thembi and Pamela cook a cabbage they boil it and tip the water out, wasting the vitamin A. Tomatoes and green peppers are a rare treat. Like the cabbage, they are cooked, destroying vitamin C. All carbohydrates are refined; B and E vitamins and fibre have all been removed.

Nor have the villagers of South Africa abandoned their subsistence agriculture to take jobs in the commercial economy. Unemployment is just as bad now as it was when the apartheid government was overthrown, up to 60 per cent in rural areas (Cousins 2007: 222). The communal cropping land in the villages has often reverted to weedy growth (bushing) as in North West province or been taken over by the richer minority of rural villagers who can afford large herds of cattle, as in Eastern Cape. These richer villagers do not need any help – their success does nothing to improve the lives of the poor.

The South African situation is unique. No other African government can afford such generous welfare provision. Accordingly in other African countries the continuation of subsistence agriculture is not negotiable for the poor. There is no welfare support and no employment to provide an income to buy food.

The economic argument for subsistence agriculture

A common argument for commercial farming could be summarized as follows. Each hour that these rural smallholders work (growing food for their families) could be more profitably spent (earn more money) if they were growing a high value commercial crop. For example, if they grew maize on their one hectare they might get $400 when they sold their crop at the end of the season, but if they were to spend the same amount of time growing cotton, they could get $500. The basic cereal crops that farmers need for their family food are being grown more efficiently in other places (with combine harvesters and expensive inputs). The value per hectare of these basic food crops is low, compared to the value of crops that require more labour. For example cotton, coffee, tobacco, cacao, tea or flowers. So goes the argument. We can certainly agree with this up to a point. If a rural smallholder farmer was to spend their season growing a basic food crop and then sell it at the farm gate, chances are that they would make less money than if they spent the season growing a high value commercial crop. Consequently, proponents of commercial farming conclude, it is a mug's game growing crops for family consumption. Your work would be worth more money if you spent your time growing a commercial crop.

The answer to this argument also seems so obvious that it is surprising it is not more widely cited. It turns on the difference between *the farm gate price* for farm products and the market cost to consumers – *the retail price*. The farm gate price is what the farmer can get when they sell their produce at the farm gate – for example $10 for a 50 kg bag of maize grains. The retail price is what they would have to pay if they bought the same weight of maize at the shop – for example $20 for a 50 kg bag of maize flour. To make it sensible to farm for the market, the farm gate price of the commercial crop has to be high enough to cover the *retail price* of the food crop that the farmer *has decided not to grow*. In reality, commercial crops are rarely worth so much. Let us go back to our example again. Say on their one hectare the African smallholder might spend the season growing two tonnes of maize (which would be worth $400 at the farm gate) or instead grow cotton (which might be worth $500 at the farm gate). Assume that to feed their family for a whole year, they will need two tonnes of maize. They would not get it at the farm gate price of $400. Instead the retail price in the local market could be $800. Having sold their cotton for $500, they would need an extra $300 for the family's maize supply. This is a fictional example, so let us look at some real figures and examples.

A study of the value chain in Kenya found that the retail price for sifted maize flour is often up to *double* the farm gate price of maize kernels. In 2008–9, the average price of maize grains per kilo at the farm gate was Ksh 21.50 (Kirimi *et al.* 2011: 38). In the same two years, the average price of maize flour per kilo in shops was Ksh 37 (Kirimi *et al.* 2011: 63). Between 1994 and 2009, the retail price was frequently double the farm gate price (Kirimi *et al.* 2011: 63). In other words, if your holding is just big enough to grow all the maize your family needs, your cash crop would have to earn you *double* the farm gate value of your maize, if you wanted to *buy* maize to feed your family. That is a very big ask.

Here is another real world example. Tschirley and Kabwe argue for the potential of cotton as a cash crop in Zambia and argue that it is a better crop than maize to enable 'food security'; 'cotton is almost entirely a smallholder crop. Its potential role in poverty alleviation and food security is, thus, very large' (2007: 1).

Where the poorer farmers are concerned, their argument is unconvincing. The bottom quintile of farmers have a median of 0.40 ha in cotton and 0.70 ha in maize. The top quintile have a median of 1.22 ha in cotton and 2.07 ha in maize (Tschirley and Kabwe 2007: 12). The poorest 20 per cent of farmers would be struggling to get sufficient yield in maize from 0.70 ha to feed a family of six. For these farmers, it would make sense to grow more maize and less cotton. In their study of six villages, Tschirley and Kabwe divided the population into four groups based on the relative size of their cropping fields devoted to cotton. The third group (42 per cent of their sample) had an average of 1.5 ha planted to cotton and were making an average of $115 per annum. The fourth group (34 per cent of the sample) had an average of 0.5 ha devoted to cotton and were making only $81 per annum. The amount earned from cotton is negligible compared to the amount they would have to spend on the food crops that cotton had replaced.

Tschirley and Kabwe miss these rather obvious points and tackle the issue by comparing the price these farmers could get for maize with the price they could get for cotton. The market returns on maize (after expenses are deducted) are only ZKW 474,000 per hectare. The comparable returns on cotton are between ZKW 542,000 per hectare and ZKW 787,000 per hectare (depending on the market). Selling maize on the market they would be getting about half the returns that they could get on cotton (in a good year for cotton) and a bit less than cotton (in a bad year). So, Tschirley and Kabwe conclude, cotton is preferable as a crop for food security! We could well arrive at a different conclusion. Given the difference between the retail price of maize flour and the farm gate price (as argued above), there would be no point in substituting cash production of cotton for *subsistence* production of maize. We know from the study carried out in Kenya (Kirimi *et al.* 2011) that the retail price of maize is likely to be double the farm gate price. The farm gate price for a hectare of maize is ZKW 474,000, so the retail price would be ZKW 948,000. The farm gate price for a hectare of cotton can be as low as ZKW 542,000. Even in a good year it is ZKW 787,000. Not enough to pay for the amount of maize flour they *could have grown* for home consumption. As a *food security* strategy, growing and selling cotton would make no sense. The argument constructed by Tschirley and Kabwe is at best relevant to *surplus* production after all food needs have been met. In that context (and in fact here we must be talking about the richest quarter of the farmers) cotton is a preferable *cash crop*. But the farmers with most food insecurity are in a very different position. Their best strategy is to use all their cropping fields to grow food for household consumption.

So let us now look at a final example. In 2014, I was researching a project in the Eastern Cape of South Africa. The project was helping local households to grow fruit trees. Many households had been in the project for eight years and their trees were producing well. Yet typical earnings were considerably less than R500 per month. These households could have been growing maize on their home stands and using it for family consumption. Their home plots were about 0.675 hectares, so at two tonnes per hectare, their yield could have been about 1.35 tonnes, enough to feed a family of six people. What would be the cost in rands to purchase 1.35 tonnes of maize meal in the shops? The cheapest maize in 25 kg bags in 2014 was R100 per bag. So to purchase 1.35 tonnes you would need 54 × 25 kg bags or R5,400 in a year. This is a monthly cost of R450. This is a rough guide to the amount that the trees from the household gardens would have to produce in cash to make a fruit tree strategy financially viable – by comparison with a strategy based on just growing maize. In fact, most families were getting quite a bit less than this from their tree crops.

So why does this obvious argument get so widely ignored? Economists' thinking is influenced by the kind of farming they know best, large scale commercial farms. Consider the farmer in Iowa growing wheat on a hundred hectares, using farm machinery, fossil fuels, synthetic pesticides and fertilizers. The amount of maize they produce on their farm dwarfs what their family needs for its own subsistence. The money they make from their farming is far in excess of the money needed to pay for their family's food needs. It makes sense for these farmers to think about the most efficient use of their time because every hour produces a lot of dollar value. If they were to use some of their time grinding their own flour, and growing foods for home consumption, this would be inefficient. The dollar value they would realize by doing this 'menial' and 'unmechanized' labour would be negligible compared to the dollar value they could realize in their main business, an expensive hobby.

By contrast, the African smallholder family is unlikely to have much more land than what they would need to feed the family. The land available for dryland cropping is usually one or two hectares and rarely more than three hectares per household (Congressi and Kennedy 2009; Rural Poverty Portal 2012). For example the top quartile of smallholder farmers in Zambia have an average of 5.81 hectares in cropping land, the next quartile 2.75 hectares, the third quartile 1.60 hectares and the lowest quartile 0.74 hectares. The average for all smallholders is 2.73 hectares (Jayne *et al.* 2006: 333; Milligan *et al.* 2011: 361). On these figures, the bottom quarter and maybe up to a half of the rural population is struggling to provide sufficient carbohydrate production on the fields they have available to them. If they do have more land they should certainly be using it to grow whichever cash crop fetches the most money for their hours of labour. But on the land they need for their own family consumption, the most economically sensible strategy is to do just that and to ensure that this farming does not just produce staples but everything they need for a diverse diet.

This argument produces a feeling of vertigo. It is very hard to believe that this obvious conclusion has not been reached many times before. One of the ways in which the economists' argument seems to make sense is this. Let us compare the efficiency of farming – the subsistence farmer producing maize compared to the Iowa maize farmer with their harvesters and inputs. Who is producing more food and economic value (what the food would cost) for each hour that they work? Well clearly the Iowa farmer. So the African farmer should buy their maize on the global market from the Iowa farmer, while spending their working days growing a crop that requires a lot of labour to produce value – say cotton or coffee. Let us say, for a fictional example, that the African farmer produces maize worth $3 in an hour of work and the Iowa farmer produces maize worth $10. Yet coffee is a crop that is hard to mechanize and the African farmer can produce $5 value in coffee in an hour, the same as the Iowa farmer. It seems like eminent good sense that the African farmer will grow coffee and the Iowa farmer grow maize.

But actually when you look at the situation more closely this argument begins to unravel. Let us consider two ways in which our fictional example may not stand up.

(a) The African family needs maize to eat. To buy the maize that the African farmer can produce in one hour, they will need to pay $6 at the shop. Meaning that it is better to be growing maize to eat than growing coffee to sell.

OR (b) The cost of maize in the shop is $4 – to buy the amount of maize that the African farmer can grow in an hour. So it seems to make sense to be growing coffee ($5 an hour farm gate price) and buying maize ($4 retail). However, and here is the catch. There is a limit to the amount of coffee that you can sell on the world market when the farm gate price is $5. If this African family (and others in a similar position) start growing coffee, the value of their hour's work will fall to $3 per hour – coffee would be a glut on the market. In that event it would again be more sensible to be growing maize, which you would have to buy for $4.

The way that situation (b) manifests itself is that there is no work for the African farmer that would pay them well enough to make it sensible to spend their time working for money – rather than growing a subsistence crop. In statistical terms, this appears as the unemployment rate. The reality is that in all these countries unemployment in the rural areas is at least 40 per cent, and a lot higher if we take into account those not bothering to look for work. Neither the private economy nor various attempts by governments to kick-start the economy have worked to change this. As Ntebeza and Hall (2007) point out, the economy 'is failing dismally to absorb the unemployed as well as new work seekers, and this is unlikely to change in the near to medium future' (Walker 2007: 134). In such a situation the African farmer has plenty of time in which to grow their subsistence crop – however inefficient they are compared to the Iowa farmer. But they do not have any option to use their time to earn more dollar value than the retail cost of their subsistence crop.

As explained in the first chapter, it has been estimated that to keep the rate of unemployment *constant* in South Africa, economic growth must be at least 6 per cent per year (Reilly 2006). Without more than a 6 per cent growth rate, the rate of unemployment will go up. Yet no feasible government intervention is likely to make the economy grow at 10 per cent and actually *reduce* unemployment. We could get into a whole discussion here about the way the world is set up so that the poor of the world are not getting what they need – but there is no work available for these same people to be paid to produce these necessities. This is a terrible tragedy but it is not the topic of this book. The question is, *in this economic context*, does it matter that the productivity (in dollars per hour) of the African farmer is lower than the productivity of the farmer in Iowa? Well actually, it is does not matter at all, the African farmer has got plenty of time to do this work and nothing better to do – nothing that would make them sufficient income to pay for the food their family needs.

Vignette B
How much land do you need?

Terry Leahy

This vignette is concerned with the amount of land that would be necessary for a rural family (of six people). I am taking it that their aim is to provide all their food needs through a diverse range of cereal, tree and vegetable crops. The vignette also considers the land requirements to provide food and space for small livestock. Finally, it includes a discussion of how much land is required as a woodlot to allow a sustainable harvest of building timber and firewood for a family of this size.

How much land is required for cropping?

The following calculations are based on quantities made use of by the Malawi agriculture department. The calculation is for a family of six – with three adults and three children. It assumes a rainfall of at least 500 mm per annum. For dryer conditions, you would need more land.

The Malawi department of agriculture estimates that to feed one adult for a year you will need to harvest 6 × 50 kg bags of maize kernels. In other words, 300 kg of maize kernels.

For a family of 6:

    3 Adults = 3 × 300 = 900 kg
    3 Children = 3 × 150 = 450 kg

Total = 1,350 kg of maize kernels is needed for the full year for the whole family.

Smallholder farmers are typically getting about one tonne per hectare in the villages. They are unable to afford synthetic fertilizer. However, it would be reasonable for a project to aim at a much higher yield, using some fairly simple low cost techniques. To be on the safe side let us estimate a yield of two tonnes per hectare.

If the yield is 2 tonnes per hectare (forty bags per hectare), how many hectares do you need to get 1,350 kg (1.35 tonnes)?

0.675 hectares is required for the cropping field.

How much land is required for the vegetables and chickens?

What is also required is a garden for vegetables and a place for chickens or other small livestock (for example a fish pond, pigeons, rabbits, guinea pigs) and for the house itself. Let us assume that the family has 1,000 square metres (a hectare is 10,000 square metres) for this purpose. A big housing block in suburban Australia. This is probably generous. They could likely do it on slightly less land.

0.1 hectares is required for the house, home garden and small livestock.

How much land is required for the orchard?

The family will need an orchard of fruit trees, nut trees, legume trees, shrubs, vines and the like. They will also use this area for free range for the poultry (probably in rotation – not all at once). Let us assume that this is also 0.1 ha. There would be plenty of produce from this area and an excess to swap with neighbours or sell to a local market.

0.1 hectares is required for the orchard.

How much land is required for the woodlot?

The family will also need a woodlot to provide fodder and mulch, fuel wood and timber, as well as habitat for pest eating species and bees. Shackleton, along with Dovie and Witkowski, has investigated the quantity of woodland required to provide fuel wood for an African household. The research is in South Africa, in Limpopo province, with a rainfall of 670 mm per annum (Dovie *et al.* 2004; Shackleton 1993: 247). Shackleton estimates the total woody mass of the community woodland as 18,907 kg per hectare. Making use of a range of other studies he estimates the sustainable annual yield as 3 per cent of this amount, which is 567 kg of wood per hectare available as fuel (Shackleton 1993: 252). For this region, household use of wood as fuel was found to be 692 kg per person per year (Dovie *et al.* 2004: 123). Estimates for other sites in Africa (and around the world in other developing countries) are close to this figure. So a family of six would need 7.3 hectares.

This is a sobering conclusion. The implication is that many rural areas of Africa are not sufficiently resourced with woodlands for fuel collection. Woodlands are being harvested unsustainably. As this research also shows, even when electric power is connected to a household, the amount of wood being used for cooking does not drop. Even when members of a family are employed and could conceivably buy cooking fuel, they do not actually do this. The use of fuel wood remains the same because it is the cheapest option for poor rural households (Dovie *et al.* 2004).

These figures are calculated for areas with the kind of rainfall typical of much of Africa. Where rainfall is higher, more woody mass is produced. The amount can well be double (Freudenberger *et al.* 2004). As well, planting with fast growing fuel wood species can improve the production of firewood. An established woodlot is more productive than the indigenous woodland that Shackleton is writing about.

56 Vignette B: how much land do you need?

In many places, original indigenous vegetation has been cleared and it may make sense to plant quick growing eucalyptus or acacia species. In Australia the annual yield from a plantation of eucalyptus has been found to be four tonnes per hectare (with a ten year rotation), even on sites with a low annual rainfall, comparable to the African villages. Harvesting dead and fallen timber from an indigenous forest in Australia, where eucalypts are dominant, produces a yield of 800 kilograms per hectare per year (Freudenberger et al. 2004). What these figures suggest is that the productivity of a woodlot can be improved by growing selected introduced species, well adapted to dry conditions.

For the purposes of this account, I will assume that the family is mainly harvesting from indigenous woodland in a low rainfall area, but has supplemented the original woodland with some woodlot plantings of eucalyptus and wattle species. These have been established on land that was originally cleared for grazing. The yield of the woodland and woodlot together will be assumed to be 700 kilograms per hectare, enough to support one person.

6 hectares is required for the woodlot.

Total area required

So the total area required would be 0.675 (cropping field) + 0.1 (vegetables, house and small livestock) + 0.1 (orchard) + 6 (woodlot) = 6.875 ha for a family of six, where rainfall is more than 500 mm per year.

The implication of these figures for the countries in Africa where I have worked is as follows.

For the most part, holdings for cropping fields are close to adequate, but only if sustainable agriculture techniques are being used to boost and maintain production.

The land required for orchards, vegetables and small livestock is larger than some residential stands but many residential areas are adequate for this purpose. In planning for rural villages housing blocks should always be at least 0.2 hectares.

Fuel wood supplies are very variable. The use of grazing land to grow wood supply is a problem in many communities, as cattle and goats impair the productivity of this resource where fuel is concerned. Other communities have adequate wooded land, but this is under pressure as wealthier villages expand their cattle herds. In many cases, all current grazing land should really be turned over to grow wood for cooking! This is a very difficult proposition to implement, given the local power of cattle owners.

Acknowledgements

Acknowledgements to Ezra Mbendera for cropping calculations from Malawi. Acknowledgements to Unathi Sihlahla for helpful suggestions where woodlots are concerned.

3 Hunger as a fatal strategy – a Zambian case study

Terry Leahy and Debbie Jean Brown

We have been tempted to call this chapter, 'The Absent Goat'. One of our authors makes regular contributions to OXFAM. Every few months, he is invited to contribute by 'buying a goat' for Africa. A smallholder rural family can breed from their goat and sell the offspring, milking the goat at the same time. One wonders why the family does not have a goat already. Rural villages in Africa usually have goats, and these are most likely to be found on the community grazing land. Why is it that a large number of villagers do not *own* any of these goats? We could ask the same questions about numerous other issues. Why are villagers short of vitamin A when traditional African cultures made use of a variety of indigenous and introduced weedy vegetables that are still available today? Why do they only get a decent meal of protein every few months when every house owns a small flock of chickens?

This chapter is an attempt to answer these kinds of questions. While a large part of this book is devoted to explaining solutions that can work to relieve food insecurity, this chapter is about the social context in which food insecurity is the most likely outcome. It is about the social landscape in which food security projects have to work. While most discussions of poverty see it as something imposed from the outside, which requires outside assistance to manage, the following discussion attempts to shift the focus. How does *local culture* get caught up in a socially constructed system that *ends up* with food insecurity as a regular and predictable outcome?

We will be arguing that the Zambian villagers have created an ideal for food provisioning which links food security to a particular kind of moral performance. What is morally appropriate is hard work in the cash economy and disciplined scientific practice (as it is locally understood) in the subsistence economy. An outcome is to constantly run short of food, something which is experienced as an unfortunate failure of reality to meet reasonable expectations. In making this analysis we are intending to use the concept of 'fatal strategy' as employed by Jean Baudrillard (1983, 1990). A fatal strategy is a reaction to an intolerable situation. It does not aim at making structural change but makes a moral claim. Victims of the situation appear to follow the advice of respected authorities but end up by making things worse for themselves. The strategy is fatal in the sense that it leads to 'fatal' outcomes. However, it would be a mistake to think of it as 'fatalism'. It demands hard work and commitment.

It is not the intention of the authors of this chapter to construct an account of food insecurity that 'blames the victims'. At the same time it is vitally necessary to consider how people react to poverty and to explain the strategies they employ to deal with their situation. Only by understanding this can you really begin to get an idea of what is going wrong and what might be done to fix it.

This chapter will be devoted to a small corner of the Eastern Plateau of Zambia, but the issues that we identify here are mirrored in other villages all over Eastern and Southern Africa. To begin to understand these issues it makes sense to seriously consider particular people and their particular problems. The land of the Eastern Plateau of Zambia is mostly flat with low hills. The rainfall is about 1,000 mm per year and almost all of that falls in the four months from December to March. Rural households are concentrated in village settlements of up to a hundred households (Phiria *et al.* 2004; Vail 1977). One of the co-authors came here just before Christmas of 2010 as a guest of a small NGO, which operates with the support of churches and Rotary clubs around the world. We will call this the Kai NGO. Adjacent to the centre was the Nyandane village, its cropping fields and grazing lands. Accordingly, it was possible to walk out and explore the village agricultural lands on foot. One of the staff at the centre, Patience, spoke good English and came from this village. She introduced us to her relatives and we interviewed them and other villagers. Also staying at the Kai centre at this time was a researcher from the USA. She was conducting research in another nearby village, looking at how older women managed their lives as farmers and as the heads of their families. The co-authors met up and decided to share research data and ideas. So some of the quotes in this chapter come Nyandane village and some from Tumba village. Another set of interviews was conducted with staff from the Kai centre. Except for senior management at the centre, the staff received only a very small income. Accordingly, most of them were still responsible for farming for their families in their home villages. One more interviewee was a white aid worker who was an engineer in a local hospital. Names of people, the centre and the villages have been changed to maintain the anonymity of respondents.

Food insecurity in the villages

The malnutrition of the rural Zambian population is well known. A Jesuit Centre study looked at three rural communities in Zambia. They found that food consumption was 'nearly half of daily calorific requirements', a truly disastrous situation (Barkworth and Harland 2009: 6). Malnutrition is revealed by the stunting of Zambian children. The rate of stunting for children under five is currently 40 per cent. The percentage of undernourished in the population as a whole is 46 per cent (Chapoto *et al.* 2017: 9–11). There are shortages of total calories, as well as protein, iron and vitamin A, all of which we will explain in this chapter.

These studies give averages for Zambia or were conducted in villages that might be worse off than the villages we studied. Yet we had no doubt that food insecurity and malnutrition were huge problems for our interviewees. The topic came up, whether we asked about it or not. Even wealthier village families did not have enough food.

An interviewee from Tumba village explained her problems: 'My living ... I find difficulties in my life, especially in finding food, so I do a lot of piecework.' When asked how many times she ate in a day, she made the comment, 'Sometimes once, sometimes twice a day, sometimes none; even now there is no food in my house. I had *nsima* [the staple meal of maize porridge] once yesterday.' On two or three days of the week she, her daughter and her grandchildren went without food. On some days, she did not have the strength to work because she had not eaten for several days. An interviewee from Nyandane village, Joshua, had a high school education and had worked in a desk job in the local hospital. He estimated that in his village of 160 households, the only people who were not suffering from hunger were those who had converted to Islam to receive gifts of fertilizer and maize (forty households). Even though his family had fourteen hectares of fields, they had not been able to produce enough maize. He said this was because he was feeding members of his extended family, including orphaned children. He had harvested in March but had run out by January. The food insecurity in these villages is typical of sub-Saharan Africa, as explained in Chapter 1.

Land shortage

The cause of food insecurity in the villages around the Kai centre is a puzzle. Few of our interviewees mentioned a shortage of land. When asked, they argued that this was not the problem. The director of the Kai NGO was trenchant on this topic, claiming that people were just not managing their land adequately.

> Most people, farmers here, they have enough land. And you see [laughs] frankly speaking, even if a farmer has two hectares, or ten hectares, when it is not managed properly, they cannot harvest enough. No. Let me tell you. They can produce a lot of food. Even on one hectare.

Another organizer claimed that further from the road, all households had at least three hectares, so there was no scarcity.

Despite these statements, it seems possible that land shortage is in fact contributing to food insecurity. The average landholding for all smallholders in Zambia is 2.73 hectares. The bottom half of the smallholders average less than 1.60 hectares (Jayne *et al.* 2006: 333; Milligan *et al.* 2011: 361). These are just the figures for their cropping land. Villagers also have access to land around their houses (their residential land) and land that is owned communally for grazing or gathering wood. We need to understand why this extra land is not used more effectively to provide food. Even so, on these figures, up to a half of the rural population could be struggling to provide sufficient carbohydrate production on the fields they have available to them.

Another way to look at this is in terms of population density in Eastern Zambia. This is currently 25 to 40 persons per square kilometre (Phiria et al. 2004: 133). In the early twentieth century, the minister of agriculture calculated the optimum carrying capacity with traditional farming methods. A cropping field would be used for several years and then left alone for fifteen years. Natural regrowth would restore soil fertility after this fallow period. The minister also included land used for wood gathering and grazing. He estimated the ideal carrying capacity at approximately ten persons per square kilometre (Vail 1977: 149). So, if villagers had adequate land to maintain these traditional methods, only a quarter of the current population could be accommodated. If villagers today are being forced to keep cropping in the same place year after year, then a likely outcome is that soil fertility is constantly dropping and so are yields.

Of course, land shortage is a delicate topic. When the British government established its rule they helped white farmers to set up plantations – coffee, tea, cotton, tobacco (Milligan et al. 2011; Tschirley et al. 2004). If you drive around the area where these villages are located you can still see these everywhere. They are taking up land, which is producing money for someone and providing a few jobs, but not significantly helping to relieve poverty in the neighbouring villages. Population growth could also be seen as the problem, with men to blame, as they want a large family to establish their status (Jayne et al. 2006: 333). Then there is the fact that some of the chiefs are selling land to people from outside, displacing locals. Finally, much of the land is being used for grazing, yet only a few families are getting any benefit. In Nyandane village, of 160 households there are only 6 that own cattle and 10 households that own goats. Yet half of the village land is being used for grazing. So all this is very political and it may be that the NGO field workers that we were interviewing did not want to recommend that the poor seize land to grow their food!

Overall, *cropping land* is *barely* sufficient for many families. It could be sufficient if they used fertilizer. To get the same result more cheaply they could intercrop with legumes and use mulch, contour bunds and zero tillage. Nevertheless, in all the villages there is land outside the cropping fields that could be used to grow food. So there are two questions coming out of this. Why are villagers failing to use fertilizers or legumes to boost production? Why are villagers letting cattle owners monopolize their community land when this land could be growing food?

As a cash and fertilizer shortage

Our interviewees did not see land shortage as the explanation for food insecurity. The most common explanation was insufficient money to buy the fertilizer they needed. They were also unable to buy hybrid high yielding seeds or to take their crop to the mill after harvest.

A worker at the Kai NGO centre explained that she did not have enough food for a large family of children and orphans:

Hunger as a fatal strategy: Zambia 61

> I have enough land but the soil is not fertile. I am unable to manage to buy fertilizer to put in the field. So I would be able to grow a lot of maize. Like last year, I had two ox carts, that's all. I harvested in March. And that lasted till September, then I had to buy some.

She went on to say that local maize stored better but hybrids gave a bigger crop. She could only afford one bag of hybrid seeds so she planted a mixture.

Dora was a resident of Nyandane village and head of a household of twelve. They had three hectares for cropping. She was receiving some support from her son, who had his own family to worry about but had managed to buy them hybrid seed in the previous year. Nevertheless they could not afford fertilizer. She contrasted her situation now with that in the past.

> OK, I was buying ten bags of fertilizer. I am failing now to buy fertilizer. Because my daughter was married to someone, who was helping us. At least he was working then, and was helping us. But what has happened is that he's now dead, there's no one to help us.

She pointed to the granary in the yard. We went up to it and she showed us the dimensions of the one they had before, when they had used fertilizer. It would have been three times as big. Without fertilizer, they had only grown one ox cart of maize, which had been eaten by October. Following that, they had survived by doing piecework and buying food, but they were often hungry.

Before going on, we could consider this explanation of the shortage this family is experiencing. If you grow a crop without fertilizer the likely harvest is about one tonne per hectare (Japan Association 2008: 10). So on three hectares of land (the amount Dora's family owns) you could expect to grow three tonnes. In Malawi, the agriculture department has calculated that in a year an adult will need to consume about 300 kg of maize kernels. We could work this out for this case. There are four adults each eating 300 kg and eight children who might eat 150 kg per year each. The total they would need would be 2.4 tonnes. So even without fertilizer, the family could get more than enough maize for a whole year (three tonnes). But instead it is only lasting them from March to October (seven months).

Dora's son Joshua has fourteen hectares of land and yet is not producing enough to last the whole year for his family of about fifteen (including the orphans). He produces only enough to last nine months. He bakes bricks to earn some income and he normally buys some fertilizer. It is surprising that he is not easily producing at least six tonnes, enough for this large family. Joshua is also a leading farmer in projects run by the FAO that promote legumes and conservation agriculture. He engages in these projects to receive the incentives connected to them. While he has planted legumes on a few of his fields to show commitment to the FAO project, his work at this is desultory – inadequate to achieve a good yield.

So one possibility is that these calculations are very mistaken – the land area is much smaller than the interviewees imagine, the yields are much less than one tonne per hectare. A more likely possibility is that people are generally cropping *less* land than they need for a year's supply. Dora's family are not planting out their whole three hectares, they are only planting out the area they would need to plant *if they had fertilizer* – roughly three-quarters of a hectare. Joshua, who can afford some fertilizer, is only planting the fields he can afford to fertilize. These households are not short of labour. In Dora's case, her middle aged daughter, a young adult granddaughter and a grandson are all helping with the crops and have no other employment. So if they are planting less than the area needed to get a full crop, it is not because of a labour shortage.

Our interpretation of Dora's situation is that she has an expectation that fertilizer *will* be available and plants accordingly. Yet it is a paradox that Dora might expect to have access to fertilizer. She is doing only subsistence farming, so she is not selling a crop to pay for inputs for the next round of production. Our suggestion is that she expects employed men in her family to be purchasing fertilizer for the family plots. She talked about two men who had provided income for fertilizer and seeds in the past. One was her daughter's husband, who had now died from HIV/AIDS. The other was her son Joshua, who had supported them in the previous year. The ideal for food provision is to use inputs from the cash economy brought in by employed men. The methods of production are not premised upon a cycle of subsistence agriculture providing its own inputs.

Our explanation of Joshua's situation is as follows. He only sows the fields for which he can afford to buy fertilizer. His other fields are left fallow. He does not engage systematically in organic strategies to boost production because these take time. He would rather spend this time baking bricks because that activity earns a cash income, a high status display of masculinity. To spend the time digging in the fields growing legume intercrops would bring in no cash income and would be perceived as low status. While his work baking bricks is intended to provide funds for enough fertilizer to grow the family's maize for the whole year, it is actually insufficient. Joshua is a relatively well educated villager who used to have a paid full time job. The scarcity of rural employment means he is reduced to part time work in his mini business, producing bricks for local village buyers.

For these interviewees, the expectation is that men might get some piecework provided by commercial plantations, or they might earn some income cutting and selling wood, making charcoal or firing bricks. There could be some petty trading. Migrant labour in the copper mines of Zambia and Zimbabwe was the main source of income in the past, with between 60 and 70 per cent of able bodied men being absent at any one time (Vail 1977: 151). There has been a downturn in mining jobs throughout the South-Eastern region of Africa since the 1980s (Englund 2008: 39). Without an employed adult male, households can easily fall into food shortage (Barkworth and Harland 2009: 4). So men are expected to get paid work and enable families to buy sufficient fertilizer. But the reality is that the paid work is insufficient.

Villagers also talked about the failure of government to subsidize fertilizers and hybrid seeds. From the mid 1970s, the Zambian government subsidized fertilizer and hybrid seeds to rural households, making these virtually free. Farmers were 'loaned' the fertilizer but rarely paid the loan back (Mason *et al.* 2013a: 613). The government guaranteed rural producers a good price (Japan Association 2008: 18). Consequently, the average yield per hectare doubled (from one to two tonnes) between the 1960s and the 1970s. So a share of the earnings from copper mining was being paid to rural households via a subsidy on fertilizer. This policy was no longer viable following a drastic fall in the international price of copper (Dorosh *et al.* 2009: 352; Tschirley *et al.* 2004: 18). By 1999 the government's budget declined by 50 per cent and the share allocated to agriculture dropped from 26 per cent to 4.4 per cent (Govereh *et al.* 2006: iv, 4). The fertilizer subsidy and floor price were dropped (Japan Association 2008: 4). Declining soil fertility was the outcome (Phiria *et al.* 2004). The average supply of maize and cassava per person fell from 198 kg per year (1980–93) to 111 kg (1994–2003) (Del Ninno *et al.* 2007: 421; Japan Association 2008: 4). The overall calorie consumption fell from 2,250 calories per person per day in 1980 to a low of 1,885 calories in 2001 (Del Ninno *et al.* 2007: 416). The area growing maize was one million hectares in the 1970s and only 0.5 million hectares from the 1990s (Japan Association 2008: 4).

More recent policy has turned this situation around to some extent, with bumper maize harvests between 2013 and 2015. This followed new subsidies on fertilizer and hybrid seeds with a boost to the farm gate price (Chapoto *et al.* 2015). These changes did not assist poorer households. Criteria of eligibility included membership of a cooperative, at least 0.5 hectare of cropping capacity and upfront payment (Mason *et al.* 2013a: 12). The total cost was 20 per cent of annual income for at least 60 per cent of rural households (Mason *et al.* 2013a: 12). In 2010–11, about 50 per cent of farmers with *more* than two hectares received the package, while only 23 per cent with *less* than a hectare received it (Mason *et al.* 2013a: 10). A government that had promised to assist the poor was only helping the more wealthy villagers (Mason *et al.* 2013b: 616). As Sitko points out, the systems of government support for rural food production prior to structural adjustment were founded on 'humanism' – 'the very legitimacy of government was in many ways tied to ensuring food availability' (Sitko 2013: 386). More recent policies fit with the 'farming as a business' model – hunger is a temporary effect that will be removed by further exposure to market pressures (Sitko 2013: 391).

So, villagers expect that fertilizer will be used to grow a subsistence crop of maize. Ideally, husbands will get work and supply the money for this. This is now very uncertain. Alternatively, it is expected that government will subsidize fertilizer as part of their responsibility for the rural poor. This is clearly unlikely in the current global context.

The utopia of food provisioning

To fully understand the logic of the food system of these villages, we must consider the ideal that informs it. We can look at this in relation to food groups.

Maize

The ideal for food provisioning starts with the preference for maize and the expectation that hard work will be rewarded with a good crop.

In comparison to more drought tolerant staples, maize is regarded as *real* food. This has not always been the case. The huge expansion of maize took place from the early twentieth century. Maize was promoted as the ideal crop to supply mining workers. It was this 'shift of maize into a mono-cropped grain staple that changed its effects on diet and transformed African farming systems' (McCann 2001: 256). Maize was also favoured because it could be harvested over a period of weeks. With any other grain, you need to harvest quickly or birds will eat the crop. With maize, the cobs are protected from birds. So while the husband is working in the mines, his wife can take her time to harvest the crop. Whether this is still relevant is doubtful. Women we interviewed were often the heads of households but none of them were working on their own – their numerous young dependents were doing a large part of the agricultural work.

So maize monoculture replaced an agriculture in which maize was just one crop, along with plantains, root vegetables, sorghum and millet (McCann 2001: 256). Accompanying this was a shift in dietary preference. Coral, a worker at the Kai centre, explained why gardens growing root crops were regarded as no substitute for maize:

CORAL: Yes, it is true, but here, we prefer maize. We are not interested in eating food from cassava. But only maize.
INTERVIEWER: What about sweet potato?
CORAL: We prefer that, when we just want to make tea and can make that sweet potato. You can drink tea with the sweet potato. Or you can put it as a relish now. So that you can take food, and that potato you can eat. Just the same as if you were putting a chicken. We eat with the food.
INTERVIEWER: So what you are saying is, nsima, maize, is the real food, [yes, yes]. That's how it looks, and then sweet potato, cassava, bananas...
CORAL: Banana it is a pleasure, just a pleasure. Not to eat it, like when you can eat food, nsima, no.

Sweet potato is seen at best as a snack (with tea) or as a side dish (relish) to maize. Coral uses the English word 'food' to indicate maize porridge *nsima*. So, in terms of the FAO definition of food security (see Chapter 1), sufficiency in maize is what makes for food security – because maize is the *preference*. Yet this preference is actually a health problem; not because of the nutritional deficiencies of maize but because of its high demands *as a crop* (McCann 2001). Maize is a very high user of nutrients and depends on a good rainy season. Within Zambia, total maize production can drop to as little as a quarter of maximum production in a bad year. These bad seasons take place every three to five years. Total production of cassava shows none of this yearly variation (Dorosh *et al*. 2009: 351).

The *methods* used to grow maize in these communities are also preventing good yields. While these methods were encouraged or enforced by colonial governments they are by now 'traditional' – villagers have learned them from their parents. In the colonial period, farmers were instructed to make a neat linear mound to plant their maize. This 'ridging' was made compulsory from the 1930s and is still close to universal (Drinkwater 1989: 299; Jones and Sakala 1991: 12). During the growing season the field must be 'cleaned' by constant weeding with hoes. These bare ridges and exposed soils are often washed away by heavy rainfall. Colonial authorities encouraged farmers to drive cattle into the fields to eat the maize stalks after harvest, providing manure. Yet the cattle compact the soil and eat the mulch that protects micro-organisms (Mloza-Banda and Nanthambwe 2010: 73). Later, colonial and post-colonial authorities recommended fertilizer. The view that a good crop cannot be grown without fertilizers has become established wisdom. Colonial authorities also advised farmers to set light to the fields after harvest, a common practice now (Japan Association 2008: 8, 32, 34; Sosola *et al.* 2011: 1). The intention was to deter termites (Mohamoud and Canfield 1998). Current thinking sees this as bad advice. The decomposing mulch left in the fields after harvest is essential protection and food for soil micro-organisms.

The method of cultivating maize that became established in the colonial period is now regarded as the proper and morally appropriate way to live. The emphasis on 'cleaning' by weeding and by burning the crop residue is morally equated to other cleaning, such as washing the hands before eating, or sweeping the yard. These regimes of weeding create immense amounts of agricultural work. All the women from Tumba village saw hard work in the fields as a virtue. When asked what would bring her joy, Naomi said:

> When I wake up fit to do any job it brings me joy because I can work and get food or money.

Grace saw her hard work as a moral duty:

> In my life, everything is just OK because when I am working it is better for society. When I wake up, in the dry season, I start by sweeping the yard, and cleaning in the house. Then I cook porridge and after we eat I go and look for relish. But at this time, the wet season, I go straight to the fields in the morning. Then from the fields, I come back and I cook porridge, then clean the plates, and then do the work at home.

They all described a daily routine like this. This method of maize production swallows time. There is not a lot left over to establish a more varied subsistence production. This method of production systematically degrades soils. The only thing that has held this system in place is the constant expansion of agriculture into woodlands. This expansion has run its course. The end result is dependence on fertilizer, which most families cannot afford.

Vegetables and fruit

Villagers have come to believe that the right vegetables to eat are European vegetables that are not that easy to grow in village conditions. For example spinach, okra, peas, peppers, tomatoes and drumhead cabbages. Assisting villagers to grow vegetables that can fetch a good price is a common strategy for nutritional projects (for example see Englund 2008). This requires a supply of water piped to the household or to a community garden. This is unlikely. These preferred vegetables also depend on pesticides, as they are likely to be attacked. Home cultivation is an option in the wet season but it is believed that inputs must be purchased. Patience explained this.

> OK, it needs money. Money can be a big problem. Because if they want to grow maybe some vegetables. They will need money to buy some seed. They'll need money to buy, maybe some chemicals to spray.

Consequently, the expectation of local people is that 'real' vegetables will be purchased in the market. Coral, one of the staff at the Kai centre, explained why villagers may sell some of their maize crop.

> If you have got no money, where can you buy vegetables, tomatoes? But if you have a little money you can buy vegetables, or tomatoes, salad, soap, salt.

Accordingly, a shortage of money means a deficiency of vitamin A (Ekesa *et al.* 2009; Japan Association 2008: 39). Vegetables like tomatoes, cabbages and green peppers are always cooked, so their vitamin C is destroyed before they are eaten.

Interviewees also mentioned the African leafy greens that are being displaced by European vegetables – grown within the cropping field without irrigation (pumpkin and cow pea leaves) or gathered as weedy leafy vegetables growing wild (amaranth, black jack, spider flower). These weedy vegetables are regarded as backward (Ekesa *et al.* 2009). Yet there is no reason for them to be in short supply. Seeds could be saved and planted around the house. These crops do not need irrigation or pesticides. This cultivation is not happening and is not on the agenda of aid organizations. The consequence is that these weedy available vegetables are not being eaten in sufficient quantities to supply vitamin A (Ekesa *et al.* 2009). Another important factor in the shortage of vitamin A is that there are few fats or oils in the diet. Without these, vitamin A does not metabolize in the body.

Wild fruit is becoming more and more scarce as woodlands are taken over by grazing and cropping. It seems that only children eat fruit – as they forage in the woodland. Fruit trees are rarely planted. Fruit is never dried and kept to supply vitamin A during the dry season. This absence compounds the problems of missing vitamins and inadequate carbohydrate. Colonial authorities eliminated large indigenous fruit trees left in the fields after clearing (Wilson 1989). They saw them as competition for crops. Current thinking is that scattered trees in fields recycle nutrients, create a comfortable environment for agricultural work and provide a plentiful supply of fruit.

Protein

In the utopia of food provisioning, meat should be purchased rather than provided by the household. But there is rarely enough money. Dora, who was typical of the poorer interviewees, explained that she relied upon piecework to buy occasional supplies of meat:

> In terms of hunger, it's a big problem, because if you don't have money, you cannot have food to eat. You cannot have anything to eat. So like, maybe you just buy a small tin of meat, then you need money to get the mealie meal [maize].

Her son Joshua, who certainly had plenty of land to grow fodder and raise chickens, claimed that his family rarely ate meat. His wife Lily concurred:

INTERVIEWER: So do you buy meat, you have to buy it.
JOSHUA: Yes, when we have got money we have to buy meat.
INTERVIEWER: So how many days in the week would you be eating meat, do you think?
JOSHUA: In a month, maybe once or twice. [Laughs]
LILY: Because of poverty.

One of the interviewees from Tumba village remarked wistfully:

> There are a lot of wishes; one is living in a good house, and enough money to buy meat.

The amount of protein supplied from livestock owned by households is minimal. A chicken every three months is typical. Dora did not have *any* chickens, though she had killed and eaten chickens in the previous year. Joshua's household, despite his work firing bricks, was no better off. He told us that they had seven chickens and rarely ate any eggs. They ate a chicken every few months. The failure to integrate animal husbandry and protein consumption within subsistence agriculture is reflected in the treatment of these 'indigenous' chickens. While very small flocks are ubiquitous, they are rarely fed. Households do not construct any chicken coops or laying boxes. Households with pigs are raising them for sale rather than household consumption. Dora had three small piglets that were not yet ready for sale. A larger pig had been stolen by a gang of young men, who sold it to buy alcohol.

As noted at the beginning of this chapter, it is only a few, relatively wealthier villagers, who own large livestock. Only 10 per cent of households in Nyandane village own cattle or goats. In any case, these animals are only sold in an emergency or killed for a ceremony. They are not eaten for the daily food supply (see Ferguson 1990: 125). Mark, a local aid worker, explained the situation:

> Yes, because the only problem is, they keep a lot of cattle and that but they don't slaughter and sell, they just keep them, like pets.

This is a somewhat demeaning characterization of what is going on. As Ferguson points out, the effect is to supply retired men with a bank, to be used in emergencies. While wives and relatives can make demands on any available *cash*, cattle are sacrosanct. Today, men who have retired and own cattle are a small minority in these villages. Yet the aspiration to *become* one of these prestigious men blocks resentment (Ferguson 1990). The use of a large part of village land for grazing by a wealthy few is not contested. Consequently, grazing land is not available to grow fodder for goats and chickens.

So it is expected that meat will be purchased. But in the daily reality, this rarely happens. Provision of vegetable protein does not make up the difference. Cultivation is inadequate and there is little cash to buy beans or nuts. Joshua said his family did not grow beans but bought some from the market. A member of staff at the Kai centre explained that her annual crop of peanuts would only last them a month after harvest. She said she did not have enough money to buy the seeds necessary to grow a year's supply; another example of the way in which the subsistence economy is premised on the input of cash from paid work. Villagers may also buy dried fish if they have money but this is infrequent. Betty said she would buy dried fish once a month, after she had been paid by the NGO.

A summary of the utopia of food provisioning

Summing up, the ideal food production system combines four elements.

- Maize is grown with fertilizers and seeds, which are purchased with money earned in paid jobs. A small crop of peanuts may also be grown.
- The successful villager owns cattle and goats. These are slaughtered for ceremonies, or sold, if absolutely necessary, to fund an emergency. Pigs or chickens may be raised for sale.
- If households grow vegetables at all, the intention is to sell them. They require irrigation supplied by projects or government.
- Supplementary luxury foods are bought with a cash income – European vegetables, dried fish, beans and meat.

Food provisioning is constructed within a moral economy. Ideally, the cash economy supplies money for inputs to grow enough maize for the whole year. There is enough money to also pay for 'proper' vegetables, meat and beans. Men earn income as the household providers and their wives do not need to do piecework.

Other elements of the utopia

Along with the ideal of food provisioning go two other aspects of the utopia of participation in the cash economy.

Villagers hope that their children will leave poverty behind as the country develops. So school fees, uniforms and soap are all necessities, if the children are to have a chance of getting a good job as adults. The director of the Kai centre claimed that households can sell *up to half their harvest* to pay for all this, knowing they would be short of food later on:

> They do that in order to raise money so that they pay school fees for their children, they buy other items for their families, yeah.

In up to about 20 per cent of households, some of the maize crop is sold and the household ends up short of food later in the year (Japan Association 2008: 21). A member of staff at the Kai centre explained how this could happen. Relatives will not lend you money if you have just harvested. They think you already have money. However, if you run short of food later in the year, they might be generous. Counting on this, families sell some of their crop to pay school fees. But then later in the year, their relatives may be unable to lend them money for food. So the family will go short. School fees are a higher priority than making sure the children have enough to eat! The thought that the children will *remain* in poverty is too hard to bear.

Another requirement for cash is a 'proper' house, not one made of mud with a thatched roof, but a brick house with a corrugated iron roof. When asked what would bring them joy, most women in Tumba village said that what they wanted above all else was a proper house. One of these interviewees explained:

> I have no house to live in, there is no food in the house, so it is hard to find fulfilment. I am living in a thatched house but in my lifetime I would like my own house with a metal roof.

Realizing the utopia of food provisioning depends on the cash economy: for fertilizer, hybrid seeds, meat, vegetables. For other items of the utopia, the cash economy is also central. Children will use their schooling to leave poverty and get a good job. Families will have enough money to buy fired bricks and a metal roof. The cash economy is the avenue to modernity, something villagers could attain if the world was *as it should be.* As Joshua explained, people were paying for their maize to be ground, rather than grinding it by hand, 'because of this modernization, people are trying to be modern'.

Gender and the utopia of food provisioning

The utopia of food provisioning has to be seen in the context of dominant concepts of gender. A common explanation of food shortage is that there is no husband to provide income to buy seeds and fertilizer. Grace, an interviewee from Tumba village, explained her situation:

GRACE: At this time I do not have energy to work in the fields, but in past years when my husband was alive he provided for us.
INTERVIEWER: Does your son who lives with you help you in the fields?
GRACE: Yes, my son helps in the fields. We both work in the fields every day. The other problem is that we do not have enough money for fertilizer.

It is not men's labour that is missing from her life, her son provides that. It is a partner in paid work. Husbands have often died from HIV/AIDS. Men are prone to leave their first wife and take their economic support to a second family. The combination means that there are a number of female headed households. These experience the most extreme poverty. Unemployment is a key problem given the mechanization of mining and much agriculture.

The ideal is that men provide cash and women labour. Yet even when men are earning they may not spend their income on the family. Income from a small business, like making charcoal or firing bricks, is the husband's to dispose of as he pleases. A diversion of family income can also happen when men sell some of the maize crop, a topic discussed in more detail in Chapter 6 (see also Barkworth and Harland 2009; Ferguson 1990). Men may spend money on alcohol, girlfriends or cigarettes. Interviewees thought that one in five men were doing this. Mark, the aid worker, was asked why these men spend their earnings on expensive *manufactured* beer, rather than just drinking a local brew:

It's like everyone in the world. It's a change. You know. They've worked for something, and they're drinking something that they can't afford the rest of the year, so they feel like they've empowered themselves to do this and they like it, you know. And next week, they'll go back to the *shubuku*, or the illegal spirits, whatever they do, and the *bangi* [marijuana].

A common event in the villages was that gangs of young men would steal goats or pigs at night and sell them to pay for alcohol. Real masculinity is to have a job and buy alcohol from a bar. Young men are angry that this path to masculine status is barred. They steal to achieve this status in another way. The outcome is to undermine the family economy. What is the point in putting all this work into growing livestock if it may well be stolen?

An alternative system of food provisioning

It is not that difficult to imagine an alternative system of food provisioning that could provide a good amount and variety of food in these villages. There are current practices that lead the way.

Some farmers are trying out more effective ways of growing maize. Projects have convinced a number of 'leading farmers' to plant some maize with legume intercrops (see Vignette A: Low Input Technologies). Yet these plots on the lands of leading farmers are just 'experimental'. It is not in their interest to plant out their whole cropping land like this. The experimental plots perform no better than the fertilized plots, and are more work. They can afford fertilizer but have been chosen by projects to be 'leading farmers' because they are better educated, can speak English and follow instructions. These leading farmers cooperate by planting out at least one of their fields in the approved manner. Their aim is to get the incentives connected to the project – the bags of fertilizer, hybrid seeds or free tractor use.

The whole of the project design based around 'leading farmers' depends on the idea that leading farmers will show how it can be done and then other farmers will take it up. Yet these ideas never get to the poor villagers. Dora's son Joshua was one of these leading farmers and yet he had never helped her to try out these ideas. Another leading farmer was the headman. Terry went with Dora to visit his cropping fields one morning. We arrived at a plot only 500 metres from her cropping fields. Each row of maize had been intercropped with a row of pruned Gliricidia trees, putting nitrogen into the soil. Around the edge of the field, these trees had been allowed to grow to provide seed stock. When Dora realized what was going on, she started collecting seeds, putting them in her pocket to take home and plant. The headman had never talked to other villagers about this technology.

Conservation agriculture (zero tillage) has recently been promoted by the FAO, NGOs and the government of Zambia (Tschirley *et al.* 2004). About one in eight fields around Katete *are* using this technique, so it is not unknown. By combining inter-planting with legumes and zero tillage, villagers could produce yields equal to those achieved with fertilizer – up to four tonnes per hectare (Phiria *et al.* 2004: 134). Seeds are planted into small basins, rather than the whole field being cultivated with a hoe and raked into parallel mounds. The technique being used here is described in detail in Vignette A: Low Input Technologies. Most villagers have not adopted this technology. It may be that what are taken to be traditional methods are regarded as more reliable. It may be that this method confronts cultural demands to 'clean' fields by weeding and burning crop residues. It may be that villagers who do not own livestock find it difficult to get manure for the planting stations. It may be difficult to keep cattle from eating the stover after the harvest. You would need to cultivate and maintain a hedge to manage this.

What villagers could also do is to grow and eat crops which are not as demanding as maize. Cassava, sorghum and millet are much easier crops where rainfall is erratic. Sweet potatoes, bananas (plantains), rice and sugar cane could take advantage of the many damp areas around these villages. Most of these crops do not depend on enriched soil fertility to the same extent as maize. Yet as we have seen, villagers do not see these as any substitute for maize – *real* food.

There are a rare few 'nutrition gardens' in these villages. These have been recommended by FAO advisors. A garden in the grazing land of Nyandane village was a quarter of a hectare. The edge was a hedge of sisal and euphorbia, to keep livestock out. This was reinforced with a few hand cut posts and some barbed wire. Inside was a mix of food plants: cassava, sweet potato, bananas, weedy vegetables, sugar cane and rice. The ground was quite damp, so the owner had dug ponds that would fill up in the wet season and provide water in the dry season. There were only three or four gardens like this around a village with two hundred households. Why so few? Colonial governments banned gardens in damp areas, which might explain why they need to be re-established now (Wilson 1989). Families expect to be able buy such 'supplementary foods' with the money earned by men. Cattle owners might oppose the siting of these gardens on the land they now use for grazing.

A new development in the villages is the initiation of women's clubs, growing food for orphans and the sick. These clubs have their own cropping plots. Such clubs could become a nexus from which improved agricultural techniques might spread. Commitment to a poly-culture of diverse species, grown without purchased inputs, is required to get this started.

Vitamin A intake depends on oils or fats being present in the diet. Vegetable oils could come from nuts, sunflower seeds, canola or olives. These could be intercropped with maize, planted near houses or established on the edges of the grazing lands. Vitamin A is present in leafy weedy African vegetables. These could be harvested from around the village or cultivated around houses. It is also present in species such as pumpkins and sweet potatoes. These could be planted in cropping fields. Many fruits also have vitamin A. Fruit trees could be planted around settlements. Fruits and leafy greens could be dried after harvest for later consumption.

Sufficient animal protein could also be provided by villagers themselves. Leafy fodder, weeds and fruit trees could feed small livestock, such as rabbits, guinea pigs, chickens, pigeons and turkeys. Some suitable fodder trees would be Leucaena, Acacia, Albizia, Moringa, Gliricidia. Suitable fruit trees would be species such as native figs, mulberries, guavas and mangoes. There is space for the trees you would need to feed small livestock. More than half of the land around these villages is now grazed by cattle or left as marshy bogs. Meat is not the only kind of protein. Villagers also expect to buy beans and do not plant enough peanuts to last a year. Suitable vegetable protein crops to grow with maize would be soybeans, cowpeas, peanuts, bambara nuts, and beans. Nut trees grown in areas now grazed by cattle could make a real difference. For example, pecans, macadamias, Malabar chestnuts, which would provide copious quantities of vegetable protein.

As we have seen, aspects of another agricultural system have already been established in pockets in the villages. These could provide resources for a widespread change if villagers were motivated – building food security without expensive donations of inputs and machinery. The failure to establish such a system could be seen as merely an information deficit. Yet living examples from a small minority of villagers have not made much impact. We need a social explanation to understand this.

The perspective of the philanthropist and the perspective of an observer

So what to do? It is not too difficult to think of an agricultural system that could work. Outside help would kick-start changes, which would allow food security through household farming – *feeding the farmers first*. The value of such a strategy is gradually being acknowledged. De Janvry and Sadoulet note that smallholders in African countries are net buyers of cereals. For example 46 per cent of smallholders in Zambia in 2007 were buying more maize than they sold, growing less than a full year's supply (2011: 475). They recommend increased production for household consumption. Peeters and Maxwell found that Guinea households growing most of their own food are protected from a volatile food market. So 'promoting household food production would assist in increasing household resilience, particularly in the face of the predicted sustained levels of higher prices' (2011: 624).

Such an approach requires a change in mindset. Villagers would have to give up the utopia of appropriate food provision we have described. They would be producing food for their households *as though there could be no expectation of income from the cash economy* – abandoning the promise of development. Such a project of cultural change would adopt the perspective of *the philanthropist*, coming to help people by convincing them that their own understandings are mistaken. From the perspective of *the observer*, present practice is a 'fatal strategy' (Baudrillard 1983, 1990). It is a mute protest against the state of things as they are, rather than an attempt to reform the deep structure of things. The Zambian villagers construct a practice that would work, and should work, if the world was a fairer place. Work opportunities *would* be available and there *would* be enough money to pay for fertilizer and hybrid seeds. Husbands *would* remain loyal to their first wives. Hard work cleaning the fields *would* produce good crops. Money *would* be available to buy supplementary foods.

As Ferguson argues, we cannot see current 'subsistence' household agriculture as a dogged traditionalism yet to be replaced with modernity. Instead, it is part of a suite of strategies that makes sense in a modern capitalist context. The ideal for food provisioning begins with maize. The family should grow enough maize to provide carbohydrate for the whole year. This main crop is to be farmed by women, using fertilizers and hybrid seeds. The men, working hard in the cash economy, will provide the cash for these inputs. Alternatively there will be a government subsidy. The other ingredients for a reasonable diet are to be purchased with the money men earn through their jobs. This ideal emphasizes hard work and puts its faith in a scientific agriculture laid down in the past and promoted by dominant elites. This virtuous action should be rewarded with an ample food supply. In fact the outcome is hunger and malnutrition, a fatal strategy. Philanthropy could never be effective without an understanding of the fatal strategy described here. In other chapters we will look at the way projects designed to alleviate food insecurity work. Some project designs dominate and yet are actually very poorly adapted to this cultural context. What *can* work, given this context?

Let us return to the absent goat. The main reason village families do not get enough animal protein is that they do not make small livestock a priority. They expect to have money to *buy* meat. The ideal is that men will have jobs and will pay for 'luxury' foods. Poor families may occasionally obtain a goat. Before it has produced kids, they will sell it to cope with some emergency, or to pay back a loan. Alternatively, some unemployed young men will steal their goat at night, drug it with poisons and sell it to buy alcohol at a bar. More wealthy households may have a small herd of goats or cattle but they will not be served up for everyday protein supply. They may be killed for a ceremony or to cover some emergency. Men in a regular job will build up their herd as insurance – for the time when they will be out of work, through illness, retirement or the sack. Many of these more wealthy families are not actually wealthy enough to *buy* the meat they need for an adequate protein supply, whether they have goats or not!

Note

Some parts of this chapter have been published in an earlier version as ' "People are trying to be modern": Food insecurity and the strategies of the poor', *Forum for Development Studies, 43*(3), 489–510. DOI: 10.1080/08039410.2016.1233136.

Vignette C
Smoothing out the bumps in food security

Terry Leahy

In the African villages, food insecurity is seasonal. There are certain times of the year when particular foods (and nutrients) are hard to come by. I will approach this from the point of view of villages that have the most typical rainfall pattern for this part of Africa, a dry winter with rainfall in the summer. The person who started me thinking about this issue was Nomokhaya Monde, a lecturer from the University of Fort Hare, in Eastern Cape, South Africa. She pointed out that vitamin A shortage is especially a problem in winter. Vegetables that depend on rainfall are hard to grow. I then read her PhD thesis, a close study of nutrition issues in two villages near Fort Hare, which I subsequently visited. I will divide these issues up according to the types of food in question.

Vitamin A and C – vegetables and fruits

In a way these should be kept separate, although some foods contain both vitamins in abundance – for example parsley. The main thing to remember is that vitamin C is destroyed by cooking or drying. The food needs to be eaten raw. Boiling and making preserves is not an option to store vitamin C. Vitamin A is quite different. Cooking breaks down plant cell walls and releases vitamin A for digestion. Drying plants to preserve them can store vitamin A. The vitamin will stay in the plant only if you dry it in the shade – it will be destroyed if you dry the plants in full sun. These dried leaves can be used in soups and stews as a 'relish' to provide vitamin A. Using dried leaves like this to flavour a stew is commonplace in the villages. However, in most cases the vitamin has been lost by drying in full sun. You can also harvest those fruits that are full of vitamin A and dry them for the winter, for example apricots.

To retain and eat the vitamin A, you have to eat the cooking water or frying oil – along with the cooked vegetable. Otherwise a large part of the vitamin A is dispersed in the water or oil and lost when you throw that away. So recipes that use all the water or put the vegetables in a soup or stew are best. For example, boiling the green vegetable in a very small quantity of water with a half teaspoon of sodium bicarbonate (baking powder) and a handful of peanuts. The baking powder will help to break down the tougher vegetables (like black jack) and turn them into a flavoursome mush!

The time of the year when vitamin A and C from vegetables is hardest to get is the dry winter. There are some vegetables that are frequently sold and popular with consumers. From the point of view of subsistence smallholders, they are not always ideal. They depend on lots of water. If it does not rain enough, they will just curl up and die. For example spinach (silver-beet), cabbages, carrots and tomatoes. Without irrigation they are totally impossible except in the wet season, and even then it is touch and go. From the point of view of providing the family with nutrition *all year round* they are useless.

How can we supply these vitamins throughout the year? I will talk about vitamin A first and go on to vitamin C later. The following sections provide some simple techniques to avoid the worst shortages and also offer some local examples of the kinds of crops that may be grown.

Vitamin A

- Preserve vegetables, by drying the leaves to make a 'relish' or making preserves in jars.
- Grow vegetables that can withstand the dry winter conditions, especially the weedy or wild leafy vegetables: amaranth, jute mallow (*Chorchorus olitorius*), solanum species, balsam apple (*Momordica balsamina*), cow peas, pumpkin leaves, spider flower (*Cleome gynandra*), black jack (*Bidens pilosa*), nettles. These vegetables often come up without assistance. They can also be established by collecting and sowing the seeds.

In 2014 I was staying in one of the dry parts of Eastern Cape. It had been an extremely dry year. The spinach and cabbages that people were growing for the market had died. Because water had to be brought in a bucket, there was no chance of keeping them alive. Meanwhile these very same gardens usually had a plot of 'imifuno' or weedy vegetables for the kitchen – two kinds of amaranth and black jack were popular. These weedy plots were always looking very healthy.

- Grow a vast quantity of pumpkins. Store them on a roof to be consumed during the dry season. A good harvest depends on water supply and compost. In turn that depends on a pond, along with a good supply of leafy branches and manure from your small livestock. Each element of the household agriculture depends on the other elements.
- Create a simple pond and direct run-off from the home stands and roads into this. Use a bucket to collect the water and water to improve the crop. Save seeds from readily obtainable and unfussy vegetable crops. A pond can be constructed using black gardening plastic, and stones to weight the edge. More expensive but more permanent ones are constructed using chicken wire and cement.
- Go for sources of vitamin A that do not have this seasonal pattern. Perennials can be harvested at any time. For example, lobes from prickly pear, and leaves from *Moringa oleifera* or *Leucaena leucocephala*.
- Grow fruit for drying, to be eaten throughout the year. Apricots, mangoes and pawpaws are good options.

Vitamin C

The vitamin C problem is more intractable because the food has to be eaten fresh (raw).

- Plant a variety of citrus trees, with different ripening periods. Lemons, oranges, mandarins (tangerines).
- Plant fruits that ripen at a different time of the year from your vegetable sources of vitamin C. For example, guavas, mangoes, pineapples, pawpaws, blackberries, raspberries.
- Feed water from the roof to a pond and use that to irrigate a small but constant supply of salad vegetables – parsley, Lebanese cress, green peppers, rocket and the African leafy greens. Get used to eating these raw.

Fats to mobilize vitamin A

Vitamin A cannot be used by the body if you are not eating what chemists call 'fats'; whether vegetable oils or animal fats. If your main source of fat is animals and you are only eating them *at one time of the year* you will have a problem that vegetable oils can solve.

- Make sure there are a variety of oil bearing plants that are harvested throughout the year.
- Olives, sunflower seeds, avocadoes are good. Likewise nuts: pecans for colder wet areas; macadamias, Malabar chestnuts and peanuts for the subtropics; almonds for Mediterranean climates.

Carbohydrate crops

In much of Africa cereal crops are grown for household consumption and also as a cash crop. Traders come around, tempting villagers to sell. Too much of the crop can be sold at harvest and the money spent before the next harvest, producing the hungry period. This is rare in South Africa because the market is supplied by big commercial growers, while villagers just grow cereals for home consumption. The problem in South Africa is that insufficient cereals are grown and stored to maintain supplies for the whole year. Despite this, there is usually plenty of land to grow a full year's consumption. There are two kinds of solutions. One is growing more cereals. The other is diversifying carbohydrate resources so supplies are available all the year.

To increase production

There are social explanations for people's withdrawal from crop agriculture in South Africa that are unique. Nevertheless, even here, there are project ideas that can work. One suggestions is to work with households that *are* growing a crop

78 Vignette C: smoothing out the bumps

and help them to produce more. If this is effective it could motivate others. If only some of the fields are being used it is difficult to expand cropping. It can be unsafe for women to go to their fields alone. Livestock owners have come to expect this former cropping land to be available and are not going to pay for fencing to restrain their cattle. In this situation, the first thing to do is to boost production on home stands. The second thing is for government or NGOs to assist people to fence their cropping fields.

What is also necessary, in all these countries, are strategies to improve production and prevent soil degradation. Companion planting with legume green manure and cover crops is important (see Vignette A: Low Input Agricultural Technologies for details).

Soil and water conservation structures, such as contour bunds planted with vetiver grass, or gabions in creek beds, can also maintain productivity. Storage for cereals is essential, either in people's homes or in a constructed household granary. For example, a large woven basket, on a platform, with a thatched roof. The posts for the platform should be equipped with metal caps projecting to the sides to stop rats climbing up. Ashes and neem leaves mixed in with the stored crop can deter pests.

Diversify carbohydrate crops

As Chapter 3 indicates, there are many parts of this region where maize predominates as a cereal crop. This has deep cultural roots. Often the preference for maize dates to a time when the people in question were living in places where rainfall was more adequate for a maize crop – before forced relocations. However, in the present context, it might well make sense to stop growing maize as the staple in dryer regions. Cereal crops that tolerate dry conditions, such as wheat, millet, sunflowers and sorghum are preferable. Some root crops may be left in the ground and harvested at any time: enset, cassava, taro, sweet potato, yams and arrowroot (*Canna edulis*). Cassava can tolerate drought much better than maize. Fruit and tree crops can also provide carbohydrate if cereal production is insufficient – for example, cooking bananas (plantains), carobs, dried stone fruit, raisins, mulberries, sugar cane, melons. Saving crops as dried fruit can accommodate shortages of other carbohydrates. Nuts are also a source of carbohydrate and are readily stored. See the list of nut species in the section on vitamin A.

Protein and animal fats

In Nomokhaya Monde's research, the one period of the year where villagers received sufficient protein was December, the month in which there were always many ceremonies and meat was distributed. To increase supply throughout the year:

1   Distribute more meat and improve pasture productivity. Large livestock owners are a minority. More wealthy villagers have much bigger herds.

They are using a community resource, the grazing land, without much benefit to other villagers. Those with a substantial herd should hold more frequent ceremonies and distribute more meat throughout the year. Pasture would be more productive divided into rotating seasonal camps. The whole herd would be moved every few days to a new spot in that season's camp.[1]

2. Diversify animal protein and ensure that women maintain control over the disposal of small livestock. Most obviously, increase the productivity of the indigenous chicken system – for eggs and meat. Roosts, chicken houses and egg laying boxes are necessary. Small runs for newly hatched chicks protect them from hawks. NGOs and governments should supply chicken wire. Plant trees for chicken food – for example Moringa, Calliandra, pigeon pea, Acacias, Leucaena, Tagasaste, wild figs, mulberries. Part of the home stand should be fenced off, so that a weedy patch of useful plants for chickens can be established. Other small livestock such as rabbits and pigeons could also work.

3. Produce more vegetable protein and store it for year round consumption. Soy beans, cow peas, common beans, broad beans, lentils, chick peas (garbanzos), bambara nuts. Dry and store in jars. Nut crops are also important (see list above). Some of these foods can be grown with cereal crops, others in home gardens.

Conclusions

African villagers *could* achieve year round nutrition, using careful design. Villagers will not be able to provide year round *irrigation* to source vitamin A and C but other methods are available. They will not be able to hire tractors and buy fertilizer to get a good cereal crop but they do not need to. They will not be able to buy enough beef for their protein needs but there are other solutions. A key strategy is legume tree and field crops; to provide mulch and enrich soils. Another is to grow what works without fuss and without irrigation: African leafy greens, indigenous poultry, easily grown fruit trees.

Note

1 See Njeremoto Biodiversity Institute website at njeremoto.wixsite.com/njeremotoinstitute.

4 Why do projects fail?
What could work?

Terry Leahy

One of the great puzzles of development work is the way money can be spent without much result. In the past, colonial governments implemented projects to deal with land degradation and food security. Very often these projects did not work (Hoffman and Ashwell 2001). According to more recent development theory, this is no great surprise. Without the active participation and goodwill of the recipients, projects will inevitably fail. It was expected that with the end of colonial and apartheid regimes, subsequent projects would not suffer the same fate. Projects were to be participatory and would be initiated by a democratic government. But this has not been the case. This chapter examines why projects are still failing. A typology of projects can permit systematic discussion. Some types of project are absolutely certain to fail while other types of project may be successful or not, depending on the circumstances. I will mention six kinds of project design that can be delivered, even though the chapter will discuss just three of these in detail:

1   Community group entrepreneurial projects.
2   Leading and emerging farmer projects.
3   Inclusive family projects.
4   Top-down service delivery.
5   Managed business projects.
6   Demonstration projects.

I will explain the first three of these project designs later in the chapter. Accordingly, here is a brief explanation of the last three.

4   A 'top-down service delivery project' provides ongoing intervention to alleviate food security problems. The project is delivered like a medical service, with paid officers appointed by government. For example, a woodlot to provide wood at subsidized prices for villagers.
5   A 'managed business project' is more likely to be run by an NGO. The NGO pays professional staff to run a business employing poor people. For example, the NGO might contract local farmers to provide honey, to be processed and sold to commercial outlets by the NGO.

6 In demonstration projects a technology is implemented on land owned by the government or an NGO. A paid worker shows how the technology can work for villagers. For example, an agricultural officer could be instructed to construct a cheap pond to irrigate a vegetable patch, on the home stand they have been allocated.

Nothing about the structure of these last three project designs predestines them to fail. Depending on the appointment process, the technologies being used, the market research and so on, they may well succeed. What these three project designs have in common is that they mirror in detail the organizational formats that are already working in the community – schools, small private businesses, government services.

I was first introduced to project design in 2003. My postgraduate students then were agricultural officers from South Africa who came to Australia as part of a 'Landcare' initiative – an aid project of the Australian government. In their research papers they were writing about the projects they had implemented. Later, staying at Lilydale in Limpopo province, I started to develop the ideas that inform this chapter. One afternoon I went to visit the agricultural officer. We sat down in the yard for a cup of tea and started to talk about the problems with the projects. By then I had visited a number of projects in Gauteng and Limpopo and had been in Lilydale for three weeks. As we talked I pulled out my notebook and started to make some notes about our discussion. What kinds of projects were most frequently set up in the villages and what were some other options?

1 The community group entrepreneurial project

Almost all projects and the vast bulk of project funding in Africa go to two kinds of projects. One is the 'community group entrepreneurial project'; the other is the 'leading farmer' project. Both project designs are about stimulating economic growth and providing poor people with cash income. As 'food security' projects, their rationale is that the poor will be able to buy food. The LandCare programme in South Africa has been just one of many vehicles of this project design. Intending to avoid the problems of projects in the apartheid period, the programme insists on participation and local ownership of projects (Department of Agriculture 2005; Holt 2005; National Department of Agriculture 2000). LandCare is to be based in a 'community' approach: 'Fostering group or community based and led sustainable natural resource management within a participatory framework, including all land users ... so that they take ownership of the process and the outcomes' (Holt 2005: 15). In practice this has meant that group based 'community projects' get more attention than projects aimed to help individual households. A 'community group entrepreneurial project' has the following characteristics.

• Usually between 20 and 60 people become beneficiaries of a particular project. A village can be as many as 5,000 or even 15,000 people. So many are left out.

- The people who join up are not all relatives of each other but of course there are subgroups of relatives.
- Typically a community leader links up with a funding body to get this kind of project moving. The project members usually hope to get at least some part of a job or some direct financial benefit.
- The aim of the project is entrepreneurial – the project aims to relieve poverty by setting up a business cooperative.

There is nothing inherently wrong with this model and in other places around the world it works. However, it is a poor fit for the cultural and economic realities of countries in this region of Africa.

The dominance of the community group entrepreneurial project model

The community group model of projects is dominant in South Africa and very common in other African countries. Richard Holt was employed as part of the team to construct the LandCare programme in South Africa and authored the government publication explaining the strategy. In a typical passage he is giving advice about project design for LandCare. He *assumes* that the community group entrepreneurial project model is the kind of project that will be implemented.

> Cash contributions are extremely important even if they are quite small because they foster ownership more than labour contributions and they provide a mechanism for the group to establish and manage a bank account … Community groups able to collect money and manage a bank account are also much more likely to attract other funding partners.
>
> (Holt 2005: 26)

Members must put some of their own money into the project (not all money should come from the government) and take control of that money through effective accounting procedures and a joint bank account.

What goes wrong with community group entrepreneurial projects?

For every working project in a village there are usually up to eight projects that have been started in the past and later fell apart. Though current examples stress participatory initiation, the design itself goes back to the colonial period. So what goes wrong? People usually attribute failure to personality clashes and laziness. Neither of these explanations is helpful. Conflicts come about because of problems of project *design*.

- The intention of the project is to supply infrastructure so that people can produce something different from what they normally produce.
- The aim is to go 'beyond subsistence' and enable a cash income.

- The project takes place on land that has already been allocated to individual families for cropping or to the community for grazing.

Common projects are to grow vegetables, grow mushrooms, make soap, raise livestock or produce eggs. When these projects are called 'food security projects' the aim is *not* to produce food for beneficiaries to *eat*. Instead it is to produce something that can be sold – giving beneficiaries money to *buy* food. The donor will supply inputs that the villagers could not normally afford; something that allows a commercial production. For instance a vegetable project will be supplied with some land, fencing materials, a brick shed, a borehole and a diesel pump to draw water. I have visited many projects like this, some of which had been recently initiated and were still operating. But most were by now defunct.

Problems of the community group entrepreneurial project model

These projects are beset by a range of typical problems.

Limited opportunities for income

The equipment, land and inputs supplied by the project are usually insufficient to give any serious amount of extra cash to forty people. For example, a vegetable project will usually occupy about four hectares. Villagers will normally have at least a hectare for their own cropping land, so you could say that the project land is enough for *four* households, not for *forty* beneficiaries. Even with the most reliable equipment to boost production, and a market to match, the resources provided are insufficient for the number of beneficiaries. There is work and financial commitment required to maintain a project. If the project does not pay well, motivation drains away.

An example is the vegetable project I visited in 2006 at Mmatau in North West province. A dedicated agricultural officer had developed the project with twelve young people. They were committed to a commercial success and were growing a healthy set of cabbages. They had a site of four hectares, but were only cropping on a quarter of a hectare. There were some typical problems. The borehole they first installed failed. They put in another one about 500 metres away and ran a pipe to deliver water. Their pump was stolen – despite being placed in a locked shed with a sharply pointed steel fence round it. They had not been able to buy a replacement and the department would not fund a second pump. So they had been getting water from a hose in the yard of the household next door. The householder was lucky enough to have a connected tap. The limitations of this arrangement made it hard to expand their production onto the land available.

There was little chance for the project to produce a useful income for participants. In one three month cycle they estimated they would get R6,000 for their cabbages. This would be R500 each or R166 per month. Out of this would also have to come the money to supply inputs. The income for participants would be a welcome addition to child support (R180 per month) or a help to a household where most income was from an old age pension (R780 per month) – but hardly a full time wage (at least R1,000 per month).

Summarizing the financial problems of the community group entrepreneurial project design:

- Forty beneficiaries are a small fraction of the total village community.
- The land allocated for a typical project is insufficient to support a commercial project that could substantially increase the incomes of participants.
- The project funding and the human capital available are insufficient to produce a commercial outcome proportional to the land supplied.

Awkward social connections

Another problem is that a typical group for farming in these communities is not a large group of unrelated people. Mostly, when people work together in agriculture in the villages, it is with members of their family. A typical cropping group consists of two sisters or female friends and some of their children. This kind of working group is typical of developing country situations and as Roland Bunch suggests, it is better to start 'building institutions' with a group like this rather than attempting a larger community cooperative (Bunch 1997: 220).

Distrust of leadership and corruption

Working together as members of a community cooperative is an unfamiliar social experience. The project design expects democratic control but it is hard to know whether to trust the elected leaders. Corruption may be suspected. If the financial structures necessary to run the group are complicated, the wealthy and educated members take control, and distrust escalates (Bunch 1997). All these points were made by Augustus, who for many decades had worked as a project officer for NGO agricultural projects. He was very much aware of how many of these projects failed. His first explanation was that members of a group expect that a project will make money quickly and that they will receive something for their efforts. When this does not happen they become disillusioned and leave the project. Second, they join a project because they hear that a certain amount of money is available for the project – for example R80,000. When there is no cash paid out, they become convinced that the leaders must be siphoning off the money, which can happen. However, what is just as likely is that the project grant has no provision for paying beneficiaries directly. Instead, the officers of the project are required to justify all expenses and keep receipts. When there is no income, other villagers will tease the beneficiaries – why are they putting in all this work for no benefit?

Community jealousy and theft

Community distrust comes from the fact the projects are established on land that is owned by the community as a whole or allocated to individual families. Those who are not participants wonder why these forty project members are getting special treatment. This creates a climate in which theft can seem appropriate. The theft of the pump at Mmatau is very typical. Such events can stop projects in their tracks. Typically, donors make a two year commitment. They supply what is required to start the project and expect future maintenance and replacement to come from the cooperative's savings. Thieves from the community will steal the broiler chickens, the vegetables, the pump or the fencing wire. Vandalism is not uncommon. Thieves might set light to a shed and its equipment. People from the community cut fences and drive their cattle onto land reserved for the project.

Theft and vandalism is not necessarily typical of these communities. In Lilydale, for example, it is not acceptable to walk on someone else's land without permission. Stealing from someone else's plot, you might be struck down by a spell; glued to the spot until the rightful owner returns to release you. One day, walking in the cropping area, I saw that someone had felled a huge Marula tree on their cropping field and cut it into pieces to be taken away later for firewood. They had stacked this wood right next to the common path. It is *projects* that provoke theft. The project's ownership of land, resources and equipment is not legitimate. The land has been taken from grazing land previously owned by the community, or from cropping land owned by particular families. The land, inputs and equipment are going to a small group favoured by the government or NGO. Tall mesh fencing topped with razor wire is always necessary – while people's individual cropping fields go without any fencing. Constant harassment drains the members of energy and financial resources.

Inadequate financial skills

Inexperience in business is another problem. Projects are designed to produce an income. Money is to be set aside for inputs, for repairs and to replace stolen machinery. The necessary accounting skills are often beyond beneficiaries. Members must keep a tally of income, put the money aside, return this cash to the treasurer and receive income back, depending on the financial situation. The treasurer must bank this money and keep an accurate account. This process has to be transparent and understood. An egg project at Voordonker in North West province, South Africa, epitomized the problems. I visited this project on a grey morning in 2006. An older woman, one of the project founders, greeted the agricultural officer. The project had been defunct for several years, after operating for two years. We walked up to the site, next to the residential area. About half a hectare was enclosed by a rusty fence with some of the iron standards (fence pickets) removed. In the middle of this bare paddock was a shed, housing cages for the layers. We could not go in because she did not have the key. As we stood outside, she explained the failure of the project.

The project had been funded by an NGO to help 'the poorest of the poor'. There had originally been eleven participants. The fence and chicken house had been supplied, along with a hundred chickens and twenty-four bags of layer mash. They were to sell the eggs and use the money to buy more layer mash. Disputes broke out. People took the eggs to sell and then did not bring the money back. People who were not doing any of the work wanted an equal share of the money. Many of the members did not trust the leaders of the project. Poor book keeping had exacerbated this distrust. Five of the original eleven members left the project. Fifteen of the Rhode Island Red chickens died from diseases. There was no money to purchase layer mash to keep the chickens. The members who were still active decided to sell the remaining chickens, closing the project.

The larger the number of beneficiaries, the more accounting issues get mixed up with issues of trust. The less educated the beneficiaries, the more difficult it is to find a competent treasurer and secretary – and the more difficult it is for members to understand what is going on. As Roland Bunch remarks, 'If only two or three people can understand the accounting, effective participation is limited to those two people. And only their goodwill will keep the organization from being run not only *by* them but *for* them' (Bunch 1997: 217). As an agricultural officer from Malawi put it:

> So most of the farmers that are into farming are primary school dropouts whose literacy level is low. And you expect these kinds of people to run big businesses! And in most of the groups you find that if they are lucky enough to have someone who has attended secondary school, they put them in the leadership positions, and these are the people that would always manoeuvre, that are usually clever and in terms of the finances they would always trick the farmers.

These organizational problems take place in projects that are not actually increasing people's income to any extent. So it is easy to give up rather than hang on through disputes and setbacks. Community groups like this do not have the business know-how necessary to operate group funding. As Roland Bunch claims, cooperatives 'are tremendously complicated structures that are difficult to understand and even more difficult to run' (Bunch 1997: 217). Failed and failing community group entrepreneurial projects were evident in every part of Africa I have visited, and every place my students have worked. Successes were always fairly recent, as these projects rarely last beyond five years.

The failed community projects of Lilydale

A good example of the situation on the ground is the village of Lilydale in Limpopo province, where I stayed for a month in 2006, walking about the village lands and talking to local people about their experiences with projects. I went with Lovemore, who was the grandson of a keen food gardener. Here I discovered a number of projects that had been put in place and were not working at the present time.

Why do projects fail? What could work? 87

The oldest of these had been called Komonani. I spoke to Julia, one of the founders of this community food garden. She was able to show me the original financial notebooks from the project. It was started in the late 1980s and there was some government assistance to create a fence. There were a few tanks put in to store water, which was drawn from a large dam in the grazing area, located about half a kilometre up the slope from the garden. To begin with the project worked well, and members kept a rigorous account of contributions and noted their decisions in the minutes. During a drought, the cattle owners were worried that their dam was being drained of water they would need for their cattle. People who were jealous of the financial success of the participants worked up the cattle owners. Because these people were powerful members of the community, they were successful in ending the water supply. By 1990 the membership had dropped to thirty people, from an original sixty. They sent numerous letters asking for a borehole, but their pleas fell on deaf ears. The group dissolved after this setback. All that remained of the plot by 2006 were the corner posts. Further up the slope were two concrete tanks that had been used to store water from the dam, the donor's name still stencilled on the side. There was only about 1,000 litres of storage in total. In a slightly different account of the Komonani project, the agricultural officer maintained that the project had been spoiled by conflicts within the group, which had split into three factions. The members were unable to submit a proper application to get a bore working. He went on to say that agriculture was very hard and required commitment. Previously, in the apartheid period, people had been spoon-fed. That was not happening now.

Since the collapse of the Komonani group project, two sisters had carved out a garden on land nearby, with the spillway from the dam running through it and providing irrigation. The fence was a makeshift of logs and old barbed wire, taken from the Komonani site. Technically the site was on the grazing land, but cattle owners had not demanded its return. This was an extremely lush garden, growing sugar cane, watermelon, cassava, pawpaws, pumpkin, squash, maize and cowpeas. When I went there first, two sisters were working together with a teenage son. Another day, a man with a utility (bakkie) came to help them carry off a load of sugar cane and watermelons. Their success was partly due to location around the spillway. It also depended on the ties between the sisters. Their un-project was not burdened by any of the financial and social complications of the previous Komonani project. Most production was for subsistence. Any sales were handled simply without a whole group to take into account.

Next to these two projects, slightly further from the creek bed, were six very large rectangular holding ponds. These were empty; there was no water despite the fact that we were at the end of the rainy season. These ponds had been installed for a community aquaculture project funded by yet another NGO. This second community project had also failed.

A third failed project in Lilydale was the community vegetable garden on land adjoining the health clinic. This was a half-hectare plot. The agricultural officer had recruited the group and secured a borehole for irrigation. Previous participants in the Komonani project were offended. He should have organized a borehole for their project. While people had worked hard at this clinic project for one season, it had fallen into disuse after that. The agricultural officer was unable to account for this failure. Some in the community blamed him, he had stopped giving the participants his help.

It was pure chance that led me to my final failed project in Lilydale. I was with Lovemore walking off towards the cropping fields when we came upon three hectares set aside on the edge of the village. Surrounding this was a very new fence topped by barbed wire. Inside was a new brick building that had been completed but was obviously not being used. Surrounding this, the grass and weeds were rampant. As we approached, two men greeted us. They were well dressed and spoke English well. They were two brothers who were the leaders of the project, which now had forty-one members. They had secured R80,000 of government money to start this project but could not get it going because funding had stopped. What they needed to complete the project was money for a borehole and a pump. The plan for the project was to grow vegetables, raise chickens and grow mushrooms – for sale. It might have been premature to write this project off but I was not optimistic.

After we passed this project we met women returning from their fields, with bags of maize or greens on their heads. None of these farmers had been told about the project I had just seen, and they had not been consulted. They were disturbed that this community land had been allocated to a project when they did not have enough cropping land for their own families. They also complained about cattle intruding onto their cropping land. This made it difficult to protect their crops from damage before harvest. The cattle also packed down the soil and prevented a winter fallow from being established. The community forum and the tribal authority had ignored their complaints. In other words, community group projects are instituted in situations where fairly simple changes might help to increase the productivity of family subsistence cropping on people's own fields.

Recent projects in Malawi

In 2013, I conducted interviews with agricultural officers from Malawi. Eric started out by saying that though projects are called 'food security' projects, at least 80 per cent are 'agribusiness' projects. I asked Eric why these projects are called 'food security' projects:

> I think the idea was that for the farmers, if they were able to get at least some income from the enterprise, then they can be able to maybe buy some food.

All the projects that he had experienced like this were in fact community group entrepreneurial projects. For example, a chicken layer project:

> I will give examples to show why I am calling them business projects. One is supporting farmers with layers. Basically we are supporting the farmers.

Why do projects fail? What could work? 89

But we don't support them once the chickens are laying eggs. By then they should be selling the eggs. And then, whatever incomes they get from selling the eggs, they should be able to reinvest it in the business. And part of it they can share as dividends.

The project would begin by enrolling the farmers in a group. The group would construct a fenced off enclosure and a house for the chickens. The beneficiaries would supply the labour, the sand and the bricks. The government would supply the roofing iron, the fencing wire, the iron standards and the cement. The structures were intended to be identical to those used in commercial production:

Generally you have a standardized sort of structure. As would be in a commercial set up. The house would fill all the major needs required for a house for poultry. Even the windows, ventilation. They would borrow all the specifications.

The farmers would be supplied with chickens and layer mash to get started but as soon as they produced their first round of eggs they would be on their own. The expectation was that they would be able to afford layer mash after they sold the eggs.

The projects with this design failed. Eric explains what happened in the two groups he was monitoring:

After the feed that was supplied with the project was exhausted the farmers only managed to buy feed for the next three months. After that the farmers started to mix the feed with maize bran and they would supply this mix to the layers and we would start noticing the drop in egg laying because of the type of feed. In the long term both of them collapsed.

For the first one it was because the farmers did not accept our advice that they should not share the money until the business was on solid ground. They thought oh no, we should at least need some money to support our families. So secretly they would start sharing the money that was needed for the business so you would find they are not buying drugs for the layers, not buying feed, maybe they are just feeding maize bran. So you would find there is a lower egg production. So they are not able to get enough money.

The other group, what they were doing, they were sharing the actual birds. They would take them home and eat them and what they would do is they would maybe pluck off the feathers and say a fox had come in. And we would think maybe let's buy them some bars so a fox will not get in. So they knew the department would not let them share the money, so they shared the birds. So the amount of money they were getting would start declining.

Eric also talked about projects that were intended to help villagers to keep dairy cattle with a view to setting up a cooperative to process and sell the milk. These projects also failed. To begin with the department insisted that the beneficiaries keep the cattle in a common kraal and share them. The project started out with three groups. The beneficiaries resisted the idea that they should share the cattle. In one group they point blank refused to share. Because the cattle had already been purchased and were expensive Friesians, the agricultural officers decided to let that group own the cattle individually. In the other two villages, the project insisted on the cattle being shared. In these villages the cattle were not being properly fed:

> The farmers wouldn't want come to feed the animals. You find that maybe they are feeding the animals lesser amounts. So the animals' health deteriorated, the animals were so thin. Some were even dying because they couldn't get enough to eat. There were always quarrels amongst themselves you see because others, in a group setup, others wouldn't come to feed, others would find all sorts of excuses. And even in terms of managing the animals, before the animals came the farmers were provided with training to provide quality feed that the animals would be given. But you'd find that those that were trained were not the ones who would come to feed the animals. Maybe they'd just send a child. They would just send the young daughter. OK, go and feed the animals. This is a daughter that has never received any training and they would expect that when she goes to check the animals, she would do it properly.

The farmers who were in the third village and raising the cattle individually were generally doing better. They were getting about twenty-five litres of milk a day, which was considered by the project to be acceptable – with forty litres as the target. But the groups that were raising the cattle together were only getting three litres a day. Finally, one of the two group projects decided to rebel and share out the cattle:

> But when we heard that we rushed there and we shouted at the farmers, you cannot share these animals! And the farmers said, but look here, we are failing to feed these animals. At household level, maybe if it's surrendered to an individual, at least you will be feeding them. But no, we said you were given these animals as a group, so we will not accept you to divide or to share these animals. If you don't want to be in the group you are better off leaving.

I asked Eric why the ministry was so insistent on a group project model. He made a number of points, all of which relate to two aims: to help the greatest number of people without playing favourites; to create a commercial project.

1 Running cattle as a business requires money for ongoing expenses. If the cattle were given to individual households, there would be little chance that any money returned from selling the milk would be saved. Cows could be

Why do projects fail? What could work? 91

slaughtered to pay for some household expense, rather than maintained for ongoing profit. If a group owned the cattle together they could decide to save some of the proceeds.
2   The department did not want to give a very expensive dairy cow to every individual villager in the project. Instead, there were to be more villagers in the cooperative than dairy cows donated to the project.
3   Ultimately the project intended a cooperative, a milk processing factory and a cooling plant. This ownership would have to be shared.
4   With a group project, it would be easier to demonstrate successful outcomes.

> Because the projects wanted to sort of like create an impact, to get a result, OK? In such and such a district we implemented these projects and these are the results. When the ministry level guys come, they always want to see evidence to say, these people are making money. The good evidence will come from their bookkeeping records or their bank accounts.

As sensible as all this may seem, these community group entrepreneurial projects *do not work* in the African villages. Something else must be found, as Eric concluded:

> We are better off just assisting the farmers from a subsistence angle. Let's say for giving the cow, or giving the goats, or giving the pigs. Let them raise them on a subsistence level, not on a commercial level. At least that works. But if you want us to bring the farmers on a group level, the experience that I have so far had is that most agribusiness groups, they do not work.

In the focus group discussion, these agricultural officers also talked about the failures of community group projects for mushrooms, chickens, goats and pigs. While projects always start with a Participatory Rural Appraisal (PRA) that is meant to engineer bottom up control, the reality is that donors want and expect *group* projects. All concerned know this:

PHIRI: We tend to act like the projects are what are wanted by the people. But when we go there to conduct PRAs we tend to push our own ideas, what we want without necessarily getting what these people want. So when they get the project you will find that the people do not fully own the project.
PATIENCE: The community will even demand these projects without seeing whether they can make money.
PHIRI: Yes, donor driven ideas sometimes play a very big part. Because the donor will want the project to be a group project. They want to be seeing the structure.

Why the community project model dominates

It may seem something of a puzzle to the reader that such an unsuccessful model for community projects has been so persistent. I trace this to a number of ideas that feed into this model.

The first is that these projects are seen as bottom up and participatory. One of the things that actually prevents them from working well is the large number of participants that are recruited. The rationale is to involve as many poor people as possible, demonstrating the participation of the community.

A second is the desire to 'go beyond subsistence'. It is believed that development must be founded on market participation. These projects are seen as useful training. Foods must be produced which could be sold – and not just those that people grow on their own land and can get for nothing. A *group* project is necessary to justify donation of the infrastructure required for a commercial business. This implies all the difficulties of money management. It also means that people are measuring these projects against other options for paid work.

A third reason why funding bodies favour community group entrepreneurial projects is that it is considered easy to provide 'evidence' that the funding money has been well spent. The group establishes a bank account and it is no problem to establish that the cooperative has earned money from their enterprises, saved it for future expenses and distributed it to beneficiaries. By contrast a subsistence project on land owned individually by beneficiaries is much more difficult to monitor. The same applies to the visual surveillance of projects. A group project depends on infrastructure that is visible and located in the one place. When someone comes from the central office it is easy to show them something has been achieved. In 2009, I met a development worker from South Africa who made this point very forcefully. He had been employed to set up projects growing herbs in the villages. He knew that the only way to make these projects work would be to establish herb gardens in the home yards (the home stands) of villagers. Yet the people who were funding his projects would not permit this. They wanted to be able to visit and send back photos to overseas donors. The photos would show a large plot of herbs and the beneficiaries standing together demonstrating their commitment. In the development worker's experience, group projects like this had failed again and again.

Finally, the group entrepreneurial project is seen as an ideal way to develop 'social capital' (Putnam 2000) in order to accomplish a take-off in development. In 2006 I was staying in North West province. It was twilight when I went for a constitutional walk with Maggie, my host in the village. Several blocks from her house, we came upon a large paddock overgrown with weeds. Surrounding it was a high mesh fence. Inside was a windmill leaning over in rusty disrepair and a tank, also rusty. Rows of trellises had been installed to take plastic irrigation pipe. I asked Maggie what had happened. She explained that this was a project about ten years ago, which had failed. The aim was to involve local women in growing vegetables. It went really well in the dry season, but in the summer the women stopped coming to the project and went to plant maize on their home stands. They could not do two things at once. The project was never revived. I wondered about what she had said. After a pause I asked her whether the project might have been more successful if it had supported women's agricultural work on their own home stands. Perhaps, Maggie replied, but that way the women would have been learning nothing about working together as a group. Without that, there is no possibility of development, she concluded.

The idea behind this thinking is that 'social capital' (Putnam 2000) is necessary for people to be ready to enter into the market economy. Social capital is defined as the capacity to make social connections that is brought into play by voluntary social engagement. It is thought to be necessary for market economies and representative democracies to operate. It is considered that projects like this are the ideal way to create social capital, for people who do not have a tradition of market involvement. This rationale is problematic for a number of reasons. One is that social capital is actually abundant in the villages if you know where to look. More formal examples are the numerous churches and local football clubs, linked to global networks. Less formal examples are groups of men who get together to drink at bars. Then there are groups of kin, which share food and other resources. These also organize weddings, initiations and funerals. The second problem with the theory of social capital deficit is that it is a myth that villagers are not already participants in the market economy. Despite unemployment, most villagers have had some experience of working for an income. Organizations such as schools, health clinics, motor garages and shops all function very adequately, employing local people who work together effectively.

While the ideas behind the community group entrepreneurial model are understandable, these projects fail again and again – a waste of money that makes people feel they are incompetent, rather than capable. The common belief that 'our people are lazy' is a myth that gets to seem like good sense when projects do not work. Actually there are a number of more useful explanations. We have to look to other models for successful project design.

2 Leading and emerging farmer projects

The term 'leading farmer' is often used to describe a common type of project in Africa.

- The 'leading farmer' is given support because they are likely to successfully implement the strategy that the project is promoting.
- The aim is for this farmer to pioneer a commercial farming technology which will go 'beyond subsistence'.
- The intention is that this farmer will inspire other villagers to copy their example.
- A successful outcome is that the technology works for the leading farmer. It *also* must inspire other villagers to become successful entrepreneurs using these ideas.

94 Why do projects fail? What could work?

Because it is important that the project work in the first instance, it is really common to choose a better educated, somewhat wealthier villager. They are more likely to understand the necessary instruction and get the technology to work. They are more likely to be able to run a successful business. They are still poor by any international standards but they can be regarded as 'middle class' in the context of the villages. Often the technology is quite expensive from the village perspective. The aim is transition from subsistence into the cash economy. To enable a marketable product the leading farmer is provided with equipment and inputs that are expensive – but absolutely necessary to begin a commercial operation competing with large industrial farms. The project cannot *really* be copied by the poor. They cannot afford the technology. Nor could the project roll out this technology to all the poor who need support to achieve food security. It would be too expensive. As well, the leading farmer has a degree of education and a capacity to engage in business that is not shared by their fellow villagers.

So this model for projects embodies an unfortunate dilemma.

1   Looking at one side of this dilemma, the project may work but will only fund an entrepreneurial elite of villagers. It does not actually *reach out* to help the ordinary villagers who have food security problems.
2   Looking at the other side, the project selects a poor, less educated farmer and does not provide expensive inputs. Funding is insufficient for a successful *commercial* operation, which in any case could not be run successfully by the beneficiary.

A leading farmer project might make a lot more sense if donors dropped the idea that their project was intended to help the poor. Instead they would be aiming to assist some few people to set up businesses to compete with commercial farmers. The leading farmer would not be someone to be copied by the poorest villagers, but someone intended to drive commercial development. The term 'leading farmer' would be misleading in cases like this. Instead, these beneficiaries would be better called 'emerging farmers', a term often used in Africa to refer to black people who are entering commercial farming.

The term 'leading farmer' is also sometimes used to refer to an aspect of projects I will describe in the next section – inclusive family projects. These are projects which are *really* available to everyone in a village and use technologies that even the poorest can afford to operate. Such projects can nominate the leader of a village group of beneficiaries as a 'leading farmer'. This person is chosen to lead the other farmers because they have mastered the technologies and are passing on their knowledge. A project may even call *all* the village beneficiaries 'leading farmers'. They are villagers who have demonstrated their interest and commitment in making use of what the project has to offer.

For clarity it would be better to scrap the term 'leading farmer' altogether and instead talk about 'emerging farmers' on the one hand and 'model farmers' on the other hand.

In all *emerging* farmer projects, the help is offered directly to an individual or family and the action takes place on land that the family effectively owns.

- The government or NGO supplies materials and advice.
- The expense of the project for *each* household is too great for the government or NGO to make it available to all comers.
- The project selects local people who are most likely to be able to manage the technology and make it work to start a successful business.
- The beneficiaries are seeking some private benefit for their own family.
- In most cases all the profit goes to the family.

What are the possible disadvantages of offering government provisions to individual families in the way that this project model envisages? As explained, it is not a lot of help to the poor and is unlikely to do much to relieve food security problems. Another is that the selection of particular families for support can cause community jealousy which may end up with theft and vandalism. Yet this is less likely than in the case of community projects. When people steal from a community group project they can feel as though what they are stealing is really 'theirs' anyway – since they are members of the community. Such action is much more difficult to justify when the theft takes place on the land owned by a particular family.

The central advantage of the emerging farmer project model is that the emerging farmer is given support to work *on their own land*, rather than on a community plot. They have a strong incentive to make the project work. The failed vegetable and poultry projects that litter the African countryside might have worked quite well if all this infrastructure had been given to families rather than to community groups. In 2010 I visited a windswept village in Eastern Cape. I had been taken to see a small vegetable project run by three brothers. One was also developing a poultry project. He had funded this from his own savings. He had constructed an incubator and was hatching and growing chickens. Other villagers would buy them to raise as broilers on their own home stands. He had made the incubating closet with some scrap wood and a light bulb. He wanted to expand his operation but was unable to afford the materials for another incubator. This young man had passed matriculation but been unable to get a job. In every village in Africa there are people who are developing some small business and need financial support. Governments pour vast amounts into cooperatives that can never work. They could do better by assisting such people with small grants.

An emerging farmer strategy is implicit in the leasing of community grazing land in some villages of South Africa. Villagers lease community land and fence it. In the Komspruit collective of North West province, South Africa, members are all related to an original group of friends. Every year a calf is allocated to each member and sold, contributing to retirement income. The members are almost all people who had middle class jobs and were able to pay for fencing and cattle in the first place. In Khayakhulu in the same area, a professional employee runs his leased plot to develop his capacity to become a fully commercial grazier. This leasing is an effective strategy for commercial development in the villages. However, it cannot do much for the poor. The people who take up these options are those with jobs or those who have had jobs; people who can afford fencing materials and cattle.

The most ambitious instances of this project design have been the land redistribution schemes of South Africa and Zimbabwe. These have redistributed white owned farming land to 'emerging farmers' for commercial operations.

Let us consider this strategy in the South African case. The land redistribution schemes implemented by the majority government were intended to redress the racial inequities of the distribution of commercial farming land. The first was called SLAG (Settlement Land Acquisition Grant) and the second LRAD (Land Redistribution for Agricultural Development). Under SLAG, farms were bought by cooperatives. The aim was to 'provide the disadvantaged and the poor with land for residential and productive purposes' (Sibanda 2001: 2). Grants were a maximum of R16,000 per household so households had to join together to afford land. Up to 1999, applicants had to receive an income of less than R1,500 per month to qualify, meaning that the programme was targeted at the working class and the poor (Sibanda 2001: 5). These group ownership arrangements were generally unsuccessful; their failures similar to those of 'community group entrepreneurial' projects. The new LRAD land redistribution scheme (from 2000) was also promoted as a solution to rural poverty. However, there was a new emphasis on establishing black commercial farmers (Lahiff 2002). The requirement for group ownership was dropped. The maximum for grants went up to R100,000, so commercially viable farms could be acquired (Aliber 2001: 55; Sender and Johnson 2004: 156). Yet even this maximum grant was but a small part of the cost of a viable commercial farm. A business plan had to be produced to demonstrate the commercial potential of the project. A considerable financial deposit had to have been saved. There was a sliding scale of government contribution – 70 per cent for small projects, 40 per cent for medium projects and 20 per cent for large projects. Only middle class black South Africans had any chance of participating in this second version of land redistribution.

The total number of farmers assisted by these schemes was 19,762 by 2004, with 387,485 hectares redistributed in total. The average number of hectares per farmer was 20 hectares (Lebone 2005: 3; see also Lodge 2002). These redistributions failed to achieve their objectives because of the small amount of land changing hands and the small quantities of land allocated to each farmer. They also failed in other ways. People with an eye to a good opportunity could apply for a farm, hanging on to it as an asset until the value went up. They had no real intention of working the land (Lodge 2002: 78; Sender and Johnson 2004: 158). The white owned farms purchased by government were often run down and had ceased to operate profitably. Whites often sold only their worst portions of land – after waiting for political pressure to force the government into buying their land at inflated prices (Borras 2003). The new owners found it difficult to make their farms financially viable. For example, salaries paid to the owners ate up the profits of the farm. There were insufficient funds for labour and inputs. The people chosen to be emerging farmers had little familiarity with how to run a business. Often the beneficiaries were not familiar with commercial farming. Some lived in town. LRAD was more likely than SLAG to work, because it was targeted to emerging middle class farmers. Yet the size of the farms was rarely sufficient for a middle class standard of living. So the new owners were unlikely to persist with their farming.

Beneficiaries under both schemes rarely had any experience of agriculture as a business and there was insufficient extension available to remedy this. Post-purchase support services were handled through the support mechanisms already in place for agriculture in South Africa – hardly adequate for this special situation (Borras 2003). For example, Amos Zitha's family was one of ninety-two, which together acquired a dairy and mango farm. He blamed their difficulties on the absence of government support: 'The government just took the poorest of the poor and just left them on farms without training. The idea may have been good but the implementation was fundamentally flawed' (Molefe 2006). The black farmers who had been helped to acquire farms were up against all the problems of commercial agriculture in Africa. During the apartheid period, agriculture had been protected and subsidized. After majority rule and the accompanying neo-liberal policies, these protections vanished. South African farmers were competing against other developing countries (also with low wages) and rich countries (with agricultural subsidies).

Policies of land redistribution in South Africa have been policies intended to create a new black middle class of capitalist farmers. To make any such programme work, the people to be targeted should be the emerging middle class. They should be funded with the infrastructure for a globally competitive operation. They should be given land that makes that a realistic possibility. They should be supported through extension programmes in business as well as agriculture. None of this was forthcoming. This explains the failure of the scheme. While such a scheme makes sense to adjust the racial balance in South African agriculture, it could never have been support for the poor. Even in the minimalist version that *was* implemented, it was very expensive per capita, not the kind of funding that could be rolled out to the vast mass of the rural poor.

Emerging farmer projects cannot make much impact on rural poverty and food security. The trickle down model has failed over decades of attempts in Africa. The poor cannot all become successful business entrepreneurs. Nevertheless, emerging farmer interventions could challenge the disproportionate ownership of agricultural business by whites. Beneficiaries should be those with professional qualifications and experience. They have to be well funded and supported. The best approach is to completely separate these interventions from food security projects. Trying to do both at once is not working. More discussion of leading farmer projects on the ground can be found in Chapters 3 and 6.

3 Inclusive family projects

The aim with this type of project is to extend the benefit to all members of the community – or at least to any family that shows commitment to the project. Accordingly, there is no danger of community jealousy, theft or vandalism. The emphasis is on cheap improvements to current production, with infrastructure that is easy to manage.

- No one is excluded. Usually, only some households will be interested.
- Offers are small scale so that everyone could be given the infrastructure or materials if they requested it.
- These projects provide materials or education, with the family doing the work to set up the infrastructure.
- These projects are usually on individual household land, aiming to benefit participants directly in their own production.
- These projects can also address a whole community on community land – for example on the community grazing land.

Projects like this can assist people in their food production for household consumption or can assist people to make an income. In either case the project does not depend on people sharing income and production in a cooperative.

An example of a *subsistence* project like this might be inviting families to apply for the materials to collect water from their roof to supply their home garden. Projects like this often have an educational focus. Householders are invited to learn how to grow a fruit tree, how to dig contour bunds and so on. The low cost (per household) allows such projects to be rolled out to whole communities – no one can feel resentful that they are left out. Beneficiaries show their commitment by engaging in some task. Any villager who does this can be included. Projects with this design are more often associated with 'food security' than LandCare or 'agriculture'. We are arguing that *subsistence* projects of this kind have the most potential to deal with food security problems – feeding the farmers first (for more examples see Chapters 7 and 8).

To illustrate this project design and its application to subsistence farming, I will give an example from South Africa. In the villages of the ex-homelands in South Africa, the housing blocks in residential areas are often quite large – more than a thousand square metres. It is common to have home gardens to supply the household with vegetables and fruit. However, the only people who can do this are the ones who have enough money to *buy* fencing wire. Otherwise chickens, goats and cattle will destroy your crop. In Ramokgolela in North West province, I was shown an agriculture department project to distribute wire mesh to villagers who asked for it. Rolls of ten metres were donated to contribute to fencing to protect vegetable gardens from livestock. This project dealt with a real problem for farming for household food security. Every rand spent was going towards useful improvements in food security.

Other projects like this make less sense. For example, in Lilydale I discovered a project to supply villagers with drip irrigation systems for household food gardens. This project was implemented across the country. A small plastic barrel was supplied with plastic hoses and taps so that households could water their home vegetable plots. However, this technology was quite expensive and could not really be rolled out to all eligible families. In Lilydale the agricultural officer had been supplied with *only thirty* of these irrigation kits. Yet he was working with six villages. In each of these, hundreds of households had a home vegetable garden. These systems were unlikely to be used by the households that did install them. Households did not have their own taps but used a community tap, queuing up and filling plastic containers, bringing the water home in a wheelbarrow. This water was used for cooking and washing. Villagers were not going to go through this laborious process several times more to fill a tank for drip irrigation. Accordingly, where I saw these irrigations systems installed, they were never actually functioning. To make an inclusive family project work, it is necessary to adapt it to the situation in question rather than to sit in an office and dream up something that may look good on paper.

Let us now turn to examples of this project design that involve households in common tasks. When projects like this work with a whole community group, they do not set up an entrepreneurial cooperative, owning and producing marketable goods together and sharing the profits. Instead the work that is done for the whole community may enable individual households to produce more for their own subsistence or to be more effective in their own household businesses. They are still 'household projects'. For example, an inclusive family project might construct a contour bund across the fields of many farmers. While the work would be carried out by a group, the motivation would be to assist each household in *their own* farming enterprise. An example of a successful project of this kind is the perimeter fencing for cattle constructed at Selwane in South Africa. The fence protects the grazing land from opportunists from neighbouring villages, who will steal cattle or run their own cattle on Selwane land. It also protects the Selwane cropping fields from trampling by cattle – an effect that was very evident in lush stands of tall grass on fields that were being fallowed. A vigorous group of cattle owners is organizing the project with government support. While the work is being carried out by a group, the benefits are to individual households in their own cattle or cropping enterprises.

Business projects that are inclusive and targeted to individual households are hard to develop. Most businesses take quite a bit of capital to start up. Donors working with the poor have to be able to roll out their project to *all* families that could possibly benefit, if they are going to make an impact on poverty. These two requirements are usually in contradiction. However, there are some strategies to square this circle. An example of a successful business project was described by an agricultural officer from Malawi. In central Malawi, people keep larger livestock for sale. The agricultural department began a project to give selected households a male and female goat. It was the responsibility of these households to look after the goats and to 'pass on' the gift – by giving the first two offspring to another household. In this way, all the households in the village were supplied with goats and eventually passed the gift on to another village. This is a subtle application of the principle of small gifts available to everyone. Initially an expensive gift for the donor (two goats) is given to *just a few* families. But the donors save their money as the villagers pass on the goats, ultimately making the gift available to everyone. The high risk of theft made it impossible for the government to insist on common ownership. A common kraal would have been very vulnerable. Instead, households kept their own goats in their house at night. The villagers also set up a small community-policing group to deal with theft.

A committee of beneficiaries monitored the project in each village. This group was to supervise the care of the goats and ensure the gift was passed on. The group included those who had not yet been given a goat, who were keen to see the goats passed on. The monitoring group was also to make sure that any villagers on the list to get a goat had constructed a kraal of stones to keep their goats. In other words there was a barrier put in place to exclude people who might be unlikely to maintain the project in the long term. Potential beneficiaries had shown commitment by constructing their kraal. The role of the community group in this project was *not* to join people together to share resources, they were not producing a marketable product and distributing earnings to members of the group. The money side of things was all handled *at the household level*. While this is a commercial project it does not have some of the problems typical of commercial projects in the villages. The main reasons why it has been relatively successful are as follows.

1   The project is addressed to individual households.
2   The project can be rolled out to any family and does not cause community jealousy.
3   The project does not depend on villagers selling their produce and using the money to buy inputs for the next round of production.
4   There is no joint control of money.

Villagers fed their goats by allowing them to free range on the community grazing land. So they did not have to sell goats and use some of the cash they received to buy food for the next generation of goats. Projects that depend upon cash from sales to purchase inputs for the next round of production will fail. We can see this in the fate of a related project for 'passing on a pig'. The pigs had to be fed with pig mash. The idea was that beneficiaries would sell a pig and use some of the money to buy mash. In fact it proved impossible for families to save the money they received when they sold their pigs. Consequently, all the remaining pigs starved or were sold.

A project model that offers assistance to any family that will adopt the technology can work extremely well. It has to supply materials or educational supports that are genuinely useful to assist people's current agricultural practices. This assistance has to be cheap so the project can supply it to any household.

Successful *food security* projects will assist subsistence agriculture to be more productive. These will be considered in detail in Chapters 7 and 8. A *commercial* project cannot depend on villagers saving money from sales to fund inputs. It must be premised on a realistic assessment of markets and of the technologies that villagers can manage.

Conclusions – what to do for the future

The community entrepreneurial group model for projects is only one possible strategy. Its constant failure should not be ignored. The problem is not laziness, pointless conflicts or human nature. The social strategy of this project model does not fit with the cultural, social and economic realities of the communities. All of the other five project models have more chance of working in the long run. This chapter indicates what kinds of *business* projects might work – emerging farmer projects, inclusive family projects and managed businesses. At the same time, the basic argument of this book is that spending the same amount of money on *subsistence* projects is likely to translate into more food for the dollar, and more food for the poor. The key model for successful subsistence projects is the inclusive family project. Two other models that may be implemented to support subsistence agriculture are top down service delivery projects and demonstration projects.

Vignette D
Working for food – working for money

Terry Leahy

In 2010, I gave a talk on project design to the ARC-ISCW in Pretoria – a government agricultural research organization. A researcher from the audience quizzed me about my support for subsistence projects. He had worked on cattle projects in Buluwayo. In his experience people would not work for food but only for money. So to get a project going you had two alternatives. One would be to pay people directly for their work on the project. The other would be to convince them that working on the project would enable them to make money by selling their produce. This understanding has become a guiding nostrum for much development work in Africa.

One variety of project which reflects this viewpoint is a project which *pays* people to work on infrastructure for their community. However, as everyone knows, this strategy causes a typical problem. People enrol in a project to get an income but do not really have any commitment to the project goals, leading to problems in the long term. For example, villagers may be paid to put in contour bunds – but after the project is finished the bunds are not maintained. In the end, storms and roaming livestock break the bund and it ceases to hold water. Another kind of project design which reflects this analysis is an 'entrepreneurial project'. Projects with this design are intended to create a commercial enterprise that will make villagers a cash income to relieve poverty. Yet these entrepreneurial projects rarely work. The beneficiaries cannot actually run a commercial project, especially if it is a cooperative.

Let us assume that this nostrum about work and money is true to a certain extent. This constraint creates a barrier for projects that expect people to work without pay, carrying out tasks that will assist subsistence household production. How can we work around this?

Find the ones who will work for food

One solution is to work with *anyone* in the village who is prepared to work on their own agricultural projects, without being paid to do so. Find the few who are. This is the method used by many successful long term interventions. For example the extremely successful CELUCT project in the Chikukwa villages of Zimbabwe (Chapter 7). The project was initiated by a small gardening club of villagers who met together to work out ways to improve their own household food production. They also faced a problem that required a community solution. Their spring had dried up. The achievements of their gardening club helped them to recruit other villagers to work unpaid on this community project. Voluntary working parties of villagers dug contour bunds, built fencing and planted woodlots to restore the village water supply. This project design depends on *finding the few* who are keen to improve their circumstances *without* being promised a cash income. Begin by working with these few volunteers and others will join later.

It is mostly men who will only work for money

This nostrum makes a lot more sense if we are talking about men in Africa, it does not apply so strongly to women. Men will only work for money – arguably, it is considered beneath their dignity to work for food at the instruction of a professional advisor. By contrast, women feel a responsibility for the family food supply. Their usual practice is to do a lot of work for food for their families, without expecting income. They can be involved in projects that do not promise a cash income – if they believe that the family food supply will be increased.

What is realistic and what you say to get people going

It is not *realistic* to promise villagers that they can get a real job by using their small agricultural resource and turning it into a business – what is realistic is to use this small resource to provide most food for the family. Yet perhaps this realistic analysis is not the best thing to be *saying* to villagers as you initiate a project. Maybe the best thing to be saying is that you can use this technology to develop a cash income. By creating an *expectation* that there will be a surplus for sale, the project can encourage households to work on food security. This is not too misleading. Any successful project to increase household food production will generate a small surplus for sale. In addition, there is no doubt that *some* people will always become successful entrepreneurs if you improve the productivity of a whole village. The adult education required for effective subsistence production creates a skill set that can assist market participation.

How this mindset comes out of the failed promises of development

The insistence on working for money, and not otherwise, is a self-defeating strategy. It is an angry response to years of broken promises of development, jobs and affluence. It can also come from media exposure to global modernity in the guise of affluent high tech lifestyles. Potential beneficiaries are likely to think as follows. You western development agents and advocates have been telling me that subsistence is old fashioned and stupid for decades. You have been insisting that a good cash income is the only route to happiness and modernity. So do not come around here asking me to work for nothing and pretending it is for my own benefit. If you really want to help me, give me a job and an income.

The effect of this mindset is to treat subsistence agriculture as a chore that signifies poverty. In cases where welfare payments allow some minimal food provision, it may be abandoned altogether. In other cases, it is hard to generate enthusiasm for improvements to subsistence productivity. This is a problem that can only be dealt with over time. If governments are not actually prepared to give people jobs or adequate welfare payments, then the only answer is subsistence production. The practical answer for those running projects is to work with the people who *are* interested in improving their subsistence productivity. Their health and happiness will become apparent to other villagers, who gradually start to copy their strategies.

Another tactic that can work is to encourage school students to see subsistence agriculture in a new light, as glamorous and up to date. The way to do this is to employ permaculture methods to establish a food forest on the school grounds. Instead of a dry and depressingly barren yard, the whole of the school grounds from one fence to the other can be planted out with a mixture of food plants. This has to be done by everyone in the school taking part, bringing mulch and plant stock, working in school time to construct cement lined ponds and tanks for water harvesting, planting trees, making compost. Ultimately some classes can be held outside under the shade of large fruit trees. Lessons in science, maths and agriculture can use the school grounds as a resource. School lunches can be created out of the school production. Schools need to start to treat subsistence agriculture as an aspect of modernity, rather than as an alternative to modernity. These school strategies have been pioneered in Malawi, by permaculture activists linked to the department of education. They should be taken up more widely.

5 Teaching them to fish – entrepreneurial ideology and rural projects

Terry Leahy

> Initially, there's huge government inputs, but over time, the government input becomes less and less and then the community becomes more and more. The purpose must be to teach them to fish, not to give fish to them every day, every day, every day, like that.
> (Marcus: Agricultural Officer interviewed in 2006)[1]

The saying quoted above is often used in the context of development work. It encapsulates the idea that aid should not create dependency but instead equip people to manage their own lives more successfully. In the South African context, this saying is interpreted in a particular way. It is taken to mean that aid projects initiated by the government start off by providing inputs which *cost* money. However, the aim of such projects must be to equip villagers to *make* money through their own business enterprises – teaching them to fish. This entrepreneurial interpretation of the purpose of aid has considerable purchase in the agricultural offices and in South Africa's new middle class more generally. The intention of this chapter is to document this and to attempt to understand why this way of thinking appears to make sense.

In South Africa, government development work in rural villages is oriented to food security and sustainable agriculture. As in other developing countries, the neo-liberal approach 'advocates "development through enterprise" and emphasizes business models driven by a profit motive that engages the poor as producers and consumers' (Karnani 2009: 76).

In the former 'homelands' of South Africa, rural poverty is entrenched. As we have seen, unemployment in the rural areas, taking into account all those who need employment, is about 60 per cent and this shows no signs of changing in the near future. Over 70 per cent of poor people live in the rural areas and half of these are 'chronically poor' (Cousins 2007: 222). Rural poverty is also experienced as food insecurity and nutritional deficiencies; in 2000 about 35 per cent of the total population were suffering from food insecurity and up to 27 per cent of young children were suffering from stunting as a result of food insufficiency (Department of Agriculture 2002: 22–23). In this context both government and charitable NGOs intervene to relieve poverty. The approach taken to village

106 *Entrepreneurial ideology, rural projects*

projects can be characterized as 'entrepreneurialism'. The aim of projects is nothing less than to turn every poor villager into an entrepreneur, running a (very) small agricultural business, competing on the market to sell their agricultural products. Typically, this aim is to be realized by a small cooperative, whose members are recruited from the 'poorest of the poor' within the village.

This entrepreneurial approach comes out of long standing policy settings, as discussed in previous chapters. Growth in the agricultural commercial economy is expected to provide the poor with income and employment, and it is believed this can only happen with a change from subsistence to commercial strategies. As previous chapters have explained, these entrepreneurial projects have not relieved poverty or ensured food security. This book has argued for the necessity of initiatives to support subsistence strategies and increase the productivity of subsistence. This chapter considers the ideological barriers to such a policy change.

The most common form of project in the rural villages today is the 'community group entrepreneurial project', an attempt to relieve rural poverty by engaging the 'poorest of the poor', as they are often described, in an agricultural enterprise to be carried out on their own community land. The intention is to initiate a market based cooperative that can provide jobs and wellbeing and relieve dependency on the welfare system – in this way developing capitalist enterprise, providing poverty relief, maintaining community ownership and bottom up participatory development all at the same time.

The unfortunate reality is that these projects are rarely successful in the long term and more often fail with great acrimony and bitterness all round. As this book has argued, there are a number of fundamental causes for this failure. Despite this, attempts to make this model work continue unabated and it is useful to look at the 'entrepreneurialist' ideology that informs these continued failed attempts. In looking at the viewpoints of members of South Africa's new middle class we can see the tensions between a genuine desire to help the rural poor, and a tendency to reach for solutions which would appropriate community land for small business entrepreneurs. This approach can be understood by reflecting on the formative experiences of South Africa's new middle class. We can also note the powerful cultural forces that work to support this ideology, not just for this middle class itself but for the community more broadly.

Entrepreneurialism as ideology

In the context of this chapter I am considering 'entrepreneurialism' as an ideology in a variety of ways. Within the Marxist canon, an ideology works in the interest of a ruling class, and is 'deceptive or distorted' in some way. An ideology legitimizes the status quo (Pasternak 2005: 35). For example, entrepreneurialism suggests that anyone can create business success by hard work and intelligence, and by taking note of market opportunities, which are always available for those who are creative. This is a *partial* understanding of reality (Hall 1986). What it leaves out are factors such as the necessity to have a market, good start up capital, the 'cultural capital' required to make a given business work, not to mention luck if everything else is stacked against you. In relation to class, the ideology of entrepreneurialism justifies and rationalizes the power of the capitalist class. It makes it look as though their wealth is an effect of their hard work and intelligence. It obscures the origin of their wealth in the exploitation of the hard work of their employees. In the context of this chapter, what is more relevant is the function of the ideology of entrepreneurialism in relation to the 'professional-managerial class' (Ehrenreich and Ehrenreich 1979). Entrepreneurial ideology creates a moral justification for the relative power of this employed middle class. It establishes a framework for their role – instructing and assisting the poor.

My use of the concept of ideology is also meant to include some aspects of Stuart Hall's broader use of the concept (Hall 1986). An ideology becomes an aspect of the *common sense* which people use to understand the situation in which they find themselves. The point of this examination is to trace the way entrepreneurialist ideology operates as common sense and closes off other ways of thinking about things. Furthermore, taking up an idea present in Gramsci's writing, 'common sense' also includes elements that are not easily reconciled to the dominant ideology (Gramsci 1988: 326). We will find that the agricultural officers responsible for implementing entrepreneurialist projects have a quite genuine desire to assist the poor and to make South Africa a more equitable and inclusive society. They are not just operating to promote the narrow interests of their own middle class section of society. They are aware of the problems that repeatedly come up when they try to implement entrepreneurialist projects in the villages. Their efforts to improve the lives of the poor are hijacked by 'entrepreneurialism', which seems to them like the only sensible way to move forward.

Background to the chapter

The research for this chapter was carried out between 2003 and 2015. One part of the data is a set of field research projects (eight in total) carried out by agricultural officers in widely dispersed sites across five provinces in South Africa (2003–5). It was these studies by my postgraduate students that started to inform me about what was going wrong with the village projects in South Africa. To follow this up I went to South Africa in 2006 and my ex students helped to introduce me to the work being done by the agriculture departments in the villages. In this way they became key informants for this research. I stayed in two of the villages that they had written about (in Limpopo and North Western province) and went to look at agricultural projects with these students and other agricultural officers in Gauteng, Limpopo and Mpumalanga (Leahy 2009). It was during this visit that I interviewed quite a few of these students, who were now back working in the agriculture departments, along with other agricultural officers and talked to them about agricultural projects. Subsequent trips to Africa (2009, 2010, 2014) have certainly confirmed what I found in 2006. Conversations with a wide range of middle class Africans in many countries have backed up the analysis given here. While this chapter concentrates on the ways in which agricultural officers and the middle class contribute to entrepreneurial ideology, it is also the case that agricultural officers are very much aware of the typical problems that entrepreneurial projects face. Working directly in the villages they are reminded every day that projects are not working and become aware of what goes wrong with the kinds of projects that are being rolled out from higher up in their departments.

The entrepreneurial state

In previous chapters I have considered the way in which entrepreneurial perspectives on rural projects are 'hegemonic' in the sense of being endorsed and promoted by the state as the proper way to run the great majority of projects to relieve rural poverty. The promotion of entrepreneurial success is a key to policy at all levels of the government departments of agriculture. The LandCare programme run by the national and provincial departments provides a typical example of the entrepreneurial approach. Explaining what is required in a LandCare project, Holt writes: 'The community must gain an income through long term sustainable job creation and development of an economically viable infrastructure' (Holt 2005: 16). This does not provide much leeway to fund projects that spend government money on household subsistence agriculture, whether on home stands, cropping fields or community grazing areas. The metaphor 'teaching them to fish' declares the intention of the state to withdraw from ongoing financial support to the poor while business (run by the poor) takes over. In this respect, the entrepreneurial project is a typical instance of the neo-liberal theory of development in action (Chang 2006).

This state decision-making narrows the scope available to agricultural officers. The state mandates entrepreneurial projects. The task of extension officers is to carry them out. On the other hand, there is always some leeway in how a project is represented to villagers. For example, the officers who are running a project to produce eggs and sell them might suggest to villagers that they grow some fodder trees to help to feed their chickens and to reduce the expense of the layer mash. Officers could also talk to villagers about eggs as an important source of protein in the diet for young children, suggesting that at least some of the eggs be kept for home consumption. The state commitment to entrepreneurialism can be manifest in quite punitive sanctions if agricultural officers stray from the path. Eric from Malawi told me the story of a senior member of staff who had been in charge of a project to get villagers to raise goats in a common kraal. It was considered that a more commercial project was possible if villagers pooled the income and raised the goats in common. This project was not working, so the senior officer permitted the villagers to divide up the herd and allocate the goats to individual households. He got the sack. The other agricultural officers took the hint and carried on with the project as instructed, despite the fact that they knew it was not working. Local knowledge is dismissed if it does not fit the ideology of entrepreneurial development.

Entrepreneurial success as a measure of project outcomes

Pressure to create an entrepreneurial outcome was a feature of the Koringkoppies project and its evaluation by the department (ISDA 2002). Fencing off a wetland area to prevent damage by cattle was the central task. With this, a concrete channel to carry water to a dam was installed. These aspects of the project could be seen as assisting subsistence grazing. There was also a 1.44 hectare garden for vegetable production. Forty-three local families were members of the vegetable production team. To irrigate this garden, a pump was installed to fill three 5,000 litre PVC tanks. The aim was to extend this garden to 60 hectares. This part of the project could also have been seen as a supplement to food security – growing vegetables for consumption in the dry season.

The departmental report did not present the project as a contribution to household subsistence agriculture; it stressed the commercial options. The fence construction was to start up an 'income generating enterprise constructing wire fences for other communities'. The renewed wetland was to attract tourists. With that was a proposal to build accommodation rondavels. The report regretted the necessity for external funding. It would have been better to have 'a greater initial contribution from the community in cash and kind, as well as a gradual phasing-in of improvements to irrigation infrastructure, fencing and livestock water, funded in part by the community' (ISDA 2002). So it was a failure that government money had to be spent and that the community did not generate funding through its own entrepreneurial activities. Ideally, the report went on to declare, businesses enabled by the project should in future provide income to pay back the amount invested in the project. At the very least, the expensive infrastructure that has been installed should be maintained at community expense: 'Some of the funds generated from the development of the vegetable enterprise, as well as from the other planned enterprises should they eventuate, could be utilised for this purpose' (ISDA 2002).

What is problematic in this is not the idea that some of these enterprises may begin to generate a cash income. The problem is that the infrastructure that is being supplied *can only be maintained if a cash income is created*. There is no intention to continue to supply government money for maintenance. If the infrastructure cannot be maintained out of profits from the vegetable garden, the rondavels and the fence making, the project will fail – and will be seen by the department as a failure. Yet all three of these cash making options are very uncertain.

In fact, conflict took place in the vegetable garden, as different groups from the community were unable to work together. Vegetable sales could not pay for the fuel and maintenance of the pump. In 2005, the beneficiaries were constructing a 20 km fence. However, no money was available to maintain the fence – if it was vandalized (Mojela 2005). This extension of the original project was *designed* to depend upon a cash income from the sale of vegetables – and yet this is most unlikely.

Ideas and pressures feeding into project design

As detailed in the previous chapter, the typical entrepreneurial project in South Africa is explained in relation to a number of ideas. Not all of these ideas are examples of 'entrepreneurialist' ideology. The most common form of project involves up to forty people in a cooperative. This is because big cooperatives are seen as bottom up and participatory. Such a large number of participants is a barrier to effective work in projects; people are frequently uncomfortable working in such large groups with the purpose of making money together and distributing it. However, the rationale is to involve as many poor people as possible and so to become an expression of the needs of the 'community'. So what is feeding into this aspect of the entrepreneurial project model is a genuine desire to assist the poor.

A second important idea behind entrepreneurial projects is the desire to 'go beyond subsistence', a phrase commonly used in South Africa, and which goes back at least to 1987. At that time the Development Bank of South Africa followed World Bank suggestions and created 'Farmer Support Programmes' for emerging farmers with the aim of 'promoting structural change away from subsistence agricultural production to commercial agricultural production' to increase efficiency, food security and entrepreneurial activity (Williams 1996: 141). Today there is also the belief that projects which go 'beyond subsistence' train ordinary people for participation in the market. So there is an emphasis on producing foods to be sold – and not just those that people grow on their own land and consume.

Finally this model works on ideas about the necessity to develop 'social capital' in order to accomplish a take-off in economic development. The belief is that people need to learn to work together to be able to develop successful enterprises and participate in the economy at large (Luiz 2009: 61; see Chapter 4). As explained in Chapter 4, this rationale for community projects ignores the social capital that already exists in villages. For example, people cooperate and create social capital as members of extended kinship groups. People with an income provide purchased goods to relatives who are cash poor. In turn the relatives provide services in kind, usually from subsistence agriculture. For example, the relative with an income invites the unemployed relative to use their electric oven on one day. On another day the unemployed relative supplies a meal of cowpeas from their cropping field.

Political pressures also drive this model. Ruling parties are concerned with rural discontent, and hope to be seen doing something about rural poverty. White commercial farmer lobbies worry that their land may be distributed to poor villagers. They do not want programmes that promote subsistence agriculture as a viable way forward for poverty relief. The success of such programmes might create pressures to distribute more white owned land, for subsistence farming. Elites in the villages prefer noticeable projects that are visible on designated sites and involve many villagers – rather than to have money spent on small less visible improvements to household gardens or cropping areas. Similar pressures work on ministers of government and international donor organizations.

Entrepreneurialism as a distorted view

Marxist conceptions of ideology have always stressed that ideologies are a partial view of reality. Entrepreneurialism as an ideology for rural projects does not really come to terms with the high rate of failure of projects based in entrepreneurial designs. The constant effort to create entrepreneurial success legitimizes current power structures and the neo-liberal policy settings established for the economy. What these projects imply is that anyone who works hard and is intelligent can make their own success in the new South Africa. All that is needed is a bit of start up capital, a good idea for a business plan, and some expert guidance, which the developmental state can help to provide.

Why entrepreneurial projects fail

To understand why entrepreneurial projects are almost certain to fail in the villages, we can look at two issues. One is the difficulty faced by smallholder entrepreneurs in South Africa in translating their limited capital and skills into economic success on a large scale – the kind of success that could mean a real shift into employment for the rural poor (Bryceson 2000a; Koning 2002; Mather and Adelzadeh 1998; Timmer 2005; Watkinson and Makgetla 2002). Related to this are the more local difficulties faced by entrepreneurial community projects. The problems with projects that attempt to involve a group of villagers in an enterprise that will make money are legion and have been discussed in detail in the previous chapter. The infrastructure supplied with the project is rarely sufficient to initiate a business that will provide substantial income for the forty or so villagers who are recruited. Villagers are not used to working together in such a large group where agriculture is concerned – most agricultural work (unless it is employment on a commercial farm) is carried out by a working party consisting of one to three adult women, who are friends or sisters, and some adolescent children. Rather than trusting democratic control of the group, members become suspicious of their leadership. Community antagonism to the group is very likely and comes out of the fact that grant funding and the use of some community land has been vested in a small group, relative to the whole community. Problems with accounting bedevil projects depending on commercial success and the purchase of inputs.

Entrepreneurialism as the 'common sense' of agricultural officers

The policy settings of the government resonate with dominant thinking in the South African middle class – the 'professional managerial class' (Ehrenreich and Ehrenreich 1979) and the petit bourgeoisie of black South Africans – and consequently within the agriculture departments themselves. As Gramsci (1988) and Hall (1986) point out, an ideology is not a top down imposition of ideas. It has a purchase and becomes part of common sense. In this case, agricultural extension officers who help to implement the policy settings of the state also produce and are caught up by entrepreneurial common sense. While we can argue that such ideas express the interests of members of their class fraction, this is not always an easy coincidence and there is also much disquiet at the failure of rural projects to deliver. Entrepreneurialism is ideology but also stands as a barrier to making projects work – also a real concern.

The following interviews were conducted with agricultural officers in 2006.

Agricultural officers talk about rural projects

David

David began by complaining that of the projects he is supervising there are very few that could be used to demonstrate a successful project:

> We wanted a project that has got beneficiaries, where it has got natural resources protected and people derive their livelihoods from that area. There is not even one project where people are making money out of it. We are looking for something that has the potential to give back to people the money that was spent.[2]

So, projects can only be regarded as 'successful' if they generate a cash income – improved subsistence is not an outcome of which the department can be proud. Ideally, the money that people generate later equals the money initially spent on the project by the government. This income maintains the equipment and inputs as well providing a job. David went on to talk about a project where 100 villagers had been allocated a cattle farm sold by a white grazier. The fencing supplied by the government had been vandalized by people who claimed the farm had belonged to their 'forefathers'. They had cut the fences to move their own cattle onto the farm.

INTERVIEWER: What do you think is the solution for these other people who are excluded – the ones who are running their cattle illegally?
DAVID: South Africans still have to go a long way. They need to identify who is a farmer and who is not a farmer. Now one owns one or two cattle and another does not. They are not satisfied with the benefits from their few cattle and as a result they don't look after them carefully. I think those who are ready to farm should be given the land. Help to let those who don't want to farm to come out of their farming completely and work elsewhere and then we are left with people who have farming in their blood. If they identify students who are from the universities, colleges and this land is given to those students and if they make use of the principles of farming that they have learned from the university. That will relieve the government of many headaches ... I believe these issues can be solved if farmers are well identified and preference is given to those who use farming to make money.

Entrepreneurial ideology, rural projects 113

My initial discussion with David features projects that are designed to help impoverished villagers. Yet these projects cannot turn villagers into entrepreneurs. The discussion then took a new direction. The answer is to deprive most villagers of the land they so clearly cannot use effectively – the land they are using only for subsistence. Yet such a policy is far from a solution to the problems of the South African poor – 'helping them ... to come out of their farming completely' is not a realistic option with unemployment in rural areas running at 60 per cent.

Viewing this discussion as an aspect of 'entrepreneurialist ideology' we can say that the logical conclusion would be to appropriate the land now used by villagers for their subsistence and present it to the black South African middle class of which David is a member. Professional farmers would receive the land that villagers are unable to farm properly (commercially). While this could be a nightmare of the neo-liberal strategy of 'accumulation by dispossession' (Harvey 2005: 157), it is an extremely unlikely development in South Africa today. While village projects are always directed at helping villagers to become entrepreneurs on their land, a full scale appropriation of this land by well educated middle class farmers, with the government's blessing, would meet very serious resistance. More interesting is the way that entrepreneurialist ideology closes off consideration of more effective ways in which village land could be used to relieve poverty. The failure of village entrepreneurialist enterprise paints David into a corner – the politically unlikely solution of appropriating the land for commercial farming, illustrating 'the hegemonic grip of the "efficient commercial farmer" narrative within South Africa' (Cousins 2007: 238).

To get a sense of the kind of people who might be helped by an entrepreneurial strategy of the kind David proposes, we can look at the examples that Marianne provided.

Marianne

Marianne offered a number of examples where land or farming infrastructure grants had resulted in a successful farming enterprise and the emergence of a new black farmer, though she also noted that these were rare outcomes:

> For example, there was a farm that was owned by a lawyer and he was blind. He hired a certain boy who was trained at the college and understands things very well. That boy used to manage everything on that farm and the farm was working very well. Even this other one that was outside the town. The lady who oversees the project was a teacher and the husband works for the department of agriculture and rural development corporation. They got packages of 2.5 million rands [about $500,000] from the government and now that guy is running the farm with the wife and the farm is promising. They are educated and I think that is why the farm is well.[3]

In the first case, the beneficiary of the land grant was a lawyer and his assistant was educated in farming. We can note in the second example how much money is actually necessary to get such a successful farm going. Not only did the husband and wife own the farm in the first place, they were both well educated professionals. While these examples can illustrate the potential for funding black entrepreneurs to become 'emerging farmers', such successful farmers cannot do a great deal to relieve the poverty of the vast majority of rural villagers.

Diana

Diana began with a common view, that the way to help poor villagers to become successful entrepreneurs was by assisting them to add value to crops which they were already growing, or which they could easily grow on the land they already had available for subsistence – for example eggs, chickens, vegetables (such as chillies, taro, okra), fruit, peanuts, cattle, even reeds for basket weaving. While extra cash is certainly important for villagers, it does not do a great deal to relieve the food security problems of the villages. As well, simple value adding in the villages can lead to a glut – for example an oversupply of chutney made from mangoes. I put these objections to Diana who replied that it was up to the community to 'think of a niche market'. Following my suggestions that *subsistence* production could be useful to supplement cash incomes, she agreed with this and related it to some of the projects in the departments that are tailored to household food security. Yet what is interesting is the way she so quickly moves towards entrepreneurial solutions as the most central and important project design:

DIANA: If people are food secure, then that money will be used for other needs like school fees, development of the house. That is why we are encouraging people to have backyards because that addresses food insecurity.[4]
INTERVIEWER: You don't think the idea that communities must gain income through long term sustainable job creation rules out projects which are mainly to provide subsistence products?
DIANA: I think it's twofold in the sense that if somebody is not having a long term job, he will always think of leaving here and going somewhere else. But if he has some kind of purpose ... It's an ideal situation where somebody, say he starts a project the same as the one he visited in Kwa Zulu Natal. How did they start and where? Like any other business, you won't make money immediately, you have to work for some time before you can get money.

This discussion begins with the problems of assisting poor people in the villages and rapidly moves to talking about setting up businesses for emerging farmers. In the beginning of this passage, Diana relegates strategies for subsistence to the home stand locale – it is what we are doing in backyards. 'Food security' means backyards while cropping and grazing land are always the target of entrepreneurial strategies. In fact, funding for this backyard strategy is actually a minute portion of the total budget of the agriculture department (National Department of Agriculture 2005: 157).

When Diana begins to talk about starting rural businesses, the focus shifts to the male head of the household, and away from women who are the target of backyard food security funding. Diana speaks about a demonstration project in another province – in other words a visit to a project that has by now demonstrated its success by generating a real income. The male villager visits this project and is inspired to start one like it. He realizes that he will not make money in a hurry, but in the long term this will be possible. However, such a time frame for establishing a successful farming business would cut out most poor villagers. What they lack is the capital to back them over this period in developing their business. The people most likely to be able to realize this scenario are precisely those emerging farmers that Marianne's accounts have described – their start up funding is the income provided from a middle class business or professional job. This scenario has little applicability to poor village families.

Stephen

This discussion began with a programme that had been recently initiated by the government. Named RESIS (Revitalisation of Small Irrigation Schemes) it was intended to revive infrastructure that had been put in place by the previous apartheid government and fallen into disrepair.

STEPHEN: They were agricultural projects, mainly funded by the government. Where blacks were farming there. So, provided with infrastructure, pumps, electricity. So, all that they were doing was just to farm. Local subsistence. But the problem with that was dependence. Those people couldn't look at their activity as a business. Because the government was assisting them and paying their electricity and all that. So people didn't run the projects as businesses. So now, this new government is in the process of revitalizing those irrigation schemes. With the objective of enhancing ownership. Management, control and all that. To enhance agriculturally sustainable agribusiness.[5]
INTERVIEWER: The idea of ownership. Does that mean people will pay for their own electricity or diesel if they need those to run the pump?
STEPHEN: Yes. Basically that's that. In fact to run the irrigation schemes as business. Be able to pay their liabilities, you know.

Steven begins the discussion by describing the situation in apartheid South Africa, where some village cattle owners were supplied with boreholes and electric power to assist their cattle businesses. After the collapse of apartheid these schemes fell into disuse. So the intention of this new programme is to supply the actual borehole or dam, and the pump, with government funding. However, the maintenance and the day-to-day costs are to be provided by the villagers. The money is to come from profitable agricultural businesses. So the government actually has two complementary tasks. One is to re-supply the infrastructure that

116 *Entrepreneurial ideology, rural projects*

has fallen into disuse. The second is to set up agricultural businesses that can maintain the infrastructure. Stephen explains the rationale behind this approach.

INTERVIEWER: Can people afford to pay those ongoing costs of maintenance, electricity and diesel?

STEPHEN: I think the approach if its commodity based. People can be able. I mean we must start adding value to what people are producing, you know. Unlike production for subsistence. You know, and only sell the surplus. After subsistence. So that should be changed. To say, now you must look at the market, what the market wants. And the kind of product and the quality of that particular product.

INTERVIEWER: But these small farmers would be competing with large agribusiness concerns owned by white farmers.

STEPHEN: Well, my understanding is that a thousand miles begins with a single step. Though the market has been predominantly dominated by commercial farmers, we need to have a focus and say we are starting now and we will ultimately reach that. Fortunately for now, there are a lot of transformational laws that are enhancing equity in the country. One of them is agri BEE which is agricultural Black Economic Empowerment. Well, you cannot force us to drink water, but all that is said is that these black emerging farmers should try and secure a place in the market. And how should they secure a place in the market? Through buying shares and whatsoever. Of course, with the assistance of the government.

In this final part of the discussion, Stephen elaborates an alternative to rural projects for village communities. This is that contracts to supply government with food will go to companies that can show that blacks have a stake as owners, shareholders or managers. This is how Stephen sees BEE as working. Another option is a land grant for black workers on white farms to gain 'share equity' (Lahiff 2007: 1581). While BEE is an understandable strategy as affirmative action it has a number of problems as a recipe for village poverty. First, the BEE programme is unlikely to be pursued very vigorously by the ANC, which is firmly committed to 'a market friendly and non-interventionist set of economic policies' (Ponte *et al.* 2007: 948). Share equity schemes have in fact done little to relieve the poverty of farm workers who have been a party to them (Lahiff 2007: 1581). Second, the people most likely to be helped to become shareholders or managers would be the middle class and well educated blacks. Finally, the impact on villagers is unlikely to be profound – wages will remain low in commercial agriculture, where companies compete with each other and on the world market (Mather and Adelzadeh 1998). Unemployment in rural villages will not be reduced by the addition of a fragment of the black population into shareholding and farm management.

In all these interviews there is a commitment to the entrepreneurial model for the relief of village poverty. The obvious problem with this model – its continued failure – is widely understood but does not lead to a critique of it. Instead the most likely move in dialogue is to begin talking about the cohort that could actually make an entrepreneurial policy work – the emerging black farmers (members of the educated middle class) who are the current target of the land redistribution policy (see Chapter 4). Here the relationship to village poverty relief becomes obscure. One option is to suggest that village community land should be appropriated for the use of commercial farmers. Another is to focus on farms redistributed from white to emerging farmers. The only way to imagine these solutions could possibly help the rural poor is to suppose a massive trickle down effect from new agricultural employment. The fact that the government is extremely unlikely to come up with the funding for infrastructure support necessary to make this policy real is not acknowledged. This is an ideological view. It works to legitimize the relative power of an emerging black middle class. Proposed solutions fit the interests of that class, recommending the professional middle class as best suited to manage farming land. It is also ideological in failing to fully comprehend the situation that currently exists.

The new middle class and entrepreneurialism

So why is the ideology of entrepreneurial success so entrenched? One explanation is that entrepreneurial ideology helps to justify and account for the extraordinary success and social mobility of the black middle class today. It can be taken as an aspect of 'common sense' coming from the experience of members of this class. Given the fact that up to 1994, blacks were effectively excluded from the middle class by apartheid, very few black South Africans come from a middle class background. Even those who were employed in government jobs under apartheid were paid pitifully low wages by the standards of the international middle class. It was estimated that by 2002 there were 3.7 million members of the black middle class in South Africa (Terreblanche 2002: 32–35). This is very rapid social mobility.

It is probably easy for those who are caught up in this mobility to believe that their own success can be copied by anyone who works hard. It would be disconcerting to think that their success had partly come about through luck. Families that I met that combined middle level government work with successful small business enterprise lived in nice brick and tile houses with picturesque gardens, had two door fridges, large screen TVs and up to date audio equipment, two recent cars and a maid. Their children went to a private school or at least to a good school in a good suburb. Expensive toys such as quad bikes were not uncommon. Sometimes, these families took international holidays or business trips.

This middle class lifestyle is heavily promoted in popular television programmes in South Africa. Soap operas such as *Isidingo* and *Generations* typically show young professional black workers, engaged in large urban companies, enjoying a very up to date, international lifestyle. Advertisements on television promote the same image. Houses are elegant and stylish with all modern conveniences. There is no doubting the pull of this image of social advancement

118 *Entrepreneurial ideology, rural projects*

within the villages themselves. The ambition of young people to live this lifestyle backs up the entrepreneurial discourse promoted by the departments. This discourse is also the stock in trade of educational messages in schools – children in the poorest villages are encouraged to see their future as successful middle class employees – so long as they work hard and are 'clever'.

One agricultural officer, Malcolm, showed me a rusted iron mill sitting in his leafy garden. Malcolm's mother had used it to grind maize from the family's cropping plot when he was a boy. Thirty years ago, when he joined the department of agriculture during the apartheid period, he was earning less than 2 per cent of his current income. His wife now has a business that employs twenty people sewing curtains. She spends much time on the road, arranging contracts with buyers. She complains that her workers are lazy and that like most people, they are only waiting for the government to employ them, not realizing that you have to 'make your own job'.[6]

Of course this mythology of success through hard work has a long history in capitalist countries; the 'view that each poor individual must shoulder the blame for his/her poverty is typical of a prosperous bourgeoisie with a strong success ethic' (Terreblanche 2002: 52). This is just one version of this ideological viewpoint.

Three new middle class South Africans

To understand why the mythology of entrepreneurialism can readily become part of 'common sense', it is useful to consider some life histories in which entrepreneurial ideology seems to fit reality. What I will also stress is the way these histories of success are premised on personal luck and on broader political changes, as much as they are based in the hard work and intelligence of the people involved.

John is a successful 'emerging farmer'. Before he bought his small farm for R30,000 in the 1980s, he had worked for years in Johannesburg driving large trucks and instructing drivers. While he was working in this business, a Scottish supervisor helped him. They worked together in Johannesburg for twenty-eight years, including the first fourteen years after John bought the farm. The Scot trained John in accounting and business methods and even sold him his first tractor. John used his savings from his work to buy a small plot – nine hectares to start with and another nine hectares later. His mother supervised the farm and managed the workers while he continued his employment. He was just one of the successful children in this family; the three daughters all became teachers. There is no doubt that his mother's ambition and skills helped the family to this outcome. After he bought the farm, he saved again to buy mango trees to plant, and later broadened his operations to provide fruit and vegetables to Johannesburg in the winter – when prices were at their highest. Recently, he decided to provide sand and make bricks for local building works. Throughout all these varied stages of his business development, he used the business skills he had learned to calculate the costs and profits before he put any new development into operation. His expertise in business and his knowledge of urban life gave him these options.[7]

Charles, who now has an important position in a provincial department of agriculture, owed some of his success to an entrepreneurial father. Missionaries had given his father some education in reading and writing when he was a child. As an adult, the father worked in a jewellery business in Johannesburg. When the father returned to the village he worked his subsistence plot and was also the village blacksmith. He emphasized the importance of education to Charles, who went on from high school to a black agricultural college. Charles was one of three young men who graduated at the same time. They worked at first for the department of agriculture but two of the men decided to resign and take employment in a para-statal. This was a mistake; the para-statal collapsed. Both those men were still unemployed decades later when I talked to Charles. Charles went on to greater success within the department.[8]

One night, I visited Joan, who was a friend of an agricultural officer. Joan had one of the most expensive houses I entered during my stay in South Africa. The floors of the interior were white glazed tiles, streaked grey to resemble marble. There were impressive gates, columns and doors throughout. A two door stainless steel fridge and a recent computer were examples of high tech consumer items. A large china bowl with clawed bronze feet, smoky glass lamp bowls hanging on chains from the ceiling and regency looking furniture were set about the house. A new six cylinder black Audi was in the garage. The house was immaculately tidy throughout and looked after by a full time nanny and housekeeper. During the apartheid period, Joan had worked as a receptionist and later business manager for a hotel. With Black Empowerment, she had secured government contracts as an events manager. Her two children went to private schools.[9]

In presenting these examples, I do not intend to discount the amazing hard work of people like this. However, what I am suggesting is that many aspects of their past that have contributed to their success cannot be replicated by the great mass of rural blacks who would like to rise into the middle class. I am also pointing to the importance of luck in these trajectories. It was only luck that gave John access to his Scottish mentor. It was only luck that made Charles decide to stay in the department rather than follow his friends into the para-statal. It was only luck that Joan's previous employment in the apartheid period suited her well to take up large contracts for the majority government promotional events.

The middle class lifestyle of black South Africans is not too different from that enjoyed by the middle class in the developed countries. But what is different is that it is very recently acquired. Yet this trajectory is not open to the majority of poor South Africans in the villages. The global and national economies will not find places for another 20 million middle class South Africans. It is not just a matter of encouraging people to work hard and take entrepreneurial risks. The most likely outcome for villages is not that they will develop a range of wonderful new business opportunities that will give everyone a job. The most likely outcome is that rural unemployment will stay pretty close to the 60 per cent figure that it is today.

Beyond entrepreneurialism

One policy alternative to entrepreneurial projects involves a complete makeover of the South African economy. The large conglomerates that now dominate the industrial economy of South Africa are almost completely free, since the implementation of GEAR (Growth, Employment and Redistribution), to invest their considerable profits in whatever way they think fit. This has meant that only a small minority of black workers and entrepreneurs have been included in development that does not provide employment at high wage levels for the vast majority of South Africans. Very frequently, profits are invested outside South Africa, or in industries that produce for export. The fact that these conglomerates have a majority of their assets in South Africa make it feasible to redistribute these assets for 'alternative economic institutions, such as co-ops, community-based corporations and small businesses' which would actually employ people to relieve poverty (Carmody 2002: 274). Taxes on business and redirection of investment decisions would be the means to 'serve broader social and environmental goals such as social justice and sustainability' (Newell 2008: 1076).

Given that agriculture is now down to only 5 per cent of the GDP, it has been argued that the best options for growth are in industry, based on current strengths in energy and mining (Fine 2007). In other words, rural poverty would be relieved as people moved to the cities to take up employment in industry (Timmer 2005).

A second alternative would start from the premise that changes of the kind considered above would depend on a vast mutation of political will in South Africa. At present this seems unlikely – 'limited "state capacity" ... is not a temporary aberration, but an institutional reality knitted into the fabric of state operations' (Walker 2007: 134). While there is no doubt that the ANC is unable to deal with severe social problems within the framework of neo-liberal policies, the electorate seems likely to continue voting for a party that 'talks left while walking right' (Bond 2009). At present 'the non-agrarian economy is failing dismally to absorb the unemployed as well as new work seekers, and this is unlikely to change in the near to medium future' (Walker 2007: 134).

The main aim of an alternative that would take this context for granted would be to supplement the inadequate social security paid to the unemployed in South Africa. The meagre benefits obtained from old age, disability and child support pensions would be assisted with food produced for subsistence; money which is not spent on food would become available for other purchases – electricity, school uniforms, mobile phones, laundry soap, transport and so forth. This policy setting would take it as a given that employment solutions were unlikely to be found for the great majority of the rural poor and that the development of commercial agriculture to relieve their poverty is unlikely (Lahiff 2003). Instead what makes more sense is a strategy of multiple livelihoods; 'experimenting with diversification while retaining a subsistence fall back are complementary, reducing the likelihood of total production failure ... subsistence represents a vital safety net' (Bryceson 2000a: 8).

As a political strategy this proposal fits well with the analysis of Gibson-Graham (2006a, 2006b). They argue that current society is ill conceived as 'capitalist' *throughout*. 'Capitalist' firms, where an employer privately appropriates the surplus produced by their workers, are but one economic form. The household economy, charities and NGOs, community owned enterprises, cooperatives, government departments, family firms and subsistence strategies all fall outside of 'capitalism' strictly speaking.

An effective politics that is not premised on waiting for major changes in the political landscape can be based on strengthening alternative economies. In this theoretical context, subsistence food production is *just one* of a number of economic forms that are located in the villages. Preserving and strengthening this alternative is to work to maintain a 'diverse economy' (Gibson-Graham 2006b) that provides options for rural people – rather than assuming that the market can provide all the answers. As noted above, subsistence production has a role in binding village communities together – in creating a 'community economy' in which some villagers engage in paid work or get social welfare benefits and others contribute products from their subsistence production. These informal exchanges cement ties rather than driving villagers into separated nuclear households, split by their success or failure in the market economy.

As explained in previous chapters, there are many strategies for assistance to subsistence agriculture on home stands, cropping lands and grazing areas. Most of these should be targeted to individual households or at most to the groups of kin or female friends that help each other with agricultural tasks. To a large extent they would have to aim at women where home stand and cropping agriculture is concerned and at men where cattle are concerned. There are a number of related strategies: adequate fencing for home stands and to control cattle, water harvesting from household roofs, bunds in cropping fields, more adequate use of legume intercrops, more effective control of grazing pressure, more land reserved for fuel wood crops. These are all low cost measures that could be rolled out to villages as a supplement to the welfare payments that now exist.

One option is for an extension of land redistribution to communities. Land close to existing communities would enable people to move and use the land without breaking apart existing networks (Walker 2007: 155). Land taken from marginally profitable grazing and game farms would make the best sense to avoid disrupting commercially successful food farming (Moyo 2007: 69). There would be no attempt or need for expensive commercial farming infrastructure to be supplied.

It should be recognized that to a certain extent, subsistence agriculture is current best practice for government projects in the rural villages. This subsistence reality is masked by a smoke screen of entrepreneurial waffle – with business plans that go nowhere in practice. Two things happen here. One is that the vast majority of entrepreneurial projects fail, and most often leave a trail of bitterness and a sense of betrayal. The other is that projects can succeed but do so only because they effectively support subsistence strategies, while their intention and rationale is otherwise. To get more effective policies and action on the ground, there must be a recognition of the centrality of subsistence strategies for workable poverty relief and food security. This is not to say that surplus products from subsistence agriculture cannot be marketed, and it is not to argue that well funded and conceived entrepreneurial projects can never work. It is also not to deny the relevance of entrepreneurial strategies in creating a new class of emerging black farmers. On the other hand, successful strategies for emerging farmers cannot do a great deal for the poor.

To engage in a strategy of this kind it is necessary to make inroads into the entrepreneurial ideology that is so entrenched within the black middle class. It is these people who would be responsible for implementing alternative policies. Even now, they have considerable power to change the situation on the ground, despite the persistence of entrepreneurialism as state policy. Many minute daily decisions and the pedagogic powers implicit in their role give agricultural officers considerable leeway to develop a more effective policy – if an alternative way of thinking about these issues was to gain credibility. In turn, effective models of rural development coming from agricultural officers could link up with and aid the growth of interest groups to pressure the state for more effective policy settings.

It should be noted that effective support for subsistence agriculture is not, as commonly believed, antithetical to 'economic development', especially if we consider the situation of the rural poor, rather than fixating attention on commercial agriculture. Currently, the poor are ill suited for any kind of employment opportunities that might arise. Extreme poverty and periods of hunger are not a recipe for educational success and job readiness. In the context of the South African professional managerial class, my suggestion is that work in the rural villages be conceived of and promoted as government welfare or service. 'Common sense' is not a seamless whole and many middle class black South Africans are tirelessly dedicated to public service, whether in providing basic infrastructure, social welfare, education or health services not to mention in the churches and NGOs. Tapping into this vein of dedication would allow a more effective strategy for rural policy.

Notes

Some parts of this chapter have been published in an earlier version as 'Teaching them to fish: Entrepreneurial ideology and rural projects in South Africa', *South African Review of Sociology*, 42 (1), 37–57. DOI: 10.1080/21528586.2011.563540.

1 Pseudonyms are given for all interviewees.
2 David is an agricultural officer from the Limpopo Provincial Department of Agriculture, interviewed in 2006.
3 Marianne is an agricultural officer from the Limpopo Provincial Department of Agriculture, interviewed in 2006.
4 Diana is an agricultural officer from the National Department of Agriculture, interviewed in 2006.
5 Stephen is an agricultural officer from the Limpopo Provincial Department of Agriculture, interviewed in 2006.

6 Malcolm is an agricultural officer with the Limpopo Provincial Department of Agriculture, interviewed in 2006.
7 John is a relative of the primary school teacher with whom I stayed in Limpopo province. I visited his farm and interviewed him there.
8 Charles is a senior officer in the Limpopo Provincial Department. We had many discussions about the situation in South Africa in 2006.
9 Joan is a friend of one of my students, with whom I stayed in Limpopo.

Vignette E
What is a farmer?

Terry Leahy

A problem of terminology often comes up when I am talking with people in Africa about rural development. I make a distinction between *emerging farmers* and the *rural poor*. My view is that programmes for the rural poor have to be very different from programmes for emerging farmers. This almost always upsets people and they usually throw their hands in the air and go, well what *is* a farmer? Yet in some ways that is one of the most critical questions in regard to project design in Africa.

The way I see it as a sociologist, this is fundamentally a question about the way *social class* works, and it becomes a question of rural development strategy. Projects that make economic sense for one class continue to fail for another class. People in different classes are in really different economic situations and it is not just an economic matter. Class is also tied to what sociologists call 'cultural capital', a set of cultural dispositions and competencies that, like monetary capital, enable you to get things done. This cultural capital is much like what economists refer to as 'human capital'; economically useful skills coming out of some kind of education, formal or informal.

Who are the rural poor?

So what are the characteristics of the rural poor as a class? Well, of course they are poor by all standard measures. In Africa this means that there are health problems of inadequate nutrition that can mean iron deficiency, hunger or stunting of growth. Community members may have HIV/AIDS, they may not be treating it well and they may not have the support of their communities in their illness. They may have someone in their family who is ill from this or another disease and have to care for them or arrange and pay for a funeral. They will be unlikely to have progressed beyond primary school in their education in maths, if they are over about 20 years old. English is a second or third language and they are not fluent speakers and not literate in English.

The rural poor make up their living with what development writers have called a 'mixed livelihoods strategy'. In South Africa, some income comes from government grants. In other African countries these welfare benefits are not available. Families may get some financial help from relatives who are working, especially when they come home for a funeral or some other ceremony. They may make a bit of money by small trading or by casual employment. Some goods are exchanged within the community without money changing hands – as barter, loans or gifts. A good part of their livelihood can come from their own household production, which can provide as much as 50 per cent of the value of the goods and services they consume. This household production is first the production of their food crops and livestock. It is also the production of the resources they bring home from their village and environs: firewood, weedy vegetables, water from the stream. If they are very successful farmers on their small land holding, they can earn some money by selling a surplus from their crop, or by selling an animal every now and again.

So, there is certainly a way in which these people are farmers. Quite a number do some farming, for crops or livestock, as part of a mixed livelihoods strategy, whether to sell the produce or to eat it – usually both. But this farming is only a part of their total livelihood strategy. They are not full time farmers and they are not making most of their living out of farming. And clearly they are not making a good cash income out of any commercial farming that they are doing.

Who are the emerging farmers?

So what is an 'emerging farmer'? An emerging farmer is a black African, who is making a real income out of commercial farming. I have chosen to define a real income as more than $2,000 per year for each adult owner of the farm – husband and wife. If they employ people on their farm they would have to be paying them at least $1,200 per year. They are people who are described as 'emerging' because they have not been doing this all their adult life. Nor are they people whose parents owned a commercial farm as they were growing up.

Now, and this is the crucial point, what are the most likely social characteristics of an emerging farmer? From my research, the most likely social attributes of a black person who makes a success in commercial farming can be summarized as follows. Most usually, they grew up in a rural area and have relatives who have been successful in subsistence farming. They have a 'farming' background, though not in commercial agriculture. They have a background in business or in commercial agriculture, as small business owners or as employees. They may have used their savings from this to help them set up their farm. Their previous employment is certainly the kind of thing that has given them skills in business or commercial farming. They are literate and speak English well and can do maths at least up to high school level. They could possibly be well educated in farming, or business, with a university degree. They are quite likely to be white collar workers, such as teachers or post office workers, or they have retired from this kind of middle class work to run their farm. If they are from a village they may come from a chief's family.

Let me give two examples. John (aged fifty years) comes from a rural village. His mother is an extremely competent subsistence farmer and has always grown a bit of a surplus for sale as part of a mixed livelihoods strategy. Though she is a poor villager she can do maths and speaks some English. She is very ambitious for her children and her three daughters became teachers. John always worked hard. He went to Johannesburg and got a job in a trucking company. He learned to drive and to maintain and fix large trucks. He was lucky in that a Scot, who was employed by the company, could see his ability and taught him how to do accounting and run a business. He saved intensely and finally bought a small farm on the banks of the Limpopo river. He bought a diesel pump for irrigation and the Scot sold him his first second hand tractor. He planted mangoes and vegetables for sale. He realized that he could sell vegetables at a premium price in Johannesburg when they were out of season in the capital. He calculated in advance every new business operation – how much it would cost and what would be the profit from sale. In the first five years of operation of the farm, he continued working in his job and putting more money into the farm. He had his mother run the farm and organize the employees. After fifteen years he still only has eighteen hectares but is going well. He has developed a concrete brick making business to supplement his farming business. He employs about fifteen people.

The second example is Mary. She worked as a high school principal and retired early. She used her savings to buy a two hectare farm on the edge of a permanent stream. She decided to plant mangoes and citrus. It was a river flat so the soil is good. She got some help with extension advice and decided to plant vegetables between the trees while they are growing. She has constructed a dam and pumps to tanks to water the trees. She uses fertilizers, but because they are expensive has switched to a mix of poultry manure and trace minerals. She bought the farm in 2000 and in 2005 she married a white man who was also near retirement and had been manager of a dairy in a nearby town. He brought his business skills to the enterprise and his savings. They do not grow anything unless they have lined up a definite market and it makes commercial sense. They have put a lot of money into their farm and because the trees are only beginning to fruit they are only now (in 2010) beginning to break even and make money. Their farm fronts onto the main road between Port St John and Mthatha so they have no problem getting their produce trucked to Mthatha where they have contracts to sell it at big supermarkets. They need R70,000 to put in a borehole because the long drought has dried up their stream and dam. But the land bank will not lend to them because their farm is too small. They are using municipal water at the moment. But clearly their farm cannot be predicted to definitely make it to commercial success, despite all their hard work and undoubted capacities.

What I hope is evident from this discussion is that the social position of emerging farmers is very different from that of the rural poor. They are middle class or working towards that – before they even begin their career as farmers.

Why this class analysis is important

The key problem of most of the strategies pursued by government in much of Africa is that they are based on the idea that it is possible to turn poor rural villagers into emerging farmers. I will not say that this never ever works, but it is generally unsuccessful, even with considerable government assistance. It is almost totally impossible with the kind of assistance that is realistically likely. The reasons are to do with social class, and the competencies and economic options linked to that.

The poor do not have sufficient land to produce an income of $2,000 per year. They do not have the necessary income to allow them to start farming by purchasing inputs and infrastructure. These problems could perhaps be remedied by government funding. However, the amount of capital that it takes to establish a successful commercial farmer is so large that government could only fund a small percentage of the village population to take up this option. Even a minimal programme of assistance to help a small elite from the villages to become commercial farmers could cost more than giving *all* the unemployed a pension. Governments are unlikely to be able or willing to spend that kind of money.

In addition to this financial problem, the rural poor do not have the cultural capital that can make commercial farming a success. They do not have the necessary educational background and understanding of business to enable them to run a commercial farm and do the maths and make the contracts and negotiate with supermarkets and so on. This is not something that they can learn through a few intensive three week courses offered by a department of agriculture or an NGO. It takes twelve years of schooling to learn to speak and write well in English and to do the maths necessary to run a farming business. Beyond that, commercial farming itself is a whole field of knowledge that is best operated by people with a university education in agriculture.

This is not an iron law without exceptions. John is a good example of someone who transformed himself from a poor villager into a commercial farmer. But this example in itself shows how difficult this process is and how lucky he was to succeed in it. It also shows that he did not jump from being a poor rural villager working with a mixed livelihood strategy to becoming an emerging farmer. He spent approximately fifteen years living and working in the city and learning the business skills necessary to make his move into farming possible.

What are the implications for project design?

So what is the conclusion to all this? Let us look at this on a scale of difficulty, from the most difficult to the least difficult kind of project to get to work.

1. To turn a *community group* of villagers into a successful commercial farming *cooperative*. Close to impossible.
2. To select a few particularly well educated and wealthier people from a poor rural village and help them to become commercial farmers. Still very difficult.
3. To assist a number of village households to produce and market a small income generating addition to their production. Not completely impossible.
4. To assist a number of village households to increase their subsistence productivity. Quite feasible.

So this is about getting realistic about spending government or NGO money. If the aim of the spending is to relieve poverty in the villages you get the best result for the least money by helping villagers to improve the productivity of the agriculture that they are already doing on the land that they already own.

Projects like this take it for granted that villagers will be pursuing a mixed livelihood strategy. They are not aimed at turning villagers into emerging farmers. They are not aimed at a commercial outcome, though a surplus may be produced by some beneficiaries and marketed. The aim is to produce more food, with the likelihood that it will contribute to food security and the possibility that some of the produce will be marketed for an increase in cash income. One good reason for projects like this is to reduce the amount of cash income that poor villagers have to spend on food. On average half the cash income is now being spent on food. The other is to make sure that they are getting a good mixed diet. This is a realistic option, even on the small amount of land that villagers now own.

If you design a project to turn a small group of poor villagers into successful commercial entrepreneurs, your project is very likely to fail. Even if it works, it will do nothing to relieve the poverty of most rural villagers or to achieve food security.

Conclusions

The question – what is a farmer, and what is an emerging farmer – is a central question in working out what kinds of projects can work in the villages.

Projects to help emerging farmers are expensive for the number of people who are helped, even if you include the employees of an emerging farmer. They do nothing much to help the large majority of the rural poor. They make most sense if they are designed to target and work with those who are most likely to become successful commercial farmers – the middle class. The best rationale for this kind of project is to improve the racial balance of African commercial agriculture. Currently, in South Africa whites own 73 per cent of land. It is no wonder that there are demands to redistribute some of this land without compensation.

However, government assistance, if it is directed solely to 'emerging farmers', will do little to relieve poverty in the villages. Projects to help the rural poor must be designed to fit the situation of a very different social class. These people are also 'farmers' but they are *not* emerging farmers and are not likely to become emerging farmers, whatever attempts the government makes to bring that about. There are projects that can help these people with their farming and relieve poverty in the villages quite cheaply – but they are not aimed at turning these people into emerging farmers. They are aimed at boosting their success in a mixed livelihoods strategy.

6 Leading farmer projects and rural food security, Uganda

Terry Leahy and Francis Alinyo

In 2007, Francis Alinyo became one of the students in the Masters of Social Change and Development programme at Newcastle University. For his research project, he wanted to look at the projects that had been running in the Kapchorwa and Bukwo districts of Uganda, a district in which he had spent many years working on agricultural projects – for the municipal council, an NGO and the agriculture department. These districts are remote and hilly. There is good soil and good rainfall but intense problems of rural poverty. I visited him at the site of this research in 2009. The following discussion is a joint effort. This chapter indicates some of the problems of the commercialization strategy for rural Africa, which in the case of crop farmers, has ended up with 50 per cent in poverty. The chapter also reveals the problems with the strategy of 'leading farmer projects' (see also Chapters 2 and 4). Finally, this chapter considers the way in which gender roles can have an impact on household food security.

The economy of Uganda is dominated by the agriculture sector, accounting for 80 per cent of employment (Ministry of Finance 2008) and 22 per cent of GDP (Danida 2005: 16). Production is predominantly for national consumption and 66 per cent of agricultural GDP comes from food crops (Danida 2005: 23). Government action on agriculture has been constructed around the 'Plan for Modernisation of Agriculture' put in place in 2001 (MAAIF 2000), and revised in 2010 with the 'Development Strategy and Investment Plan' for 2010 to 2015 (MAAIF 2009a, 2009b). The key strategy of both plans has been to deal with rural poverty by increasing the commercialization of agriculture, moving farmers out of subsistence production. Whether as a result of this policy or otherwise, there has certainly been a trend towards commercialization. Between 1989 and 2004, the value of non-monetary (subsistence) agriculture fell from 55 per cent of the total economic value of agriculture, to 42 per cent (Danida 2005: 23). Nevertheless, over 80 per cent of rural families still rely on subsistence agriculture to some extent (Culbertson and Kalyebara 2008). Along with this partial commercialization of agriculture, there has also been some expansion of agricultural production. Commercial agriculture expanded by 5 to 6 per cent per year between 1989 and 2004, with subsistence agriculture also expanding by 2 to 3 per cent per year (MAAIF 2000).

Despite the implementation of the modernization plan and the growth in commercial agriculture associated with it, rural poverty is still a very real problem. While poverty declined up until 2003, it increased thereafter. For crop farmers, the percentage in poverty rose from 39 per cent for 1999/2000 to 50 per cent in 2002/3. This increase in poverty for crop farmers occurred despite the fact that food crops have become a more important part of the commercial agriculture sector in this period, and despite the increasing export of maize from Uganda (Danida 2005: 16, 21). In other words, increasing commercialization of crop agriculture has clearly failed to pull crop farmers out of poverty. The impact of rural poverty on food security and health is marked. Twelve per cent of Ugandan children die before their first birthday, and four out of ten of those who survive are stunted, with vitamin A deficiency, and anaemia being common (Bachou 2002: 356–357; Cabañero-Verzosa 2005: 1).

In this chapter, we aim to examine the ways in which the policy settings developed by the Ugandan government, following mainstream models for development, have failed to come to grips with the real drivers of food insecurity in the rural economy. We go on to suggest some alternative approaches which could be more effective. Before doing this it may be useful to explore the 'Plan for Modernisation' and its more recent incarnations in more detail.

The 'Plan for Modernisation'

In 2006, the African Union announced its Comprehensive African Agriculture Development Programme. This sets a goal of a 6 per cent per annum growth rate for the agriculture sector. With this, there is also an agreement by African governments to put 10 per cent of their budgets into agricultural development. This policy is premised on the expected economic impact of growth in commercial agriculture, seen as a recipe for poverty relief:

> Growth in agriculture enables general patterns of development that are employment intensive and hence favourable to the poor. Agricultural growth benefits both rural and urban poor by providing more food and raw materials at lower prices ... reducing poverty by increasing labour productivity and employment in rural areas.
>
> (FARA 2006: 7)

The logic and rationale of this current approach fits well with the Ugandan government's 'Plan for Modernisation of Agriculture', established in 2000. The objectives of that plan were to 'increase incomes and improve the quality of life of poor subsistence farmers, improve household food security, provide gainful employment' (MAAIF 2000: vi). The mission was 'eradicating poverty by transforming subsistence agriculture to commercial agriculture' (MAAIF 2000: vi). The intention was that farmers would orient most of their production to the market to gain higher incomes. By doing this, they could guarantee food security. Instead of providing their own food through their farms, they would specialize in profitable commercial crops and use the income to purchase food. Technological change that would increase productivity for these farmers would also 'keep downward pressure on real food prices'. In other words, farmers would use technology to produce more with less land and labour, causing a drop in food prices. This drop in food prices was expected to benefit both rural and urban poor, in their role as food purchasers. An expansion of the food market coming from lower prices and increased production was also expected to provide capital for business ventures in the urban areas. Increased income for farm households would also stimulate economic activity in rural areas. Ultimately, people would 'leave agriculture' as the stimulus from lower food prices enabled industrial growth in the towns. Land markets were to be enabled by land reforms to secure property rights. The effect would be that small farmers who left rural areas to get work in the cities could sell their land to more efficient large-scale enterprises (MAAIF 2000: vi–vii).

As has been argued in previous chapters, there are various problems with this approach to rural poverty and food insecurity. The success of commercialization for the rural poor depends crucially on *a good market* for agricultural products. This market has to be one that is available to poor rural farmers, who are intended to convert their production from subsistence. Yet it is clear that many agricultural products in fact have a very unreliable market. For example, the earnings from Ugandan coffee peaked at $2,300 per tonne in 1995 before falling to $800 in 1999 (Danida 2005: 19). This was one of the key causes of the increase in rural poverty following 2003. It is understandable that small-scale farmers who are very poor will be risk averse and will prefer to maintain much of their production in staple foods. This can lead to a second strategy of commercialization, in which staple crops become commercialized (Danida 2005). However, this is not without its problems. The increase in fish exports from Uganda has driven up the price of fish, undermining what was a cheap source of protein for the poor (Byaruhanga and Opedum 2007). As we shall see, the commercialization of maize can mean that crops are sold at harvest and there is no cash or stored food to deal with lean times. Successful technological innovation can indeed increase productivity which may just cause a fall in prices and a glut, leaving farmers without cash and without any fallback in subsistence (Danida 2005). The commercialization of agriculture and the subsequent sale of land to successful farmers can just mean that subsistence farmers are driven to urban centres looking for work without any real options to get employment.

A more exhaustive examination of the problems with this strategy is covered in Chapters 1 and 2. These issues provide a background to look at the detailed problems of agricultural interventions premised on the strategy of modernization and commercialization.

Kapchorwa and Bukwo districts

Kapchorwa and Bukwo districts are in eastern Uganda, on the slopes of Mt Elgon. The two districts are occupied by people of the same historical and ethnic origin – the Sebei. The two districts have seventeen sub-counties. Five sub-counties that have widely benefited from external agriculture interventions were selected for this study. The five sub-counties are: Benet, Kaproron and Sipi, in Kapchorwa, and Kabei and Suam in Bukwo district. This part of Uganda is widely recognized as suffering from land degradation and food insecurity, despite good soils and rainfall (IRIN 2010). The first part of this chapter looks at the shortcomings of the government agricultural interventions in the study areas. The second part looks at the roots of food insecurity and the last part considers alternative strategies. In 2008, Francis Alinyo conducted a set of interviews with key informants, as well as focus groups and PRA (Participatory Rural Appraisal) sessions with local residents. These have provided the quotations cited here.

Approaches to food security

Ziegler (Chilton and Rose 2009: 1204) explains the 'rights based' approach to food security, claiming that food security is 'the right to have regular, permanent and unrestricted access, either directly or by means of financial purchases to quantitatively and qualitatively adequate and sufficient food corresponding to the cultural traditions of the people to which the consumer belongs'. Food security is considered in this chapter in terms of access to food at individual and household level. This chapter argues that the barriers to successful food security projects are rooted in social systems that systematically disadvantage some sections of the community in accessing food.

In recommending a variety of strategies to deal with food security we are adopting a sustainable livelihoods framework with its focus on 'human wellbeing and sustainability rather than just economic growth' (Foresti et al. 2007: 1). We are recommending the promotion of a sustainable livelihood that combines a fluctuating cash income with an assured provision of household food from the subsistence economy, a strategy of 'multiple livelihoods' (Walker 2007: 133). Marketing agricultural products for cash is just one part of what can make food security a reality. Bryceson hits the nail on the head when she writes that 'continued reliance on subsistence production represents a vital safety net' (2000a: 8). As Shackleton and colleagues point out, an attempt to go beyond subsistence and commercialize all production 'can lead to the neglect of opportunities to enhance current livelihood strategies' (2001: 596). More broadly, as Gibson-Graham argue, it is a mistake to regard industrial capitalism as 'the pinnacle of economic and social evolution' and non-capitalist economic units as 'primitive, backward, stagnant, traditional, incapable of independent growth and development' (2006a: 40–41). Non-capitalist subsistence agriculture is a response to current problems, rather than a traditional relic of past practices. Food provision through subsistence strategies is perfectly possible if projects pay attention to what might work in this economic and cultural context, rather than writing off subsistence agriculture and bypassing it completely.

Recognitions of food insecurity

Food insecurity in Kapchorwa and Bukwo districts exists in the form of hunger, malnutrition and insufficient income to purchase food. Female and orphan headed households, the poor and those without any land ownership are the worst affected. This is despite the numerous food security projects that have been implemented, both by government and by foreign donors. Discussion of the problems of hunger was a constant theme in the interviews and focus groups for this research:

> The majority of families here suffer from severe hunger and they have to rely on selling labour in order to survive. Many will live on one meal in a day. The situation is terrible. Some of them get loans from the moneylenders and pay them back after harvesting their produce. July to October is the peak of hunger.
>
> Right now, there are several families that are experiencing hunger. Most households eat once a day because they lack enough food to live on. That is why if you look around you will realize that people are gloomy and weak. Beans are the main food now in many households. This is causing problems like diarrhoea.

Food insecurity is having an effect on health and the education of women. Women in Suam and Kaproron are aware of the risks associated with prostitution, but they are forced to sell sex when there is no food. As Chilton and Rose put it, 'the more food-insecure a woman is, the more risks she may take to get food on the table' (2009: 1206). PRA participants noted the HIV/AIDS deaths in their villages. Food insecurity is also having an impact on girls' education. Girls join their mothers to fetch firewood for sale, or to sell agricultural labour for food or money. As a result, enrolment for girls is lower than for boys in the primary schools in the two districts. The disparity is highest between July and October, when food insecurity is at its peak:

> Those who do not have food provide labour in the gardens of those who have money and food, in exchange for either money or food. This is very common. And then there are those who collect firewood from the forests to sell. These are women and children, especially the girls. These are young girls of between 8–15 years. They are enrolled in school but they have to help their parents when there is no food. How do they attend school when they have not eaten anything? Some women 'sell' themselves to get money to buy food. Several people have died of HIV/AIDS in the area and the lack of food is bringing this problem.

Shortcomings of current food security projects

Community group projects

Community group projects in Kapchorwa and Bukwo tend to end up being dominated by those who are already leading members of the community. To start up a 'community' project, development agencies and government extension workers call representatives of the community to meetings to identify food security problems. These people are usually leading men. They are provided with sets of proposed solutions and the corresponding financial resources sourced. These local leaders are then expected to take feedback to the communities and prepare them for implementation by forming group projects that include 20 to 40 people as members. Each project is headed by a local committee, dominated by 'prominent' people. The process of group formation is hasty, causes suspicion and relies on existing power structures in the community that many find marginalizing (Oakley 1991).

The criteria for recruiting members to community projects disqualify those in dire need of food assistance. The projects require membership fees between 5,000 and 20,000 Uganda Shillings annually (between two and eight US dollars). While membership fees are a good idea to promote ownership, those who are hungry find sums like this too much to pay. Members are also required to be a resident or own land in the area where the project is operating. This requirement discourages women, who are not likely to be the owners of land. Another excluded group are those with uncertain land tenure. A leading member of the Tuikat group explained his perspective:

> For one to be a member of our group, a membership fee of 5,000 shillings per year is needed. Another consideration is that you must be a resident or own land in the locality. So far 43 of the 113 households in Tolil village are members of the Watershed group. External support from government or NGOs does not benefit non-members because how do you extend support to somebody who has not shown interest? Some time ago, ActionAid supplied coffee seedlings to everybody in this area but most of the poor people sold the seedlings at half the market price because some of them did not have land to plant while others sold the seedlings to get money to earn a day's living. You know, dealing with poor people is not easy.

This account suggests that the poor use whatever they can sell to purchase food. They cannot afford community group membership fees if they are so poor that they have to sell coffee plants when they receive them, rather than selling the beans later. The middle class who dominate group projects view the poor as people who have 'not shown interest'. They see the poor as causing their own problems because they waste resources and money. Leaders, such as the speaker, appear unable to empathetically relate to the situation of the poor or to devise strategies for food security that would be effective where these poor people are concerned. Their preferred response is to exclude them from projects and assistance.

These project models also fit with the preferred mode of operation for government programmes based around the 'Plan for Modernisation'. Although the plan is intended to move subsistence farmers into commercial operation there has also been a decision to target only the 'economically active poor' in government projects such as those run by the National Advisory Agricultural Services. These are farmers who have access to productive assets, such as a plough and oxen, and some skills and knowledge (Danida 2005: 43). The outcome is that poorer subsistence farmers are left out of the picture (Danida 2005: 41, 46, 58). As we have seen, this bias is exacerbated by local realities that influence the design of bottom up community based projects and ensure dominance by leading members of the communities.

Lead farmer projects – targeting the local middle class

Leading farmer projects are an extremely important part of government and NGO interventions in the rural villages in Uganda. In this model, extension workers identify 'lead and model' farmers to champion the commercialization of agriculture. These are almost always the more middle class residents of rural areas. These wealthier farmers are given agricultural inputs to create demonstration farms that the poor are expected to copy. The following is typical of the way lead farmer projects work:

> I am a model farmer in this parish. I was given potato seeds, fertilizers and herbicides by the National Advisory Agricultural Services programme to establish a potato multiplication garden. In total, the inputs I received are worth 2 million shillings. The potato garden I have established is supposed to serve two purposes; one, as a learning unit for other farmers who want engage in potato farming and two, as a centre where other farmers will get improved potato seeds. I like this programme because it has helped me to access planting materials and inputs, which I would not have otherwise accessed.

Interviewees chosen to be lead farmers and develop commercial cropping were typically people with more land than most of the poor. In most cases they also had a job outside of farming that allowed them to pay for some inputs and supplement their livelihoods when their farming income was insufficient. One recipient was a secondary school teacher with what is considered a large holding (fifteen hectares):

> I was given the chickens and materials as a grant under a government programme. The programme's focus has slightly shifted from training farmers to providing inputs. Inputs are important because most people here are very poor and unable to purchase inputs. I received 100 chickens worth 1 million shillings and the poultry house cost 2 million. There are very few farmers here who are able to raise 3 million to start a farming project. Therefore the idea of giving farmers inputs is very good.

What is clear from this account is that there is no way that other villagers could actually copy the model of farming that the lead farmer is pioneering. As the interviewee makes very clear, other villagers could never afford 3 million to start a poultry project of this kind. Even as a fully employed secondary school teacher she does not have that kind of capital. That is why it is argued in Chapter 4 that such projects are better known as projects for 'emerging farmers'. They are designed to help middle class blacks to enter the commercial farming industry, which has been dominated by white owned farms. These leading farmers are chosen to pioneer a change in the racial makeup of the farming business. This policy could make sense in attacking the racially skewed constitution of the African class system, but it does not alleviate the problems of food security faced by the poor.

It is important to note that these commercial projects produce food that the poor could not afford to buy. As interviewees pointed out, the maize grown in this area and sold commercially is not marketed to local poor people but is more likely to be exported. In fact the export market drives up the local price of maize making it even harder for poor people to buy the maize produced in their own locality.

The projects that were discussed by the interviewees fit with the philosophy of 'development through enterprise' and emphasize 'business models driven by a profit motive that engage the poor as producers and consumers' (Karnani 2009: 76). These leading farmer projects are not likely to lead to a meaningful increase in work opportunities for the poor. The emphasis on commercial projects can just have the effect of helping the minority, who may benefit, while the vast majority are confirmed in their poverty. Meanwhile government funds that could go into more effective food security strategies are unavailable.

Encouraging dependence

Another problem associated with current food security projects is the way they encourage dependence on external resources. Farmers from the projects in Kaproron listed banana varieties developed in agricultural research stations as an item they needed to improve banana farming. Yet farmers in the neighbouring sub-county, Sipi, have been able to improve production from local varieties using mulching and intercropping. Another example is the provision of improved livestock breeds to wealthy farmers by projects that are directed at leading farmers. Now farmers think they need expensive improved livestock to augment their herds, when in reality, problems of fodder and pasture care are more relevant.

As a result of such approaches, farmers come to believe that their problems can best be solved by external agencies. The solution is seen as providing external inputs, reinforcing the notion that 'only outside experts can give help' (Kretzmann and McKnight 1997: 4). Traditional farming systems and indigenous knowledge that could deal with food insecurity are fast disappearing. The ability to attract external funding is becoming a measure of performance for local leaders. Yet externally motivated development projects are very likely to fail when outside funding ceases (Oakley 1991: 18).

Roots of food insecurity

An effective approach to food security has to break decisively with the orientation to middle class farmers that is the de facto outcome of the Plan for Modernisation of Agriculture and similar strategies coming from NGOs. It has to depend on resources that can realistically be accessed and maintained by the poor, rather than on expensive external inputs. Above all, it must be premised on a close social analysis of what is driving food insecurity. Food insecurity in this region comes out of the patriarchal division of labour and domestic power, the intimate link between these arrangements and the harvest cycle, and in problems of insecurity of tenure and land poverty.

Gender dynamics

A key cause of food insecurity is the way gender roles impact on family economies. Women play a pre-eminent role in agriculture in Uganda – they are 90 per cent of the agricultural labour force for both subsistence and cash crop production but own only 7 per cent of productive land (Danida 2005: 63). In these districts, men and women have different and complementary roles in agriculture, yet women do the bulk of hours of agricultural work. This became very apparent when we compared the workload diaries produced by the interviewees. In traditional Sebei culture, women are viewed as analogous to household property, a tradition expressed in bride price and men's ownership of property. Women are 'visitors' in the family. Such a view undermines women's capacity to make decisions concerning agricultural production. In farming, women perform agricultural roles like weeding and harvesting while men undertake the clearing of the land and harvesting. However, selling the produce and making decisions on the use of accrued income is exclusively men's affair. Women have no authority to say when and how much farm produce should be sold, let alone what the income should be used for. Efforts to involve themselves in such affairs can provoke a battering or divorce.

Food insecurity is directly related to these gender issues. Sales of agricultural produce peak soon after harvesting season. Middlemen come to the villages to buy the maize harvest from the men who are the heads of their households. In many cases, these men sell the harvest and then spend much of this income on alcohol and other luxuries. The burden of providing food rests with women. This gendered construction of farming and the market makes it unlikely that a strategy of commercialization can deal with food security problems. Helping a family to grow crops for sale will not necessarily mean that they have more food. In fact the reverse outcome is more likely. In the past, they would have grown food to feed the family. Now they have grown no food for their own use *and* they do not have the cash to pay for food when they need it.

A second gender factor is the exclusion of widowed women from land ownership. While married women have access to land through their husbands, this can vanish if the husband dies. The husband's relatives will claim 'their' land back and the widow will have no land to grow food. These practices are actually against the law in Uganda today. However, the interviewees did not think the law was relevant in the local context.

As a farmer from Kabei explained these issues:

> As women, we face unique farming problems. As a widow I have lost all the land that my late husband left us with. The relatives of my late husband claimed that I am not a member of their clan and grabbed all the land. Now I have to brew and sell to earn money to buy food. If I don't do this, my children will go hungry. For other women, their husbands sell all the produce they get and leave the responsibility for feeding the family to the woman. When the man has sold everything and there is nothing to eat, the woman must sell her labour in exchange for food. That is why most of the people you see in the gardens are women. They are providing labour so that they will be paid money to buy food. Otherwise, when their husbands return home in the evening and find no food, they will be in trouble, they will be beaten.

Another gendered constraint is that women are overloaded with household and farming work. So they rarely participate in sessions offered to develop farming skills. Men dominate community projects and training opportunities, leaving out women who are the actual practitioners. Those given skills by the funding organizations are not the ones involved in production.

These three factors mean that food insecurity in Kapchorwa and Bukwo is a structural problem related to gender. As Facio (1995: 17) argues, women's food security issues arise because of their subordinate position to men at the domestic and community levels. Furthermore these issues have serious effects on the food security of other family members: children and even the husbands themselves, who are unable to source food after the harvest income has been spent.

Incomes and the harvest cycle

The problems with the harvest cycle are not just an effect of gender. They are also tied into the way poverty interacts with the market in food. Smallholder farming is the main source of income and livelihoods for the communities in this region. So households sell their harvest to purchase goods and services that they need urgently. At a later stage they are forced to buy food at higher prices. One of the local leaders in Suam sub-county explained that pressing household demands force people to sell their produce when the prices are low:

> We produce a lot of food in a year. Kapchorwa and Bukwo are actually the food basket for the country and surrounding areas. The problem is we sell almost everything, especially soon after harvesting when prices are very much lower. People are under pressure to pay for a variety of needs, it is not their choice. The problem is they have to buy food later at even higher

prices. There are also households that have nowhere to cultivate and yet don't have any source of income. It is a problem for them to buy food when prices rise so high.

Hunger becomes an issue when households do not have income to purchase food as they wait for their crops to be ripe for harvest. A common coping mechanism is that farmers acquire loans from loan sharks that charge them exorbitant interest rates. In the process they have been trapped in a vicious cycle of food insecurity and poverty. Middle class farmers are in a better position. For example, farmers who earn a salary from government use the income to smooth out the ups and downs of the harvest cycle. They sell their produce when the supply is low and prices for their produce are high – because they can use their salary income to purchase household needs. This civil servant explains his strategy:

> It depends on the products. Milk is basically for home consumption. I sell part of the maize and keep the rest for consumption. I will use most of the eggs to generate income. Another important factor is the fact that I and one of my wives are civil servants. We are able to buy inputs like seed and fertilizers on time. Our salaries act as a supplement when there is no other income generated from farming.

For the poor of Kapchorwa and Bukwo, the commercialization of agriculture takes place in relation to their condition of poverty. A very likely outcome is that they will sell all their harvest to get cash and then spend the cash. As we have seen, this pattern is also linked in to the patriarchal division of labour and domestic economic power. An effective programme for poverty relief has to take this context into account, rather than simply assuming that commercialization will solve problems of poverty.

Land tenure insecurity

The issue of land tenure also has an impact on food security. Many farmers in the study area come from groups that were excluded from what is now Mt Elgon National Park. Those who missed land during the resettlement process in 1983 complained that in the absence of secure tenure, they have no motivation to work on their farms. There seems to be little point in putting work and money into farm projects that will only pay off in the long term, when you could end up losing your land (Pretty 1999: 36). Communities in Yatui and Kisito sub-counties, regions which border the park and where ownership is contested, complained that they are not allowed by the management of the national park to grow long term crops like coffee, bananas and fruit trees. This makes them vulnerable to food insecurity and poverty. As we have seen, land tenure insecurity is a perpetual condition for women in these districts. As they are the main part of the agricultural labour force, this has a particularly dire effect on strategies for labour investment in practices that pay off in the long term – including of course, many actions necessary to sustain soil fertility, as well as the planting of perennials for food, fuel or fodder.

Proposals for dealing with the gender issues

We are not the first to have noticed the problems of food insecurity that can come out of the patriarchal division of labour and domestic power. The Danish government's evaluation of the 'Plan for Modernisation' notes that women do most agricultural work and have control of and responsibility for subsistence crops, 'whereas men, who own the land, tend to grow cash crops and raise livestock for cash income – which they often spend for their own personal needs' (Danida 2005: 63; see also O'Laughlin 2007).

The Danish government report suggests that these problems could be alleviated by improving women's ownership of land. They note that there has already been some legislative progress with this – for example, women's rights to inheritance are now recognized. They recommend further changes so that women become the legally recognized co-owners of family land. At the present time, this seems unlikely to take place. At any rate it is unlikely to become effective. The new inheritance law has not stopped seizures of widow's lands. Men's customary control of cash income for agricultural products is not likely to be altered by a law that states that women have legal co-ownership. As Kimani (2010) points out: 'Gender relations are the most difficult social relations to change.'

We support the attempts to empower women to own land and recommend government funding to enable legal cases for poor women. On the other hand, it seems likely that a strategy that works more closely within the framework of gender practice in this region could be effective. We propose treating the gendered division of power and preference in farming as an asset to be used strategically. Projects should promote and encourage those kinds of farming that are more likely to be controlled by women and provide food for household consumption.

Towards food security – strategies to make a difference

As we have seen, the causes of food insecurity in Kapchorwa and Bukwo are complex and structural. Any attempts to improve the situation must depend on a deep analysis of these. In an apparent move to address food insecurity, external institutions are instead contributing to the problem – supporting the middle class and marginalizing those who are hungry, poor and landless. In the light of this critique of existing programmes we will make a number of suggestions.

Securing land tenure for the poor

Where the poor do not have adequate access to employment income, control over at least some land is vital. A full analysis is beyond the scope of this chapter but the following suggestions could be useful. Funding should be applied to enable women to claim their rights under Ugandan law to maintain their ownership of the farm after their husband dies. Land should be restored to widows where members of the husband's clan have taken it. The land insecurity of those excluded from Mt Elgon National Park should be resolved. Government funded land redistribution is an option for the landless poor.

Strengthening participation

Whereas all the development projects in the districts emphasized participation as the mode of delivery, this research found that the form of participation practised is what Pretty (1995: 1252) calls passive participation – 'a form of participation where people are involved merely by being told what is to happen'. The outcomes of food security interventions would be more successful if all the people in a specific neighbourhood were actively involved in the analysis and implementation of food security projects for their neighbourhood. As Pretty remarks, long term economic and food security can be realized when 'people's ideas and knowledge are valued and power is given to them to make decisions' (1999: 172). Full participation could bring ownership and sustainability to food security projects – something missing from the projects that we studied. Those who are food insecure would be able to access external assistance. Full participation and consensus building would enable projects to identify and build on community assets.

The need to involve all farmers in food security and land care interventions is recognized even by the elite who are the beneficiaries of the current arrangement. The actions of those who are not recruited into projects can have negative impacts on other farmers:

> I have been categorized as a lead farmer in this area by the National Agricultural Advisory Services. I have received 100 chickens and materials to build a poultry house. It is expected that people who want to learn poultry management will come and learn from my unit. I have also established contour bunds to check runoff water. But some of the problems I experience in my garden are caused by the activities of ordinary farmers, who are not presently a target of the interventions. Such problems include water runoff, theft of farm products like firewood and fruits, as well as roaming livestock. These people leave their livestock to roam around destroying whatever is in the garden. All the contour bunds and trees I planted have been destroyed.

So, some of the common agricultural problems spill over to affect all farms. Water runoffs, thefts and free grazing of livestock, are problems that can best be addressed through collective action. The 'catchment approach' has the potential to target and involve communities living or farming in a particular catchment (Mitchell 2001: 96). It would mean targeting all people within the given catchment to develop a food security project (see Chapter 7 for an example of a successful African project using this strategy).

Promoting 'women's crops'

In these districts, there is a gendered segregation of crops. Women prefer and make decisions for crops like sweet potatoes, sorghum, millet and vegetables. Men prefer and predominantly control maize, coffee, barley and wheat. The interviewees often referred to sweet potatoes, sorghum, millet and vegetables as 'women's crops'. The men acknowledged that it is uncommon for them to get involved in these crops. There are no men selling these crops in the local markets. The situation is no different when it comes to livestock. Women prefer and have control over poultry while men have control of cattle and goats. Men are concentrating on crops with a high market value and women on crops that are most relevant to home consumption (and food security).

The link between gender segregation of crops and market relevance has also been noted in Mukadasi and Nabalegwa's study of Uganda tree cropping:

> Marked variations were reported in tree species preference according to gender needs. The fruit tree species with a high market potential are the most preferred by men. This is due to the potential revenue likely to be obtained through selling the products. Our survey results show that women preferred those tree species with a lesser market potential, and effectively having more products available for domestic use.
>
> (Mukadasi and Nabalegwa 2007: 10)

We consider the gender segregation of crops and livestock as an asset – a local social setting that can be built on to combat the food insecurity situation. As often noted, 'resources transferred to women are more likely to be used for feeding children than resources given to men' (Devereux 2001: 292). Men and women's expenditure preferences differ. The women Alinyo talked to were concerned with ensuring that their children did not go hungry while the men were keen on business opportunities.

Against this background, we suggest that promoting crops and livestock over which women have greater control will address household food insecurity. A good starting point is to support and expand the kitchen gardening activities that have been established for farmers in Sipi and Tegeres – one of the rare effective project interventions in these districts. Aid projects should assist villagers to construct water tanks or garden ponds to supply water for the house and kitchen gardens. Interventions should promote the traditional 'African dark leafy green vegetables' which are nutritionally superior to commercial vegetables and require fewer costly inputs (Ekesa *et al.* 2009). For example amaranth, spider flower, jute mallow, black jack, pumpkin, cowpea and sweet potato. Projects should emphasize the root and cereal crops controlled by women. They should strengthen production of local varieties of poultry, rather than larger livestock grown for sale. They should promote tree crops for fuel wood, fodder, fruit and nuts. The crops that are known as 'women's crops' are unlikely to be harvested by men for cash income – projects that target their support to these women's crops are more likely to make an impact on household food security. This is because women, who have the responsibility for feeding the household, control these crops. They are also the crops that are hard to market for cash income.

Rather than an attempt to redefine development 'to include the elimination of discrimination against women' (Facio 1995: 17) this suggestion approaches the gender power dynamic in a tactical way, using existing cultural resources as assets. The segregation of men's and women's crops is clearly an operation of patriarchal power in Uganda today – with men's crops being the ones that bring a cash income. One strategy would be to demand an end to this discrimination – to try to enforce women's rights to control commercial crop resources. Another approach is to treat this crop segregation as a cultural asset, which may be used tactically to achieve some empowerment for women.

Neo-liberal agendas on the part of governments put commercial farming as the target of development work. Yet in cases like this, this agenda ends up by diverting almost all land to a commercial crop that actually is unlikely to produce a reliable income with which to purchase food. Turning this arrangement on its head, we are suggesting that growing foods that are *not* likely to enter the commercial economy is a more secure route to food security for poorer farming families.

Securing women's rights to the cereal harvest

Rationing of agricultural produce is a strategy that the Sebei community historically used to address hunger. The harvested produce would be divided and stored separately. One of the granaries – the one controlled and managed by the wife – was used to store food for household use. Another granary stored food for other purposes. This practice was recommended by some of the women Alinyo spoke to:

> In my opinion, we should go back to the old days where there was a granary for food and another for sale. Those days the food granary would even be called the women's granary. Those granaries with stuff to sell were called 'men's granaries'. The village councils should pass a law that every household should have at least two granaries: one for food and another for sale. This should be the demand of all the women.

It appears that the collapse of this arrangement has increased conflicts between men and women and led to food shortages. The interviewees proposed new by-laws to restore this practice. This is possible if projects mobilize communities and their local leaders. We note that this strategy is the opposite of that proposed and funded by the Bill and Melinda Gates foundation. They want to maximize commercial production of maize in this region and are intending to establish a state of the art grain storage facility for 2,000 tonnes of maize (IRIN 2010). Instead our proposal is to retain more of the maize crop to enable local food security, storing it at each household.

Crop diversity for maximum food security

A key issue in food scarcity is the fact that cereal crops are harvested and then sold without being stored for later use. Later on, families go hungry, as there is insufficient cash to purchase food. We are recommending that a diverse suite of carbohydrate crops be grown. The ideal crops to add are those that are not usually marketed. They are crops that can be stored for lean periods or harvested at different times of the year. These are, for a start, the root crops such as sweet potato, arrowroot, cassava, potato and taro. Many of these store themselves in the ground and can be harvested at will. Some can be stored after harvest. There are also a variety of nut crops that can be grown here – peanuts, macadamias, Malabar chestnuts, pecans and walnuts. These crops can be readily stored. Bean crops can be dried and stored – the obvious cropping beans such as soya beans, lima beans and broad beans, but also carobs, a tree crop. Fruits can be preserved by drying and eaten at lean times of the year – mulberries are a particularly easily grown fruit crop that is rarely sold because it does not travel well. However, it can be dried and stored quite readily. Aid projects should develop these crops and assist people with storage technologies.

Conclusions

The food security projects we have examined in Kapchorwa and Bukwo have been oriented around the 'Plan for Modernisation' of agriculture, established by the government in 2001, and still providing the rationale for most interventions by government and NGOs. On the ground, the reality is that these interventions have benefited the middle class. Lower class people have been marginalized. We need a strategy adapted to the particular problems that are causing food insecurity in the first place. Land shortage and insecurity is one problem. It can really only be relieved by strong government action. Another set of problems relates to gender and the role of the market economy in food. Maize is often sold straight after the harvest, leaving none to eat later in the year. The money is soon spent so there is no cash to *buy* food. Men control the income from the harvest. It is quite likely that they will sell the maize crop rather than storing it. Within the local culture, they are not expected to take responsibility for feeding the family. Strategies to deal with this context would promote crops which are not likely to be sold; would maximize the spread of crop harvests and crop storage so food is available throughout the year; would prioritize the crops that are culturally regarded as 'women's crops'; would secure women's ownership of part of the cereal harvest for storage. The participation of women and the poor would be essential to make these strategies work. This is a menu of suggestions. Community groups would be invited to choose from this list and develop particular projects relevant to their own needs. Projects should not depend upon purchased agricultural inputs; cash for this is what is most lacking. Projects should not be targeted at those who are already middle class with the aim of increasing the productivity of local commercial agriculture – this will do nothing for the poor.

Note

Some parts of this chapter have been published in an earlier version as 'Designing food security projects: Kapchorwa and Bukwo, Uganda', *Development in Practice, 22* (3), 334–346. DOI: 10.1080/09614524.2012.664620.

Vignette F
A permaculture design for a Ugandan household

Terry Leahy and Karen Stewart

Uganda continues to experience high levels of poverty. The World Bank (2013) estimates 24.5 per cent of the population live in poverty and a similar proportion experience hunger and malnutrition (see Chapter 6). Our aim in this vignette is to design a smallholder farm for a family of six in Eastern Uganda in the Mbale/Moroto region. Thirty per cent of people in Moroto are food insecure (Shively and Hao 2012). This model is an example of permaculture design and copies many aspects of working farms in successful permaculture projects running in rural Africa (see Chapters 7 and 8).

The design presented is intended to provide food security for a household through permaculture. For the purposes of this design we are going to assume that there are *no cultural barriers* to adoption of any part of this design. Other chapters deal with these cultural barriers and have helped us to see what might work despite them. The aim of this vignette is instead to establish a feasible farm plan that could provide all necessary nutrients for good health, on the smallest possible plot, with the smallest possible investment of time. We are going to explain methods that would be sustainable for the indefinite future and could be achieved with a minimal initial cash investment. While our design is presented as a completed unit, the time to establish a fully self-sufficient farm using permaculture principles is significant. It can take land up to five years to recover from the damage caused by artificial fertilizers and pesticides. It would take time to well and truly establish the legume trees, shrubs and vines for mulch and nitrogen fixation. Fruit trees can take even as much as ten years to grow to fruiting. Making changes like this to an existing holding would also take time in educating households in these technologies. Yet at any stage of this process, yields of food would have improved compared to current conditions.

The plot of land we are going to assign to the family of six (three adults, one teenager and two children) is five hectares (see Vignette B: How Much Land Do You Need?). This is considerably more than the amount of land that is often considered typical of smallholder plots in Uganda. For example, Shively and Hao state that 80 per cent of smallholder families own an average of only two hectares (2012: 8). However, such calculations are probably estimates of the *cropping land* owned by households. Other agricultural land uses do not figure because the land is often used communally, rather than owned by individual households. The figures given in an FAO report confirm this interpretation. They state that the 'arable and permanent cropland per agricultural inhabitant' in Uganda is 0.3 hectares (FAO 2012: 4). In other words, a family of seven people would, on average, own 2.1 hectares of arable and permanent cropland – an approximate amount similar to that given by Shively and Hao for land owned by 80 per cent of households. In this FAO table, land used *for other purposes* is not included. Another page of the FAO report gives the percentages for *all* land uses – 47 per cent is arable land and permanent crops, 31 per cent is permanent pasture and 22 per cent is forest (FAO 2012: 12). On this reckoning, an average household's 2 hectare plot for crops might be supplemented with access to 2.25 hectares of pasture and forested land. So 4.25 hectares for an average family of seven people. The total amount of land we are assigning (5 hectares) is accordingly only a bit more substantial than the average.

The climate of this region is tropical, though the altitude (1,100 metres) makes for cool nights. The annual rainfall is about 1,200 mm, with peaks in April to May and July to August. Maximum daytime temperatures vary between 27°C and 31°C and minimum overnight temperatures vary between 16°C and 18°C (Climate-data.org 2014). The prevailing winds alternate between warm, moist south-easterly winds, which bring the rains, and dry north easterlies in November–February (Matete and BakamaNume 2010). Although eastern Uganda is generally flat, the Mbale region is marked by hills and valleys. The main soil type are 'Andosols' which are highly fertile. However, they can be low on phosphorus available to plants (Nakileza 2010).

Organization of a permaculture holding

Principles of permaculture suggest a household design based around six zones from the house and kitchen garden (Zone I) to a biodiversity/conservation area (Zone V) with other functionally numbered zones in between (Morrow 1993). The aim of the zone strategy is to place things around the farm for maximum convenience, so less time is spent walking to undertake tasks. Because of this, the compost heap and washing up stand are placed closest to the house, along with the house for the chickens (Zone I), with the orchard and vegetable patch in the next zone (Zone II), the crops further out (Zone III) and woodlots and wild areas (Zones IV and V) the most remote. Our design uses this zone approach.

Around the house – Zone I

Within permaculture writing, Zone I is taken as the house and the immediate kitchen garden area. As we will suggest, we are varying this to put the kitchen garden in Zone II, for reasons that will be explained. We are taking it that the house and yard will occupy 500 square metres (10 × 50 metres).

The house is oriented east–west to take advantage of light, while minimizing westerly sun. The house has a roof area of 90 square metres and wide gutters leading to two tanks – each 2.5 metres high and 3 metres in diameter. Gutters are made of colour bond waterproof iron. They could also be constructed using locally fired pottery pieces. The tanks are constructed on a concrete base, with locally fired bricks and concrete mortar. Tanks like this can be repaired and maintained indefinitely, unlike plastic tanks. They will be able to hold 17,670 litres each. On average 99,000 litres of rain per year will fall on the roof (with 1,100 mm rainfall). Rainfall is consistent throughout the year in Eastern Uganda, so these tanks will provide sufficient holding capacity for dry spells.

A pergola and plantings of fodder trees (*Leucaena leucocephala* and *Sesbania sesban*) around the house and kitchen rondavel will support climbing edible plants – such as passionfruit (granadilla), cherry tomato and climbing beans. These plantings will keep the house and kitchen cool in summer, as well as provide food for chickens and vegetables for the kitchen. A freestanding kitchen rondavel is adjacent to the house and allows easy access to the household chickens. Nearby are racks for drying fruit and leafy vegetables. A shade house is used to establish cuttings and seedlings. These structures are constructed of bamboo with a thatch roof to keep direct sun off the drying crops and fragile seedlings. Containers of dried food and seeds are stored in a cool, dark room in the house. The entirety of Zones I, II and III will be fenced with bamboo fencing, reinforced with a hedge of *Plectranthus barbatus* and *Gliricidia sepium* to keep livestock out.

Open grazing of large animals requires significant access to land. Large livestock are also expensive. In most cases, the large livestock owned by village households are for sale rather than consumption. The design proposed here seeks to meet the family's animal protein requirements through poultry, fish and guinea pigs.

Thirty chickens will be kept for meat and eggs. The run and chicken coop are at the bottom edge of the house yard. This way the chickens can be monitored and readily fed with kitchen scraps. For most of the day the chickens will free range in the orchard. At night they will be herded into a raised chicken coop, fitted with roosting perches. This is to protect the chickens from pythons and other predators. Along the shady side of this coop are ranged the nesting boxes. There is a run for the chickens, which is to be five metres by five metres. There will also be an enclosed covered cage for hens with young chickens, to protect chicks from hawks (about one metre high by one metre wide and three metres long). The chickens will each produce 50 kilograms of manure per year – making a total of 1.5 tonnes (McCall 1980). Much will be collected from underneath the chicken coop and the rest will fertilize the orchard as the chickens forage. The manure collected from under the coop will be used to make compost, or added to the fish pond for fish food. Several large trees (tamarind, avocado, mango, mulberry, native fig, moringa) are planted on the border between Zones I and II. These are to provide accessible fruit for the children as well as shade and fodder for the chicken house. Moringas will supply a continuous stock of leafy vegetables for the kitchen and the chickens. Within this zone, the compost heaps (two bays used alternately and a bay for the collection of plant materials) are placed downslope and downwind from the house. These are on the upper side of the banana patch in Zone II so that people can carry a bucket from the toilet to the compost heap.

Orchard and kitchen garden – Zone II

A stand of plantain bananas is situated below the house yard and chicken house. This site receives runoff from the yard and grey water from the kitchen. This patch will be twenty by fifty meters – 0.1 hectares. Fermont and Benson (2011) estimate crop yields for banana in Eastern Uganda of 13 tonnes per hectare. So we would get 1.3 tonnes from this patch. At 0.6 kilograms per person per day, this is close to a daily supply for six people. Including the cropping fields, there is effectively a double supply of carbohydrate. Banana leaves and stalks are good livestock fodder, and can be used throughout the property for compost and green manure (Heuzé *et al*. 2013). The banana patch would also be planted out with nitrogen-fixing legume ground covers, for example Amarillo peanut, or vetch (Firth 2003). Pineapples are a good option for planting between rows of bananas.

This is the zone for a moveable guinea pig hutch. Lammers *et al*. (2009) found that guinea pigs are an efficient source of protein, can survive on a 100 per cent forage diet and are easily cared for by older children. We are suggesting a pen two metres by two metres for 20 to 25 guinea pigs. The pen should be enclosed with a floor and roof to protect from predators (Lammers *et al*. 2009). Wire mesh around a bamboo frame would be suitable.

The toilet is the simplest possible. A wooden seat over a twenty litre plastic container. A handful of mulch is thrown in after the toilet is used. When the container is three-quarters full, the mixture is taken out and placed on a compost heap, with about half a bucket of extra mulch added. There are two compost heaps, each about one cubic metre in size. These are rotated. The first compost heap is built up for one year. After that you switch to the second compost heap. Meanwhile the first heap is left to mature. At the end of the second year the compost in the first heap is removed and can be used in the cropping fields, supplying nitrogen and phosphorus (Jenkins 2005; see Vignette H: Composting Toilets in Africa). To respect African cultural conventions, the toilet must be hidden away in the bananas. It should not be visible from the house or from the path to the vegetable patch. The path from the toilet to the compost heap should also be hidden. Thickets of clumping bamboo could achieve this. A tippy tap at the compost heap is for washing your hands to prevent disease transmission.

The rest of the orchard for Zone II is further down the slope, with the tallest trees (such as mangoes and avocadoes) at the top so that they do not shade out the smaller trees growing below on the northern side (such as tangerines or lemons). The orchard size is twenty metres by fifty metres or 0.1 hectare. A diverse mix of tropical and sub-tropical species will be successful. These include guava, macadamia, Malabar chestnut, mulberry, Mexican apple, mango, passion fruit (granadilla), choko (chayote), tamarind, pineapple, avocado, jackfruit and citrus (tangerine, lemon, orange, grapefruit). The guavas, pineapples and citrus will provide vitamin C. Surplus fruit will enable a small cash income. The orchard would also be intercropped with shade tolerant legume ground cover crops, such as Amarillo peanut and Namoi woolly pod vetch.

Below the orchard, and receiving full sun, the kitchen garden is located. We are taking it that this garden will be 500 square metres – 10 metres by 50 metres. From the point of view of permaculture, it could make sense to put this vegetable patch closer to the house. This is because frequent visits have to be made to collect vegetables and look after the vegetable patch. However, in this plan we are placing the vegetable patch below the orchard. The main reason is that we are reserving the wettest area, that immediately below the house yard, for plantains which require a lot of moisture. Having made this decision, we want the vegetables to be growing in full sun, rather than being shaded by the orchard. We have also provided a dam immediately below the vegetable patch so that seedlings can be watered with a bucket.

Within these kitchen gardens, beds one metre wide and five metres long will be constructed. Each raised bed will be protected from chickens by a seventy-five centimetre fence, slanted outwards so that chickens find it hard to get above the fence. These beds will grow vegetables such as marrow stem kale (*Kovo*), canola (rape), cucumber, carrot, spinach (silver beet), eggplant, cauliflower, onion, okra, peppers, lettuce, leek, yams (FAO 2010). African leafy vegetables will also be grown, including black jack, spider flower, jute mallow, and amaranth species. These weedy vegetables will be grown in abundance so there is always a plentiful supply to add to cooked meals as a 'relish'.

Cropping area – Zone III

Zone III is the cropping area. Planted below the vegetable garden and the orchards, this area receives full sun. We are suggesting a variety of carbohydrate crops, inter-planted with legumes to add nitrogen to the soil. Along with this we propose to grow some vegetable crops in with the cereals, maximizing the usefulness of the cropping space. At the top of this area we are including a dam.

The National Agricultural Research Organisation Uganda (Agona and Muyinza 2013), Ugandan Ministry of Agriculture (Fermont and Benson 2011) and USAID (Balirwa 1992) all estimate an average yield of 1.5 tonnes per hectare for Ugandan maize cropping areas. The Ugandan Ministry of Agriculture estimates the same yield for millet, and 8.2 tonnes per hectare for cassava (Fermont and Benson 2011). However, this figure of 1.5 tonnes per hectare of maize is an average. It includes the yields of impoverished farmers who are likely to be getting only 1 tonne per hectare because they cannot afford fertilizers and are not using organic methods to boost production. At the other end, the average takes in more wealthy farmers who will be using synthetic fertilizers. Our design here assumes that with a successful application of permaculture design it would be easily possible to get 2 tonnes per hectare (see Vignette A: Low Input Technologies). For a family of six requiring 1,350 kilograms of maize per year (see Vignette B: How Much Land Do You Need?), this requires a cropping area of 0.7 hectares (70 metres × 100 metres).

The manure fertilizer requirements for a cropping area this size are estimated to be just over seven tonnes per year (Biovision Foundation 2010). An impoverished family is unlikely to own any large livestock, making the cattle manure option impossible. Instead we are going to suggest soil fertility methods that do not depend on cattle manure or synthetic fertilizer. The cropping fields will be planted using 'conservation agriculture', with compost made with mulch and chicken manure in the planting stations, supplemented by legume intercrops to fix nitrogen (see Vignette A: Low Input Technologies). In Central and Southern Uganda, maize can be cropped twice a year but our design assumes only one crop per year. To rotate crops to avoid pest plagues different crops will be rotated with maize – wheat, potato, cassava and sweet potato (Fermont and Benson 2011). Alley cropping with *Calliandra calothyrsus* and intercropping with *Mucuna pruriens* will fix nitrogen and provide organic matter (Fischler and Wortmann 1999; see Vignette A: Low Input Technologies). Complementary food crops to grow with the cereal crops are pumpkins, squash, cowpeas, beans, bambara nuts and peanuts. As part of the design, bunds also run through the cropping area along contour lines running across the slope. They are to infiltrate water and prevent erosion (Morrow 1993). These will be planted with Napier grass to consolidate the bund, and as a source for mulch for the floor of the chicken coop.

The cropping area will have to be protected from roaming cattle. An affordable fence can be constructed from living plants, with a supplement of barbed wire. *Gliricidia sepium* is a good foundation. This quick growing legume tree can be planted up from cuttings. Barbed wire can be woven through these living fence poles. Supplementing this, a hedge of *Plectranthus barbatus* deters livestock, which find the leaves unpalatable. This living fence will allow households to establish fertile soil using intercrops of legumes and laying mulch. A hedge will also be established on the northern and north-eastern edges of the property to block the dry north-easterly winds that prevail from November to February. To get the hedge established quickly, lablab and clumping bamboo will be planted. Lablab provides edible beans and leaves, can be used for livestock fodder and fixes nitrogen. Bamboo is a fast growing timber for fencing, trellis and animal hutches. It can also provide mulch for compost. The hedge will be pruned so it does not shade the crop fields.

The design includes a dam at the lowest point of the residential area and in the top of the cropping area: to capture water, silt and nutrient runoff and to provide water for livestock and crop irrigation. If there is clay below the top soil, the pond would have clay walls and would not be lined. Otherwise it could be lined with clay or black plastic. A bund would be constructed leading water into the pond from the sides.

This dam will also be used as a pond for aquaculture. It is proposed that Blue Nile Tilapia fish be stocked as they are indigenous and do well up to elevations of 1,600 metres (Biovision Foundation 2012). The pond receives full sun, ensuring a water temperature suitable for the fish. Rocks placed around the pond also trap warmth. Tilapia have an average harvest weight of about 250 grams per fish. The proposed pond would contain at least fifty fish. They reach reproductive maturity

152 *Vignette F: a permaculture design, Uganda*

at 5 to 6 months, multiply quickly and have to be harvested often to prevent overcrowding. An ideal food source. The pond is also useful to crop water hyacinth, a prolific plant. The leaves can be eaten and provide various nutrients; vitamins A, B1, B2 as well as protein (18.7 per cent), fibre (17.1 per cent) and carbohydrate (36.6 per cent). Water hyacinth is also an excellent animal fodder and food for the Tilapia. It also makes a good mulch for compost or garden beds (Deane 2012).

Woodlot and wilderness – Zones IV and V

This is a region with high rainfall. A woodlot planted out with fast growing fuel species could sustainably yield one tonne per hectare. Average consumption of fuel wood is about 690 kilograms per year. So a family of six would need a four hectare woodlot (see Vignette B: How Much Land Do You Need?). The woodlot, along with its water harvesting structures, is also intended to capture and slow runoff, limiting erosion and increasing soil moisture downslope. A mix of trees should be grown. Some useful species for the woodlot might be Black wattle, *Faidherbia albida*, *Calliandra calothyrsus*, Blue gum, Croton, Mexican cypress, Neem tree, Nandi flame, *Sesbania sesban*, Wild date palm and Whispering pine (Biovision Foundation 2013). The trees would also provide fodder for livestock and leafy branches for mulch for the cropping fields and gardens. Much of the woodlot would remain undisturbed, so small wildlife and indigenous plants would proliferate.

Conclusions

The design of this smallholding is based on working models operating in the Chimanimani district of Zimbabwe (see Chapters 7 and 8). It is also informed by a variety of agricultural research experiments, giving us some of the figures we have used. While it is a fictionalized and schematic example, all these elements could be readily created in the African countryside. The main challenge in getting this model going is not money, but the will to put this strategy in place. As I have shown in other chapters, the problems with this are manifold. They need to be tackled through a programme of social and cultural change, informed by effective project design.

Reading the map and plan

The following diagrams show the map for our proposal. This is a simplified design. For example, we have shown everything laid out in neat rectangular boxes lined up with the direction of the slope. Reality would usually be more complicated. In many districts, it is quite common for communally accessed woodland to be situated at some distance from the residential area. Likewise, cropping fields may all be located outside the village. Joining them together as we show in the diagram and maps (Figures F.1, F.2, F.3 and F.4) makes it easier to see what elements households will need. Permaculture design suggests that the things attended most frequently should be closest to the house, and all elements of the farm should be as close as possible. The ideal arrangement would be like the one shown in these plans (see Figures F.1, F.2, F.3 and F.4). Yet for social cohesion it might be better to situate the residential blocks (home stands) next to each other. Each residential block would include house, plantains, orchard and vegetables. Householders could then walk to the village cropping fields and a communally owned woodland.

The contour bunds (as shown in Figures F.1, F.2, F.3 and F.4) are raised long mounds. These hold water on the slope, ensuring a gradual infiltration of water into the soil. The swale is the ditch on the upper side. Bunds and swales should be at least 1.5 metres wide, with the mound being about three-quarters of a metre in height and the swale the same depth (see Vignette A: Low Input Technologies). In the top of the banana patch just below the house yard, it makes sense to dig some deeper pits within the swale, to ensure that all the household runoff is used in the garden.

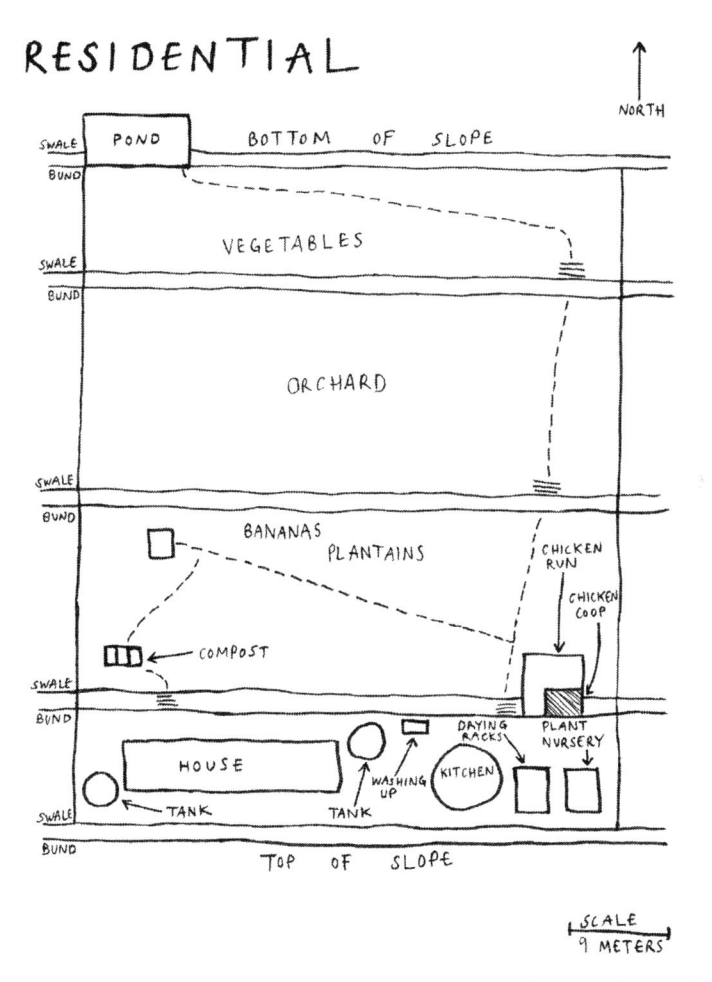

Figure F.1 Residential area – map. This map shows the area close to the house.
Source: Illustration by Miriam Joan Montgomery.

Figure F.2 Residential area – three dimensional diagram. This diagram shows the area close to the house.

Source: Illustration by Miriam Joan Montgomery.

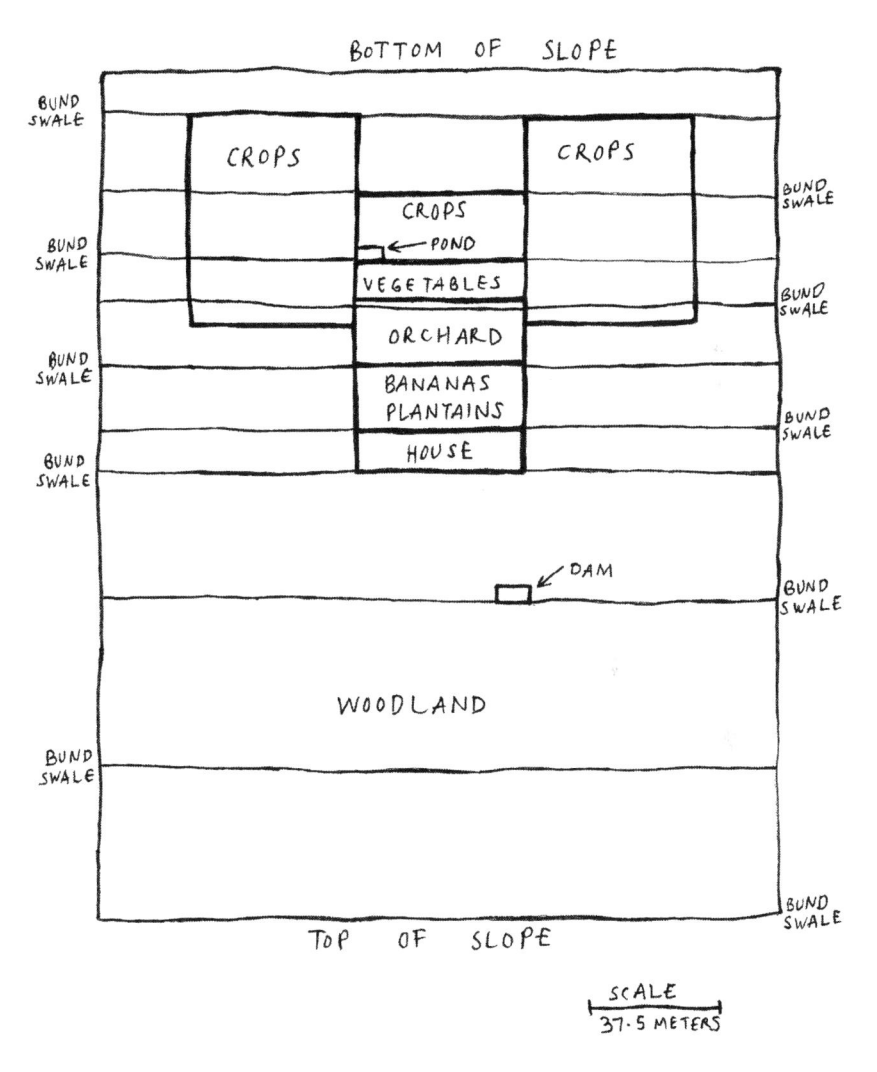

Figure F.3 The whole farm – map. This map shows the whole area of the farm, including the residential area.

Source: Illustration by Miriam Joan Montgomery.

RESIDENTIAL
CROPPING
WOODLAND

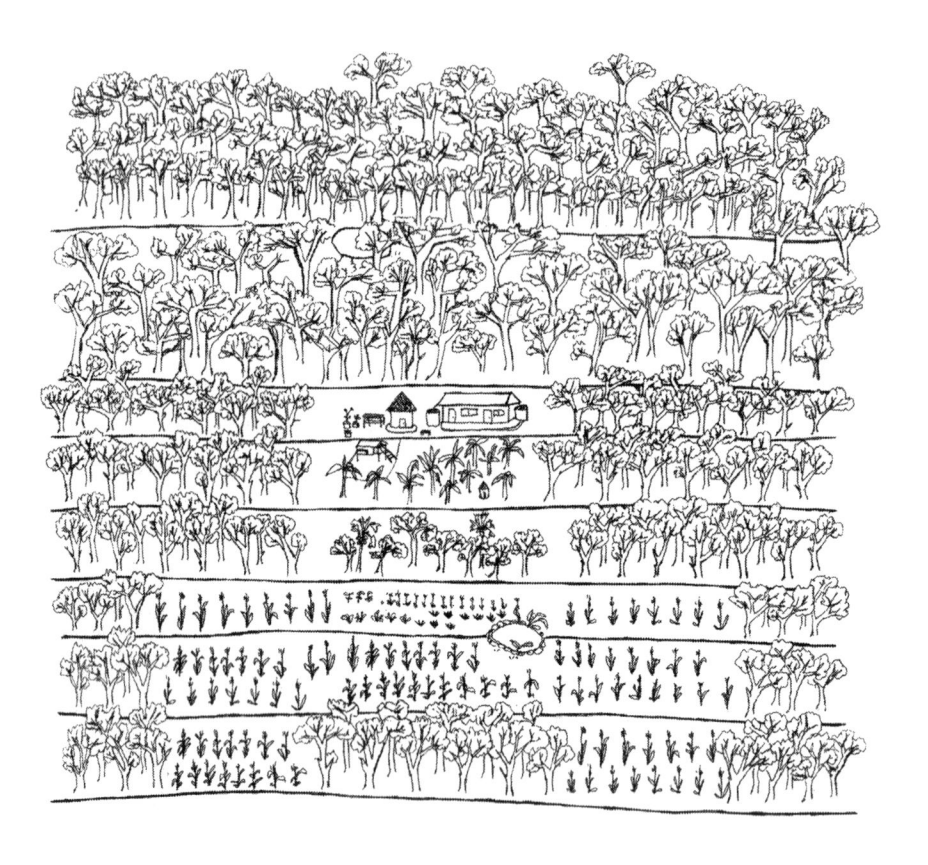

↓ NORTH

Figure F.4 The whole farm – three dimensional diagram. This diagram shows the whole area of the farm, including the residential area.

Source: Illustration by Miriam Joan Montgomery.

7 An embedded project – Chikukwa

Terry Leahy

> So we were saying, now what are we going to do? So we worked very hard ...
> (Jessica Chibharo, interviewed at CELUCT headquarters 2010)

Introduction

Jessica Chibharo gave this summary of the Chikukwa project in Eastern Zimbabwe in 2010, almost twenty years after its initiation. She was one of many project members who explained the formation of the project with this phrase. The statement indicates ownership of the project, the collective 'we' referring to the whole Chikukwa clan of six villages. It acknowledges the crisis they were facing in the early 1990s and takes pride in the work they did to turn their situation around. The Chikukwa project combined a social transformation with a transformation of the agricultural landscape to achieve long term food security.

After working on rural agriculture projects between 2003 and 2009, I was aware that most projects in rural Africa were failing. I was keen to see if any projects worked in a different way from the unsuccessful projects I had seen. In 2009 I attended the international permaculture convergence in Malawi (IPC9). Presenting a workshop at the conference was a group who were involved with a permaculture project in the Chimanimani district of Eastern Zimbabwe. The project site was the six villages of the Chikukwa clan with a population of seven thousand. These six villages occupy a fifteen kilometre stretch of hills and valleys. I made arrangements to go and see their project in the following year. The team at the conference explained that they were seeking someone who could document their project on film. My sister volunteered to come to film the project in 2010. We had a hectic schedule of filming, taking in the project in the Chikukwa villages and the TSURO project in the whole Chimanimani district (see Chapter 8). The film was completed in 2013 and is available through the website www.thechikukwaproject.com (Leahy and Leahy 2013). This chapter includes interviews transcribed from the thirty-five hours of film that were recorded in 2010.

In 2014, I went back, spending several months at the project, going around to interview local people, observing the workshops organized by the project and getting a first hand experience of people's agricultural strategies. Altogether, more than forty people have been interviewed to provide their insights for this analysis. I am also making use of photos taken in the early years of the project, along with minutes of meetings taken at that time. More recent photographic material provides a point of comparison. Permission has been granted to use the real names of interviewees for this chapter. They should be honoured for being activists in such an effective project.

While the definition of 'permaculture' is contested, a working guide to permaculture in practice suggests the following summary. Permaculture is the design of sustainable agriculture and sustainable settlements. So it takes in agricultural technologies, the built environment and the human inhabitants as parts of an integrated interrelated landscape. This project is an exemplary instance of permaculture in that sense.

This chapter is to explain this project in Eastern Zimbabwe, to understand its success and consider the extent to which it could become a model. In permaculture (Mollison 1988) the edge between two kinds of plant communities is regarded as particularly productive, sharing opportunities from each ecological zone. For example, the edge between forest and pasture. Chikukwa is such an edge. It is on the edge of a mountainous region, bordering a national park, a pine plantation and the country of Mozambique. It is home to the Chikukwa clan, which has lived in this part of the world for centuries. But also key figures in the project have been people from other parts of Zimbabwe, and other parts of the world, making a social and cultural edge. The slow collapse of the Zimbabwe economy over several decades meant that Chikukwa ended up being on the edge of the global economy. This was a crisis that drove experimentation.

The Chikukwa project can be considered in relation to 'Southern Theory', which proposes the use of theoretical tools derived from the experience of the global South (Connell 2007). The Chikukwa project is founded on the recommendations of 'permaculture' or 'permanent agriculture' developed by Bill Mollison and David Holmgren in Australia. As in Mollison's canonic book, *The Designers' Manual* (Mollison 1988) permaculture has sought to develop a sustainable agriculture adapted to each of the world's climatic regions, making a break with modernist agriculture invented for the North. In the 1980s, Mollison travelled around the world to promote this new vision. In Africa, one of those he met was John Wilson, who went on to found the Fambidzanai centre for permaculture in Harare, a key moment for the Chikukwa project. As a social technology, the Chikukwa project is an indigenously produced solution to African problems. Typical models for rural projects in Africa have sought to replicate the rural industrial takeoff of European countries – attempting to build capitalist agriculture, inspiring entrepreneurs and building market skills (Ferguson 1990; Marais and Botes 2007; Mkize 2008). The experience of the Chikukwa project suggests the relevance of a different model.

How the project works

The claim that the Chikukwa project is a success is based on a variety of considerations. One is the extent of the project's longevity – twenty-six years now. Most projects in Africa do not last beyond several years. The photos archived by CELUCT and taken at the time of these events show the Chikukwa lands in the early 1990s as barren hillsides, scarred by eroded gullies with only a few trees remaining. The banks surrounding the springs are bare and have been trampled by cattle. Interviewees explained that the springs had dried up. They were walking five kilometres to fetch water. During the dry season there was little feed for cattle. Fuel wood was in short supply. Harvests were poor and hunger common. During the wet season, rainwater poured down the hills. Houses were flooded, with silt reaching up to the window ledges.

More recent photos show small farm households, each surrounded by orchards and vegetable gardens. Contour bunds topped by vetiver grass ring the hillsides. Gullies host a lush growth of indigenous woodland. The ridges and some slopes are planted with a thick woodland of eucalyptus, acacia and casuarina species – for firewood and timber. Woodlots and swales take in water in the wet season and release it gradually, so springs run continuously. The changes brought about by the project have been increased yields of cereals, more vegetables, fruits and animal protein in the diet, and accompanying good health. These are the fundamental ingredients for long term food security. A baseline survey was conducted by the TSURO Trust in Chimanimani District (Takaidza *et al.* 2011), a study of 125 randomly selected houses from five of the wards with which TSURO works. Because the Chikukwa villages are one ward of the Chimanimani district, they were included. The respondents were asked whether they have sufficient food in each month of the year.

There is a marked difference between Chikukwa and the other wards. The food shortage the other wards experience is typical of South and Eastern Africa (see Chapters 1 and 2). Three of the four other wards surveyed in the study have food sufficiency figures that are often below 50 per cent.

While the central aim of the Chikukwa Project has never been market based development, there has been a paradoxical long term effect from the project.

Table 7.1 Enough food by ward

Ward	Monthly status (%) of households reporting enough food											
	Aug	Sep	Oct	Nov	Dec	Jan	Feb	Mar	Apr	May	Jun	July
Chakohwa	40	36	28	28	32	28	36	60	64	60	60	52
Chayamiti	50	46.2	38.5	38.5	34.6	46.2	42.3	50	65.4	69.2	69.2	65.4
Chikukwa	83.3	83.3	79.2	66.7	70.8	70.8	87.5	91.7	95.8	95.8	95.8	95.8
Chikwakwa	24	8	8	12	20	24	28	36	44	48	36	40
Manyuseni	72	68	60	60	52	64	72	72	84	84	84	79.2

Source: Takaidza *et al.* (2011: 2).

Two decades of food security, adult education and community building have primed the community to engage more successfully in the market economy. The children of people originally trained in permaculture by the project are by now young adults. Raised by parents whose education was assisted by the project, parents who have made a success of scientifically informed subsistence agriculture, they entered the education system with a kind of cultural capital that is unusual in rural Africa. Now as adults, they are going elsewhere for work and further education, or growing marketable crops in nearby locations.

History of the Chikukwa project

The Chikukwa project was initiated in 1991. A German couple who had come to teach in Zimbabwe were catalysts. Eli and Ulli Westermann took a post teaching in the Chimanimani district in the mid 1980s and were granted land for their house by the chief. They met two other teachers who also became involved in the project. One was John Wilson, who founded the first permaculture organization in Zimbabwe, Fambidzanai Training Centre, Harare. The other was Chester Chituwu, principal of the Chikukwa primary school. Eli and Ulli lived in one of the six villages occupied by the Chikukwa clan, the village of Chiteketa with their two children, who grew up speaking Shona, English and German.

In 1991, the spring which had served about fifty households in Chiteketa village for their water supply dried up. This was the culmination of a growing crisis, caused by clearing of the original forest vegetation, combined with overgrazing and cropping. Eli met with some of her neighbours and a small action group was formed. Patience Sithole explained the origins of the group:

> ...at the secondary school my husband was teaching with Ulli and Eli [Westermann]. And I became friends with the Westermanns' family. So each and every day, we could sit down, and if it rains we could see erosion, soil going and so on. And then we always discuss. And then one day said OK, but we have to action. And we began by having a workshop in 1991, at Peter's place. I volunteered, together with Piti, Peter, Abisha, Eli and Zawanda.

This group of six, 'Nuchidza Dzakasimba' or 'Strong Bees', met weekly. Their first attempt on the spring was to dig for water. But with further rains, the spring silted up again. So they organized a one-week permaculture design workshop. They invited five householders from each village, traditional leaders and representatives of youth. Instruction was delivered by the Westermanns' friend from teaching, John Wilson, with Alias Mulambo. They concentrated on the use of natural resources, especially water. There was another similar workshop in 1992. The group operated in two modes. As neighbours, the Strong Bees met to plan their own household projects and help each other – collecting seeds, establishing legume trees, orchards and vegetable plots, starting nurseries for fruit trees. Second, they recruited working parties of local villagers – to fence off the springs and plant indigenous species, to plant woodlots and fence them, to put in contour bunds and swales. As Eli describes it:

> So, me, Mai B and four other youngsters decided to do something and we took the hoes on our shoulders and walked up into the mountains and worked with the people digging swales, working at the spring, and people got so motivated and just kind of came along. It was very enthusiastic. After a few years you could see the impact. Erosion was limited. Some areas were already terracing out, after the vetiver contours. So you really could see that the maize was much higher and a bigger harvest. Two or three springs were already reactivated after three or four years of our work. And that was very motivating.

These groups were totally voluntary in character. All work was with hand tools. They brought in a truckload of vetiver grass to stabilize the bunds they were creating. It was propagated for bunds in all the villages.

The methods of the Strong Bees spread to other households. Ulli Westermann describes the process:

> Seeing is believing. The home to home exchange was the main tool. And then there were other things like 'Permachikoro' – 'Permaculture School', which happened once a month. And it was basically farmer to farmer training. So you had people who were experienced in a certain thing, they would take that knowledge to the community. The demand came very quickly within Chikukwa. I mean there was so visible success after a short time really that it was just convincing.

The group helped to establish similar permaculture clubs in all the six villages. By 1995, there were training 'attachments' to teach the methods being adopted. The group were invited to receive funding from a German NGO (*Weltfriedensdienst* – WFD). They decided to accept, so long as their community organization retained control. In 1996, to link up the village groups they formed CELUCT – Chikukwa Ecological Land Use Community Trust. Members of the 'Strong Bees' club became the management team. With the money from WFD to pay for materials, working parties of villagers volunteered their labour and built the Chikukwa Permaculture Centre – a kitchen for catering, a dormitory, open sided halls for workshops and an administration office. A catering department rostered villagers to provide meals for workshops. A pre-school was established. In 1997 CELUCT started up food processing clubs to process surplus for sale. In 1998 social groups were formed for women. In 2006, following some conflicts in the organization, they established a department for conflict transformation – Building Constructive Community Relations. Local groups were set up in all the villages and people came from beyond Chikukwa to learn these techniques. 'Talking circles' were formed to counter the stigma of HIV/AIDS and to assist infected people. Each of these 'departments' consisted of voluntary clubs in the villages, sending representatives to the central organization. Sustainable agriculture had been the first and the others had followed.

The new landscape

Over twenty years a new landscape has been established. The elements have been repeated in each of the six villages as households copied other villagers. Each village has a spring, about a third of the way from the hilltops, the water source for the village. The gully around each spring has been fenced off to protect the indigenous woodland that has come back. Each spring has one or more poly pipes leading down to a community water tank. The tanks have been constructed by community working bees, with bricks produced in the villages and concrete mortar and asbestos roofing paid for by the project. Each tank supplies water to taps in household yards. A water tank committee supervises to make sure taps are being turned off and that the system is not leaking. On the upper slopes and some lower ridges, there are woodlots of quick growing trees. They maintain the health of the springs, store and release ground water, prevent erosion and provide fuel and timber. Some are owned by villagers who cull the timber and leave the stumps for pollarding, selling wood to other villagers. The community makes sure that woodlots are not clear felled.

A typical practice in this region is to burn the crop residue after the harvest. Woodlands may be also fired up to help catch mice to eat. These actions diminish soil fertility and are no longer practised in the Chikukwa villages. Another common regional practice is to move cattle onto the cropping lands after harvest – to eat crop residues. This compacts soils. Herds of goats are also allowed to range free, destroying tree seedlings. In the Chikukwa villages, cattle are usually herded to grazing areas above the tree line. Goats are mostly tethered or kept in pens. The importance placed on food security, water retention and fuel has meant that cattle (and goats) are not given priority. They have been kept out to prevent soil compaction and to allow food crops to mature. Springs and woodlots have been protected to ensure reforestation.

There is a pattern of design common to residences today. Water from the roof falls onto the yard, which slopes gently to the orchard, next down the hillside. A washing up stand is next to the orchard, so grey water can be thrown below. Utensils dry in the sun, killing germs. This is also the site for the tap. Around to the side of the house are the pens for small livestock, typically chickens (for meat and eggs), pigeons and goats. Other livestock that are sometimes used are fish (in ponds), pigs, rabbits or turkeys. To ensure the orchard is well watered, pits or contour bunds trap water. Often a cropping field next to the orchard will have a contour bund and ditch (swale) running into the orchard. Typical fruit species are banana, Mexican apple, mango, passionfruit, guava, papaya, pineapple, citrus, avocado. Vegetable matter, crop residues and manure go to compost heaps, used to fertilize the vegetable garden and the orchard. Below the orchard, unshaded by trees, is the vegetable garden. Common crops are sunflowers, kovo (marrow stem kale), rape, amaranth and scrambling small tomatoes – trouble free vegetables. These are inter-planted with legumes such as *Leucaena* and *Sesbania*. Weedy, traditionally used leafy vegetables are also grown and collected (Ekesa *et al*. 2009). The cropping fields are close to the house or on the flood plain that is owned by the villagers. For the fields nearer to the houses, good crops of wheat and maize come from the use of compost and manure and the effect of the contour bunds. Some families have cattle and use them to plough, but many use hand hoes. An open-ventilated 'Blair' pit toilet is typical for sewerage.

This system of permaculture design is well understood. For example, Gonday Matsekete explained his household's water harvesting and nutrient strategies:

> The change, is very visible. Long ago, the whole place here used to be like this [very dried out – he is pointing to the front yard of his house]. But because we are now using water harvesting, everywhere is green. Runoff from the roof is there. And the water goes into the garden there and it irrigates the bananas there. And some of the crops that are in the garden. And at the back there, there is a bathroom. We have put a ditch there, so that the water from the bathroom goes to the bananas. And over there, we've got a swale, which catches water from the road, so each drop that comes this way is used. We were taught to interrelate the field and our animals. So, we take manure from the kraal, put it in the field and the residues from the field, to the animals.

The project has created a lay scientific knowledge of permaculture design through workshops, farmer to farmer visits and field trips. This common knowledge base informs the decisions of residents in planning their landscapes.

As part of a model to be 'scaled up', this landscape design is one element. An integrated poly-cultural farm has the house as a focus. Sites requiring daily attention are close. The slope is managed to trap water and maximize sunlight where required.

The conflict workshop

An extremely challenging aspect of rural food security projects in Africa is resolving community conflicts. As I will explain later, CELUCT took up these issues systematically. Here, I will describe one of their conflict resolution processes as an example of community processes. An erosion gully was removing soil from some farms while bringing silt to others. The root cause was excessive timber harvesting. People concerned by the erosion took the matter to the local Permaculture Club and local BCCR (Building Constructive Community Relations) Club. These asked their representatives to take up the issue with CELUCT. Patience Sithole (administrator) from the management team explained the conflict:

> Some people were just saying it in their hearts. What are we going to do? This person did this. They were even afraid of approaching the person who was cutting down trees. Those who had participated in the conflict participation programme, said, but there, we are being taught how to resolve these problems. Why not sitting down and bringing out this issue.

CELUCT consulted with the local headman and agreed to hold a two day workshop. Representatives from the local clubs, the CELUCT staff from these departments and the director organized it. A local household hosted the event. The men sat on benches with the women and infants on mats at the front. Directly in front of the house an easel with butcher's paper was provided for drawings, diagrams, agenda and decisions. For morning tea, the catering staff from CELUCT supplied orange cordial in plastic cups, slices of white bread and apples on plastic plates. These were brought to the venue in the utility vehicle (bakkie) owned by CELUCT.

The proceedings opened with prayer and singing. Then delegates from the BCCR staged a humorous skit representing the conflict. The point was that all had sensible reasons for their actions. No one was directly named and there was a lot of laughter and comments. Following this, all took part in a discussion. Morning tea followed. The men were served first. The delegates from the local clubs and the members of the CELUCT management team, with the exception of the director, took the plates of food and cups of cordial to the seated villagers. After this, there was a shower of rain and the party split into two parts. The men were in the lounge room of the house and the women in a large kitchen rondavel. An action plan was formulated. They would repair the erosion gully with rock check dams and vetiver grass and plant native trees. Further clearing in the woodlot was to be prohibited. The next day the party repaired to a local path for a trial run. Then the whole group moved to the gully. The men fixed one site and the women another, twenty metres further down. All participated, including members of the CELUCT team. The director talked and joked with the older men, occasionally addressing the whole group. Local delegates coordinated the work.

Explaining the success of CELUCT

There are a number of factors that have gone together to ensure the long term success of the CELUCT project. These create a model of project design, which could well be replicated in South and South-East Africa.

An embedded project – embedded professionals

Most projects in Africa are initiated by an outside agency, which sends in a team of professionals (Ferguson 1990; Marais and Botes 2007; Mkize 2008). They are backed by a central bureaucracy. Usually, projects will run for several years, after which the intention is that the community will 'take ownership'. Typically, the community members are unable to continue. Villagers whose education is barely at a high school level are expected to run a commercial agricultural business. A recipe for failure.

The Chikukwa project is, by contrast, 'embedded'. It was generated by residents. It did not spring up to receive funds from any outside donor. Full time staff are local residents, even though a number of them have come from elsewhere. At least half of them are locals by birth. The whole of the project is geographically contained so members of the team can actually walk to the villages and villagers can walk to the centre. The formally educated professionals in the management team have mostly been teachers in local schools. Eli and Ulli Westermann were high school teachers in the local area. Chester Chituwu, who is director of the project now, was the principal of the local primary school. Patience Sithole who is the administrator for CELUCT is the wife of a local high school teacher. She was sponsored to be trained in accountancy by CELUCT so she could keep their books. From 2010, Phineas Chikoshana, a local science teacher, became one of the project team.

This is all very unusual for projects in Africa. Usually there is a division between project officers, who live in town, and local professionals in the villages. Projects work with 'the poorest of the poor', as they are referred to in South Africa, so local professionals are not involved.

Ulli Westermann explains why an embedded project makes sense:

> You have to be integrated in the community, if you want to achieve anything. You have to know the people. It's very difficult for outsiders to quickly jump in, do a quick two or three year programme and then phase out. We knew hundreds of students by name, here and that of course makes it much easier.

Chester Chituwu, the current director, made a similar comment:

> I was working in the area, as a school teacher, and school head and I was interacting with the community. So when the idea of this organization [was] coming up, we would hold discussions together. Most of them were my former students. And then some were friends. We were work mates, in education.

So the human capital needed to maintain the organization was produced from within the community. What came from outside were ideas and a small amount of funding. The embedded professionals provide links to the permaculture movement, access to agricultural and social science, the accounting skills necessary to secure funding, liaison with government departments and the literacy and IT skills to develop promotional and instructional material. Successful community organizations need these middle class skills to function in the global economy.

This is probably the aspect of the project that is most difficult to replicate. Ulli and Eli, with their connections to the permaculture movement and their work as local teachers, provided the nexus for a broader alliance of local professionals. This is a very accidental and felicitous combination. On the other hand, there are people with middle class skills in every village. They are the people who should lead their villages in local food production for household consumption, rather than depending on projects run by people who only stay for a few years.

For food security – not for cash incomes

Most projects in this region of Africa are founded on a strategy of commercialization, and fail accordingly, as has been explained. However, in this case, the collapse of the Zimbabwe economy favoured a food security approach. Urban residents were affected by the structural adjustment programmes of the 1990s, the economic problems following 1997 and the inflation crisis of 2005. Wages fell and so did remittances to villages. Wages in towns were insufficient to purchase all food necessities and remittances were not available for rural residents to top up subsistence or buy inputs. The long term effect was to strengthen rural connections. As Potts (2011: 32) writes, '... plans to engage or re-engage with rural livelihoods had become increasingly prevalent amongst recent urban migrant cohorts, although as urban poverty worsened the attraction of the city for those with any sort of viable rural livelihood had waned'.

At the height of the collapse, people were leaving Zimbabwe to get jobs paying real currency. Even the middle class was not being paid enough. People left the city to make sure they could supplement their cash income with subsistence farming. The usual exodus of young people from the rural areas came to a halt. The Chikukwa project was the beneficiary of an 'edge effect' so far as the economy was concerned.

The basic aim of the Chikukwa project has always been improved food security. Some successful local businesses have come out of the project and the project has also encouraged farmers to add value to their surplus production. Yet the project itself has always emphasized subsistence. You do not need high school maths to improve your agricultural production. The project design avoids conflicts over money. In the subsistence strategy of the Chikukwa project, people produce food for their own household on their own land and no money is required to purchase inputs.

In a meeting of the management team and community representatives, the group was asked how the Chikukwa project had gained the participation of youth, a problem for many projects. The replies emphasized the centrality of subsistence:

PHINEAS: Our local economy is based on agriculture, we are getting the produce from our land. And when the action group started, it involved different age groups. Who were much concerned about healing the land. So, that they would produce enough to feed themselves. So you will find that what is more important here, is the food security.

JESSICA: Our youth have to learn working as young people. And that's also an inheritance to them. For example, if the parents will pass away, they have to know that we were surviving here by farming.

An emphasis on subsistence should be promoted for all food security projects in this part of Africa. The success of this project shows that this is quite possible, can work culturally and really helps to provide adequate food. The Chikukwa project came out of a situation so extreme that the pressure to engage in commercial projects was relieved. People struggled to put food on the table. This was a space in which the only sensible option for rural poverty in the region could be explored in detail. With suitable encouragement, this solution could be pursued from Namibia to Kenya.

Use of permaculture design technologies

Permaculture in the Chikukwa villages has become a local folk science. Jessica Chibharo (translated by Patience Sithole) explains her garden strategies:

> And then after that, we would have small livestocks, and we can pick vegetables from the garden, and feed our small livestocks, and they will produce manure, that manure will turn then to the garden, and also we can use those for proteins.

Permaculture promotes the development of a poly-culture with links between the different elements. In much of this region, subsistence farming concentrates on maize and cattle and little else (see Chapter 3). People expect to purchase everyday supplies of vegetables, beans and animal protein. The outcome is malnutrition. The Chikukwa villagers combine orchards, vegetable gardens, cropping fields and small livestock to be self sufficient in all nutrients without depending on inadequate supplies of cash.

Permaculture recommends organic methods. All inputs are to be produced locally and there is no need to pay for them with cash. By contrast, most projects in the region exhort villagers to buy fertilizers and improved seeds (to little effect) or make promises to subsidize inputs (but only while the project is being funded). The economic logic of permaculture is well understood in the Chikukwa villages:

> Just say I want to buy fertilizer. But we don't have the resources to buy. Why not making a compost? Where I can use manure from my small livestocks or from my goats. Or from my cattle. Rather than buying artificial fertilizers.

(Questions Chikukwa)

Permaculture has always placed an emphasis on water harvesting. In the early 1990s, flooding rains in these villages washed soil off the hillsides in the wet season. In the dry season, there was no water in the soil. The permaculture technologies of swales, contour bunds and tree planting fixed all this. Permaculture's emphasis on perennial species was central. Woodlots on the ridges retained water and stabilized runoff. Orchards stabilized soils, built humus and infiltrated water – changing the diet with increased vitamins, carbohydrates and fibre. Excess fruit were fed to small livestock, which in turn provided protein.

The promotion of organic poly-culture agriculture as 'permaculture' has been successful to an extent that is remarkable. The word 'permaculture' is used to mean both the science and the CELUCT organization. For example, July Mtisi:

> A lot of water was coming from up there, and it was eroding the topsoil. So we had a poor harvest. And there is this friend of ours, Permaculture. And we got advice from The Permaculture. They have given us the vetiver grass. And we planted this so that whenever topsoil is going away it is going to be stopped by the vetiver grass. And when it comes to this, to this swale here. When water goes inside there, it stays there and it goes down bit by bit.

Strategies that depend on the timely purchase of inputs fail time and again in this part of Africa. With permaculture strategies, inputs do not have to be bought to get a good crop. If inputs are to be purchased, they are things like poly pipe and fencing wire – bought when cash is available and lasting for decades. What is required is a long term adult education in permaculture.

Participatory initiation

The Chikukwa project is based in participatory initiation. The people concerned specify the problem and undertake the work. The project assists.

The origin story of the Chikukwa project always begins with the springs drying up and the 'Strong Bees' being formed to deal with that crisis. The motto of the 'Strong Bees' was 'like bees we shall work'. The project ran for up to five years without funding. Current practice reflects these early lessons. Villagers are recruited into clubs working within the 'departments' of the CELUCT framework. These clubs mediate between CELUCT and the villagers. Villagers approach the relevant club with a problem. The club may then decide to take this to CELUCT and request a project or training. If CELUCT supports the request, they will organize assistance but the villagers themselves will do the work required – there is no payment. Any donations are of cheap long lasting materials with low technical complexity – such as poly pipe or cement.

Martha Shumba describes how this system of decision-making and project design operates:

> As a family project, if we have a fish pond or those small livestock, that's where also the children, they learn 'cause they are the ones who even cut the vegetables and feed the small livestock, but we can stretch also to have a group fish pond. Where firstly, we write a project proposal. We gather, say five families, who have a common aim and maybe they would like a fish pond, and they write their proposal, give it to the subcommittee, of that village, and from that subcommittee [of the permaculture club], they will give it to the permaculture representative of that village. And that representative will take the proposal, to CELUCT management team, and they discuss together. If there is assistance, that will be needed there, they will be

assisted. For example with skills, how they can do it, or material if it's available, and then that's how we do it.

Chester Chituwu, the current director, explains the way that bottom up initiation ensures commitment:

> As CELUCT, we are only facilitating. They must own the whole process. And therefore it's them that own and have to be responsible and they must have that culture of ownership, so that even with or without CELUCT as an organization, they are able to stand on their own two feet.

Most projects started on people's own land come out of farm visits. People visit the farms of other villagers, and are inspired. CELUCT pays a fee to farmers hosting these visits. As Chester Chituwu explains:

> Our training sites as CELUCT are not here [at the CELUCT centre], they are in the community. So when we have people who come for training, for practicals we take them into the community. And that alone is a motivator. Because if we take people to her home. The next door say, yeah, if I do so, it means people will also come and learn from mine.

The training delivered by CELUCT catches on as trainees try things out on their own farms:

> We meet at our permaculture classes, and what we will have learned there, somebody will say, ok, now I have learned this, I have to implement it. And when they see that it's working, next time when they are also learning something, they will keep on implementing because they know that it's working.
> (Jessica Chibharo)

So, permaculture can be seen as a package of technologies. People learn about a particular technology (for example a ditch in the orchard) and install that. As that works, they try another technology (for example a new fruit tree).

These forms of participatory initiation should be replicated in all rural projects in this region. Eli Westermann's response to the drying up of the spring was not to find donor money to pay locals to dig contour bunds. Instead she started a small club of neighbours who were keen to work on their own land. Their next step was to call in advice and develop a plan. Then, they went up into the hills and started work. Clearly a party of six was insufficient to put in contour bunds across six villages. They inspired others to join them. The photos archived by CELUCT and taken at the time of these events show that working parties were between about fifteen and twenty-five people. In each, the Strong Bees joined those living close at hand. This is exactly what projects need to be successful. Begin small and work with those who *will* volunteer.

So CELUCT mostly works with individual households. People call for assistance to improve *their own food production* on *their own household land*. There is no attempt to create 'cooperatives' which will produce together, market together and receive income as a group (see Chapter 4).

This is not to say that there are no joint projects. These are of three kinds. One is where different households have to solve a common problem. For example, the construction of contour bunds to stop soil erosion. Villagers come together to form a working party. When CELUCT organizes something like this, snacks and drinks will be provided. A second kind of group is called together when one household asks other households to help with some large task. It is expected that those who are helped will repay the favour on another occasion. The third kind of group work is for joint community gardens. The garden is assisted with a donation of materials (cement, poly pipe) from CELUCT and the villagers who are going to use the garden do the work. In a garden like this, each villager has their own plot. They may give some produce to families in need. All of this fits with the cultural norms of this region (Englund 2008). Households initiate most projects to assist *their own* production. When villagers work as a group, *their individual contribution* is recognized.

Bureaucratic democracy

I use the term 'bureaucratic democracy' to refer to the structure of community processes developed to run the project. They are 'bureaucratic' in providing transparent and formalized structures. They are 'democratic' in setting up participatory control. Over the years, CELUCT has set up clear-cut and defined authority structures. These enable democratic participatory control. Meetings are conducted formally and minutes taken. All accounting is open to inspection by community committees. The use of donor funds is discussed by panels of stakeholders. The democratic aspect of CELUCT is a necessity – to discover pressing needs and enable successful interventions.

The Permaculture Club Committee of CELUCT is a good example. Eugen Matsekete describes the process of selection:

> I am representing the Permaculture Club Committee and that committee is eight representatives. We have six, and we have one person from each village and there will be a traditional leader who will sit on that committee, and the professional advisor, from the Ministry of Land. We represent the village and what we do, we work with the community members within our village, and if we have a proposal there, we'll carry that proposal to the management team, and then we have meetings with the management team. Most every month. And if there are things that the community members would like, to be assisted, they can be assisted. The committee is being selected by the villagers. In its own village. And it is chosen, once in two years during a meeting we call 'Open Day', like an AGM. There's a commitment fee, one rand per member.

So the Permaculture Club Committee is the peak body. The eight representatives are the traditional leader, the representative from the agricultural department and one representative from each of the six villages. These six are chosen in their villages on open day – every two years. Each villager who wants to vote pays a commitment fee (about twenty cents). The village committee is also selected then. During the year, this village club has regular meetings and provides training sessions. If community members want assistance, they bring the matter to the local permaculture club. Their representative approaches the central committee, which reports directly to CELUCT management. Through this, villagers participate in the control of CELUCT funds – they help to decide what projects CELUCT will assist.

This organizational framework is replicated for all CELUCT departments – the catering staff; the women's social groups; the HIV/AIDS talking circles; the conflict resolution groups and so on. CELUCT works like a minor government, operating a representative democratic structure with functional 'departments'.

As a model for project design, bureaucratic democracy works. Democracy for an NGO is always limited by donors. Assistance comes with strings attached. Within these limits, you have to get long term commitment to get a successful project. The beneficiaries must participate with enthusiasm. Bureaucratic democracy reconciles these demands. The central organization vets all proposals to fit funding guidelines. At the same time, a shadow democratic government is established at a very local level. Transparent decision-making allows an accounting to be prepared for the donors. It also reduces concerns about corruption.

Counter cultural technologies of the self – linking social and personal change

CELUCT is not just focused on food security. Food security depends on social harmony. Pursuing this, CELUCT promotes 'technologies of the self' like those developed by the counter culture of the metropolis (Foucault 1988). These are 'social technologies', through which people work on their 'subjectivity', their sense of themselves and identity. Permaculture was established first in Australia to work with 'new age' settlers moving to the country for a more harmonious relationship with nature. Other social technologies associated with CELUCT are also technologies of the self, pioneered in the counter culture.

The techniques of conflict transformation now used in the villages have been adapted from the new age therapeutic movement – resolving conflict by understanding all perspectives in a dispute. The women-only social groups that the project has developed mirror the women's liberation movement of the early 1970s. Likewise, self help groups for people living with HIV/AIDS were pioneered by the gay community in countries like Australia and the US. The CELUCT pre-school has been established to reverse educational disadvantage – a method suggested by left education theorists in the 1970s. Democratic meeting process of the kind seen in the Chikukwa committees – minutes, rotation of speakers, motions – is an organizational form coming out of the union movement and promoted in the new left and counter culture.

James Mackerenje, the head of the HIV/AIDS talking circles, explained his department:

> Here, I am here to talk about HIV and AIDS. Here there are many cases of people who are infected with HIV. And the people sit down and said what can we do? And they decided to motivate people to know their status. At the end we make a programme, which we call 'talking time', *ongwaiva taurana*, where people can get together, to open their status. And we did it in the six villages. We got six people to each village, and we came here and decided to teach others. To come up with your status. And when we came back to our villages. We teach our people about what they must do, to know what is in your heart, or your body, or your own status. And at the end, we see that the sick people, we are so little. And we said, what can we do? And we made a supportive group. This helps people affected with HIV. To share him with the chores or to go and help him, with water, or to take firewood to him. Or to wash his clothes, yes.

Patience Sithole, the administrator, added to this, indicating the values of generosity, kindness and transparency which CELUCT promotes:

> OK. Maybe to add from what you are saying. People were very motivated, because long back they thought HIV and AIDS was from other areas, not here. And if one is affected, people would say. I think that person is bewitched. And maybe they will hurt each other, they will hurt the neighbour. Whereby the neighbour should help that sick person, help look after your sick person. [Now] if they know, they discuss even with the children, that we are now positive, and it's also a learning thing for the children.

Pointing out the parallels in the rich countries is not intended to prove there is nothing new under the sun. Much of this has been invented on the spot and harks back to traditional organization. A new agricultural strategy cannot work without good community relationships. Technologies of the self are the means to improve the social context.

The setting up of the Building Constructive Community Relationships department of CELUCT is an example. At the height of the economic crisis in Zimbabwe, the management team could not be paid. Some were using the CELUCT car for personal trips. This was resented. Discontented villagers stopped coming to CELUCT functions. To sort this out, meetings of CELUCT with the community established rules acceptable to all parties. Eli Westermann then travelled to Germany to train in conflict mediation. On her return, forty Chikukwa villagers were trained and later more. Ultimately up to fifty people in each of the villages had received the training. A permanent department of CELUCT was set up with clubs in each village. The mediations make use of role-play, dramatizations, brainstorming, along with working parties and setting agreements to solve problems. They deal with a multitude of conflicts – issues of land tenure, religious conflict, HIV/AIDS, agriculture and so on. From this, Eli prepared a textbook, *The Three Circles of Knowledge* (Westermann 2008) to document their approach – one that had been evolved for the specific conditions found in African villages.

Nothing that is being done here is unique. What is different is the integration of these different technologies of the self in a total package. There is an intensive, totalizing and overlapping intervention. Jessica Chibharo describes this:

> We started doing our projects in Chikukwa. We had gardens, fishponds, orchards, woodlots; we had individual projects. And we also had home designs. We also kept small livestock. And we also encouraged those who didn't like, to join others. To get in programmes. We had exchange visits with other organizations and other communities. As we introduced our attachment programme, it was for the community members to come and learn and after learning, they would go to their own village, and work with the people there. We had social groups, those social clubs, and young women would discuss together how best they could develop their homes. Because there was violence, something like that. So they discussed those issues, and openly. There were also times when age groups would meet and discuss their own issues. But there were also times when these different age groups would meet and try to discuss issues, openly, so that they would have a good relationship.

In many of the African villages there is a feeling of despair coming out of persistent unemployment. A global media promoting the high life reinforces this hopelessness. Problems like this require social technologies that go well beyond most rural development packages. What could be copied by other projects is the development of all these strands in the one place – rather than as scattered and separate programmes, agriculture in one village, dispute mediation in another and HIV/AIDS groups in a third. There is a limit to what any of these programmes can do, taken on their own. Each of them is much more likely to work in combination.

Working with traditional leadership, traditional spirituality and Christian belief

Permaculture is a good fit with the indigenous world-view of the Chikukwa villages. In permaculture, space in the landscape is to be left for an uncultivated zone. This is for harvesting some forest products and for wild species. In its ethics, permaculture recommends care of the earth. All of this goes well with traditional spiritual practices. The springs on the land of the Chikukwa villages have been sacred sites and there is an obligation to look after the indigenous trees growing there. When the Strong Bees began their work restoring the springs, they asked the traditional leadership to seek the help of the ancestors. Peter Mukaronda described these events:

This was the spring for the community, called Chitekete, the village. And since it was their only source of water, they decided to reclaim the land, up there, trying to plant different types of indigenous trees. Because the indigenous trees, they are just made to bring back the water. And because of the chiefs in Chikukwa. Then they had to come here and sit down with the other community and they brewed beer, so the spirit, and so the water would come up. Later on, then the water came.

The traditional leadership has been involved in other ways. The previous chief gave the project his endorsement, helping the 'Strong Bees' to recruit volunteers. Headmen serve on committees and are called in to consult when villagers request CELUCT assistance. The young relatives of the chief have begun a club to restore music and dances traditional to the clan. Zeddy Chikukwa from this group explained the link between traditional ideas and CELUCT:

CELUCT, we see it as a supportive organization in everything that we do. Because in our tradition, we do not allow people to cut down trees like water berries, like fig trees. They are sacred trees, which we also believe even our ancestral spirits, they go and reside there. And also we are in line with CELUCT in the use of organic agriculture. Where you are not supposed to use some artificial fertilizers because it damages the soil. So we know, it is there to sort of strengthen the rules and regulations of our community.

It seems quite possible that this appeal to traditional spirituality could be linked to other rural projects. Aspects of African traditional belief are still relevant in much of Africa. Permaculture strategies reforest parts of the landscape that have been sacred and encourage native wildlife, creating a sense of natural abundance, very much in evidence in the Chikukwa villages of today.

Permaculture has also been connected to Christian belief through this project. CELUCT begins meetings and workshops by invoking the ancestors with clapping, along with prayers and hymns, the common currency of the Christian sects. One of the members of the Strong Bees club was Julious Piti, then a youth. He is now living in the Chimanimani district outside of the Chikukwa ward and works to promote interventions in the dry western areas of Chimanimani district, as well as working on permaculture initiatives in other countries. He describes the way he and his wife chose the land on which they are now located:

We used to go to church with a lot of people, so we used to go into the mountains and pray, and one day, in around 1995, I went to that mountain and stayed there for three days. Praying. And when I was coming down, I was passing through this place. Then I felt. Ahah. I love this place. And then my wife, she started staying here, for some years and then I saw. Ahah, she loves this place. We saw with the plants around, and everything around, we felt in love.

Later in the interview he explains the meaning permaculture has for him:

> Permaculture is a system of living which takes in cognisance to natural resources and everything that surrounds us living in harmony with no unbeneficial conflicts. And socially, you'll make peace at the end of the day. Like a peace project, you will find all the links, when you apply permaculture principles. You see the principles, they link the whole community, plant community, people, whatever, insects, they are linked and everything will live in harmony. And produce enough for each other. That way, you also promote the water cycle, and even the oxygen that we breathe, and even the ozone layer can be reduced. It actually solves all the problems that we face in the human life. So it's considered to be the right approach for us to live on earth. If you want to save the earth.

This is both secular and spiritual. It locates permaculture within a broader system of understanding, summed up in the phrase 'the right approach for us to live on earth' with its allusion to the Lord's Prayer.

The presentation of sustainable farming as Christian practice is a theological response to the environmental crisis (Jenkins 2008). The earth is to be revered as God's creation. God commands us to look after the earth. It seems unlikely that a purely secular approach to farming could be successful in these communities.

The gift in CELUCT

There is much about the organization of CELUCT that depends on gifts rather than monetary exchange. People donate labour on their own land. They donate work towards community projects. They may help other community members in a tit for tat arrangement. Patience Sithole describes these arrangements:

> It can be done also in two parts, that the family can do it [a contour bund]. But also the village, or people who are round, surrounding that area. They can say, ok today we are working on Martha's field, they can work there, and tomorrow they can work on Chester's field.

CELUCT encourages households to provide gifts of food to the vulnerable. Community nutrition gardens have also been established to help them further. All these voluntary labours work directly on people's own needs, but also consolidate CELUCT as an organization that helps the community.

Donations also come from the project. CELUCT distributes gifts from international donors, providing training and materials in the community. It also dispenses social rewards. The workshops are serviced with morning tea, there are amusing dramatizations, people get to participate with their neighbours, there is joking and camaraderie. The director shares stories with the older men while the younger CELUCT team urge people on, provide explanations and do the physical work alongside the villagers. Jessica Chibharo explains the way international donors and villagers contributed together to the buildings of the centre:

> We managed to get us some funders who gave us some funding, and with that funding we bought material, that we build a community hall, which is up there. Community members had to mould bricks and carrying river sand and pit sand so that that block can be there for the whole community.

The management team (about six people in all) are paid by the international donor funding, which they also recruit. The funding is not always adequate and months of voluntary work have been required at difficult times. Accommodation and training are provided for people coming from the villages to the centre, as well as occasional gifts of materials such as seedlings or poly pipe. CELUCT also depends on international donations for their office equipment, and for their vehicle, used to convey the management team to workshops in the villages and to take trainees to field visits. Donor funds are also used to pay a small daily fee to those whose farms are used to demonstrate technologies. The catering staff, rostered from the villages, are also paid $5 a day each.

In 2010, two international NGOs were funding CELUCT. The total amount was approximately $60,000 per year. This was guaranteed for only three years. The EED (a German church fund), their largest donor, had decided to restrict funding to activities that were a part of the conflict resolution process. Sustainable Agriculture programmes were only supported through a small budget funded by the TUDOR Trust.

CELUCT can be considered a hybrid combining aspects of a market economy with aspects of a gift economy (Leahy 2011). Looking at market aspects first, farming land is owned by individual households. CELUCT is the legal owner of the funds donated by international organizations. CELUCT pays villagers to open their farms for demonstrations and pays for catering staff. It pays the members of the management team a wage – though there are periods when their work is voluntary. So it functions as an employer within a market economy. Both CELUCT itself and the community depend on some cash income to operate. CELUCT absolutely depends on skilled business management and careful handling of money. Although CELUCT puts priority on non-market agriculture, it also promotes some sale of farm products – jams, fruit juices, livestock, wood, coffee or bananas.

The non-market aspects of CELUCT are equally significant. CELUCT depends on donations from the first world. Within the villages food is produced for use (subsistence) rather than for sale. CELUCT promotes and assists this subsistence agriculture. CELUCT depends on voluntary work. Both the work that villagers do on their own land and the work that they do for their neighbours, the community or for CELUCT. On their own farms, villagers are their own bosses – they are not employed to work or constrained to produce for the market. They effectively own their means of production. CELUCT has set up processes to negotiate the use of these smallholdings. Where the needs of the community are affected, these can trump the property rights of households. CELUCT encourages people to produce a surplus and give some to more needy members of the community. A degree of community control of the resources of CELUCT is achieved through participatory management of CELUCT projects. The community can also exercise the veto of failure to participate – to demand changes if they deem this necessary. These are forms of public control over CELUCT.

One of the biggest mistakes in development work is to see the task as integrating traditional villagers into the market economy. Almost all projects in Africa are based on this premise and fail as a result. Gibson-Graham point out that the supposedly 'capitalist' global economy can be conceived as a patchwork of different economic forms (2006a and 2006b). NGOs working in poverty relief operate very differently from capitalist firms. As the Chikukwa project makes clear, they can work very well by reinforcing activities which build livelihood but which are neither market based nor capitalist.

Conclusions

The Chikuwka project is an indigenous 'Southern' solution to a problem typical of South-Eastern Africa. This is the failure of food security in rural areas. This is a problem that is acknowledged internationally. In response, elements of the middle class of the rich countries seek a solution to these problems in aid work. The approaches gaining most traction are undoubtedly 'silver bullet' solutions that aim to roll out a particular technology and scale it up to improve the lives of millions. However, in reality these problems have a *social* context and are not readily solved by just one technology applied willy-nilly. The Chikukwa project is an example of a locally produced African solution that takes this social context into account. While this solution is unique and local, it is inevitable that international donors will seek a more general formula for effective interventions. We can draw some lessons from this project that might help to produce such a formula. The failure of so many projects is not because everything has been tried. What makes sense is a project design that takes into account the social, cultural and economic coherence of a particular region and comes up with recommendations for both material and social technology.

This chapter has been concerned to explore the reasons for the remarkable success of the Chikukwa project; a success in stark contrast to the long term outcomes of most rural projects.

The new landscape of the Chikukwa villages is a landscape informed by permaculture design, implemented through a multitude of tiny decisions. The concept of a poly-culture organized around the household unit, with subsistence agriculture providing a range of complementary crops and livestock makes sense for this whole region of Africa. The Chikukwa project has been successful as an 'embedded' project. It has depended on the expertise of local professionals committed to the villages and the project. It has been oriented to subsistence agriculture rather than attempting food security by selling produce. This lesson is well overdue in the region. Permaculture design has allowed a diversity of nutrition, a synergy of multiple crops and livestock and an agriculture that does not depend on timely infusions of cash. The project is participatory. People request assistance and work on their own land. There is no payment. Rather than attempting grand transformations, the project has been content to start small with the people willing to do something. The project has set up formally constituted means for making decisions and recording transactions, reducing concerns about corruption and allowing local control. Democratic participation ensures all measures are truly wanted and will be maintained. The project has created an intensive overlapping involvement, employing various technologies of the self. This saturation of social capital makes sense to deal with the despair and anger coming out of decades of poverty and stigma. The project has sensitively adapted itself to traditional spirituality and Christian belief. Permaculture is a good fit with both. CELUCT combines various market practices with aspects of the gift economy. It is ironic that NGOs and governments, neither of which are capitalist firms, have believed that the only kind of successful development can be an extension of the capitalist firm and market relations into every nook and cranny of rural poverty. This has turned out to be an expensive mistake.

Vignette G
What to eat to avoid diabetes and heart trouble

Terry Leahy

As explained in a number of chapters, purchased processed foods have a particular symbolic significance in rural Africa – as a sign of monetary income and modern development. As elsewhere in the world, the uptake of these highly processed products is introducing health problems to these communities. In 2014 Sam Chimbarara, one of the management team from the Chikukwa project, asked me if I could write something about dietary guidelines to prevent diabetes and heart trouble. As someone who has had heart trouble and been trained in the evidence based science of healthy eating, I was happy to produce this leaflet. What I suggest here is what you might ideally do to avoid these conditions, making use of the best science. However, it is only fair to admit that there are ways in which my suggestions confront some cultural norms of the community. I was told that if a husband suggested this diet to his wife, she would think he was just being stingy with the family income – no sugar, no sweet treats, no poloni.

This is a pretty strict set of guidelines. If you started keeping to this when you were about 3 years old and kept it up for the rest of your life you would be very unlikely to develop diabetes or heart trouble. The annoying part about this is that some people will eat a bad diet their whole lives and end up quite healthy, while the rest of us on that bad diet are going to end up getting diabetes or heart trouble.

In terms of what these rules say are *good things to eat*, they are:

1 Roughage and fibre, which helps us to digest things.
2 Vitamins, which keep us from getting sick.
3 Protein, which is good for building our bodies and making us strong.

The list of *things to limit* and *the list of things to avoid* are designed for three main purposes that are very relevant to diabetes and heart trouble:

1 To avoid animal fats (like the white part of meat, or any kind of cheese, or poloni, which has animal fats minced into it). These animal fats clog up our arteries and lead to heart trouble.
2 To avoid sugar and reduce the amount of white (refined) carbohydrate. These are the things that give us diabetes.

3 To get most salt out of the diet. An excess of salt can give us high blood pressure and lead to heart problems.

All of these things (animal fats, sugar, salt) are the kinds of things that were really rare in the diets of our ancestors. The wild animals our ancestors used to hunt did not have much fat on their bodies. There was no sugar available in those days and salt was very scarce. Our bodies are not adapted to be fed great quantities of these things.

Good things to eat

- Avocadoes (help our bodies to make use of the vitamins in fruit and vegetables).
- Vegetable oil for cooking (helps our bodies to make use of the vitamins in fruit and vegetables).
- Beans, peanuts and cow peas – three or four meals a week (protein).
- Nuts and peanut butter (protein).
- Meat – chicken, beef or goat – once or twice a week – *but cut off the fat* (the white part) *before cooking it* (proteins).
- Fish – once or twice a week (protein and no animal fats).
- Eggs – one a day if possible (protein).
- Up to two litres of water a day (helps us to digest food and to have energy).
- Vegetables – eat lots – kovo (marrow stem kale), tsunga (canola), black jack, umbowa (amaranth) and so on – with every meal (vitamins and fibre).
- Fruit – eat two pieces of fruit a day, especially fruit with vitamin C = oranges, naatches (mandarins), guavas, pineapples, mangoes, loquats, granadillas (vitamins, energy and fibre).
- Rapoko (millet) porridge, whole wheat porridge or home cooked brown bread (vitamins and energy).
- Onions and garlic (good for your health).
- Chillies and peppers (good for your health).
- Sweet potato and madumbe – taro (fibre and energy).

What to limit

Don't eat more than a quarter of a plate of all of the following at any one meal.

These are called 'refined carbohydrates'. This means that all the fibre and vitamins have been taken out of them in the way they are processed. Eating too much of them makes us fat and also makes us feel tired. It is one of the causes of diabetes because the sudden energy they produce makes our energy system go haywire.

- Sadza (white maize porridge).
- White bread.
- Irish potatoes.

What to avoid

Too much of these are what is causing diabetes and heart trouble here. It is the addition of these new purchased foods that is causing the new spike in diabetes, heart trouble and weight problems.

- Sugar – try to keep this to *only one teaspoon* in *one cup* of tea of coffee in the whole day. *This is the most important message for diabetes here.*
- No juices, cordials or soft drinks – like Fanta or Coke. These are full of sugar.
- No jam – also full of sugar.
- Honey – make it a rare treat. Just the same as sugar.
- No cakes. These have lots of sugar in them.
- Poloni or sausages – do not eat any of these – they are full of animal fats.
- No margarine – these usually have trans fats, which are bad for your heart.
- Salt – *limit to a teaspoon* (for the whole family) when you are cooking dinner. Do *not* sprinkle this on your food. Salt gives you blood pressure, which leads to heart problems.
- Dairy – whole fat dairy – *don't* eat any butter, cream or cheese. Limit dairy to milk in your hot drinks. Cheese, butter and cream are full of animal fats. It is good for children to drink milk but not necessary for adults to do so.
- Alcohol – *have fewer than two drinks a day* or avoid alcohol completely. It is just like sugar. It gives you diabetes and makes you fat.

8 A winning formula – projects that work

Terry Leahy and Monika Goforth

The 'food security outreach' model

The remarkable success of the Chikukwa project (Chapter 7) surely owes a lot to the fact that it is an 'embedded project'. The German couple who were the catalysts for the project arrived as schoolteachers in the Chikukwa villages. They wanted to live in the villages and belong to the Chikukwa community. They achieved this as they helped their neighbours and friends to save their villages from hunger and environmental catastrophe. With the assistance of their own Chikukwa organization, the villagers developed their committees and clubs and took democratic control to make the project work. The management team was initially those who had formed the first village club to look at these problems. A majority of future appointments came from local professional people who had already shown their commitment. This is a far cry from the standard *modus operandi* of projects operating in the African villages. Typically, projects are staffed by professionals who live in a larger town or urban centre, not in the rural areas serviced by their project. Commonly, an NGO or government project only works with the same people for a maximum of three years.

It is unrealistic to expect that most projects will be as lucky as the Chikukwa project. Projects are not likely to have embedded professionals running the project for the long haul and living in the same communities as the beneficiaries. Most NGOs and government agencies will work from some central urban area or large town. They will be staffed by professionals who want to live where they can have a middle class social life and send their children to good schools. They will travel by car to work in the villages. They will offer the professional expertise necessary to run a project and will work with villagers who are the 'poorest of the poor'. As indicated in previous chapters, many projects of this type fail and do not manage to engage local people in long term improvements in their lives.

So this chapter is about how projects *can work* in these more standard situations. We are calling the project design explained in this chapter 'food security outreach'. These projects work from a large town or city and reach out to the rural areas. They concentrate on food security issues for the vast bulk of villagers rather than on commercial agriculture for relatively richer village farmers. The three organizations to be examined all work on 'feeding the farmer first' using low input technologies. We are arguing that the 'food security outreach' model seems likely to be best practice for food security projects in rural Southern and South-Eastern Africa. It should also be given serious consideration in other regions of the developing world. We will be looking at the following organizations.

- The first is TSURO in the Chimanimani district of Zimbabwe. This operates in twenty-two of the twenty-four wards of a district with 120,000 people. The data for this organization is the most extensive. In 2010, as part of the work making the film on this project and CELUCT, Leahy conducted interviews with twenty-one staff from the project, and with thirty-six beneficiaries. This data was supplemented by participant observation including farm visits, attendance at a community mediation and an annual planning meeting of TSURO staff. After that visit, a small survey of twenty-five beneficiaries was conducted to obtain more systematic data. Five interviewees were chosen in each of five districts. In 2014, Leahy returned to this organization and conducted further field trips to interview beneficiaries and see projects.
- The second organization is Kulika in Uganda. This organization carries out work in a variety of rural communities throughout south-eastern Uganda. The data for this organization comes from their various publications and from interviews with two of the management staff, Elijah Kyamuwendo and Albert Obukulem. Leahy met Kyamuwendo at the international permaculture conference in Malawi in 2009 and went to visit the organization, their Kampala office and their rural demonstration farm in 2010.
- The third organization is Is'Baya, which operates in the Eastern Cape villages of South Africa. It works jointly on projects with the South African government Agricultural Research Centre. Leahy met Peter Jones, one of the initiators of this project, at a rural development conference in Eastern Cape in 2009. In 2010, he interviewed Rose Du Preez, an agricultural scientist who is also on the project management team. Leahy conducted a second visit in 2014 and worked with Is'Baya for several months in the villages, going with the field officers to communities where they were having meetings with the beneficiaries. Through this he was introduced to the monitors for the projects in the villages. He spent three weeks living in two of the fifty villages where the project operates.

We have chosen to review these three projects because what they are doing is so different from the projects that have been failing all over Africa. Their common project design was *discovered* as the research progressed. The Is'Baya project was first encountered through a presentation at Walter Sisulu University in Eastern Cape. The Kulika project was presented at an international permaculture conference in Malawi in 2009. The TSURO project was also represented at that conference. Research to follow up these initial discoveries took place in subsequent years.

The substance of the assistance

In explaining how these projects work, we are making a distinction between:

- the substance of their assistance – what it is that they offer to the people that they intend to help; and
- the methods of their assistance – the methods by which they organize the project to deliver that assistance.

The three organizations we are looking at all attempt to develop food security through household farming using low input agriculture. This is the *substance* of their assistance.

Feeding the farmers first – with a surplus for sale

The de facto orientation of all three organizations is to make *the first priority* household food security – feeding the farmers first. We say de facto, because in the African context, it is not advisable to talk about subsistence. People think you want to take villagers back to the Stone Age. The phrase usually used is 'household food security'. But these organizations also appeal to the ambitions of villagers to develop a commercial enterprise. How these organizations finesse this combination varies. A fair summary is to say that they all suggest that households start by increasing food production for their own use and then go on to market a surplus as they increase their crop and develop their skills. A TSURO beneficiary produced the formula that is at the heart of this strategy:

> ...before then I lacked some certain skills and knowledge on how to farm. But through TSURO I had to attend workshops and I would implement those skills that I was trained on. I have also improved in my yield from the farm. I am now getting enough to feed my family, and surplus to sell.

A member of the Machete community nutrition garden, assisted by TSURO, explained the benefits of their initiative:

> All this allowed our children to eat till they were full. And this allowed them to become healthy.

TSURO advises farmers on how to increase their yield using permaculture strategies. They also give advice on how to get a higher price from the surplus and engage beneficiaries in specific money making projects, such as producing honey for sale.

In visits with TSURO in 2014, Leahy went to a number of the farms of beneficiaries. They were all growing a mixture of crops and livestock for household use and crops or livestock for sale. Gladys (aged fifty) was the chair of the organic farmers' group that had been established in her village under the auspices of TSURO. She has been to numerous workshops run by TSURO, at their headquarters and also in her village. There are thirty-eight members in her group. Her block is about 2.5 hectares. When we went to her house, fifteen members of her group came to the meeting. She has taken note of permaculture techniques of design and has prepared a map of her property indicating her design. She keeps a record of spending on her crops and her returns when she sells some of her produce. As we look at the detail of her farm we can see the integration of cropping designed to make money and cropping designed to feed her family.

Up the slope from her house she has established swales to block any runoff from farms above, which might contain chemical residues. There are also some ponds excavated for gravity feed through hoses to the gardens below her house. The plots above the house are for the herbs she is growing for sale. She aims to expand this enterprise as a key cash crop for her farm.

Chickens are free ranging near the house. She has a flock of twenty-one hens and six roosters and gets five eggs a day, which her family eats. Immediately below the house is a belt of fruit trees, receiving runoff from the house and water from the ponds. In this zone she is keeping some goats, which are tethered and kept out of gardens and cropping fields. These goats are being raised for sale and also for milking. In the middle of this area and below the orchard is the vegetable patch, which receives full sun and includes a variety of herbs and medicinal plants as well as various legumes such as pigeon pea. It is a complex and diverse garden. She explained that *Bidens pilosa* (black jack) is not a weed but a useful vegetable in this plot. She also has amaranth, another weedy vegetable. Mostly, this plot is for her home consumption. Below the orchard are the cropping fields. She grows maize, sorghum and various intercrops for her home consumption. She is trying out different treatments to grow maize and making a record of yields. For example, she is using Sunhemp in some beds to deter the weed Striga, which reduces yields. Other fields have an intercrop of Mucuna beans. Her group is trying out various organic treatments for typical pests in maize fields – such as stalk borer which they are controlling with burned goat's droppings poured into the crevices through which the borer enters, and with assassin bugs which they are raising and releasing.

She has almost every variety of nitrogen fixing legume on her property. Sunhemp, pigeon pea and velvet beans in the maize and sorghum fields, also *Tephrosia, Leucaena* and *Sesbania* growing in the garden around the house. So all these legumes are being grown to provide nitrogen for other crops and to create a seed stock to distribute in the community. There is also a Moringa planted near the house to supply leaves for cooking. Her group is experimenting with the production of red worms for sale and for use in their own gardens, so there are two or three large beds for worm production, using cow manure, soil and plant matter. The whole of the property from the top, right down into the cereal cropping area, is crossed by contour bunds which trap water. Big pits and ponds are also established in the orchard and at the top of her block.

The assembled group of local members of the TSURO organization were very enthusiastic about the potential of these strategies and showed great interest in the work Gladys is doing. While she is a 'source farmer', as TSURO calls her, she is not a leading farmer who is just attending to her own commercial success. She is totally committed to the development of commercial farming and household food production in her neighbourhood.

Elijah Kyamuwendo, the CEO of Kulika in 2010, explained its origins in 1981, and its decision to concentrate on food security issues, given the hunger in rural areas. Its research in 1992:

> ... proved that there were enough food resources unutilized and yet they can cause great effect towards people having food enough to eat and having some surplus to sell.

The project shows people how they can use the materials they have to hand and gradually improve their farming output. For example, the poorest farmers might be encouraged to store water by using discarded plastic containers, by digging a hole or a contour bund. By increasing their agricultural production through these methods they could sell some surplus and buy polythene for a pond. Going further they might buy concrete for a tank:

> If you are in a community, members will look at where you are. Then after that we start talking to people. Why don't you visit this person, she or he has lining it with the polythene. This one has lining with polythene; this one has made a concrete pond! So they see the progression. So we show you where you can go if you work hard.

The project attempts first to increase the household food provision for the poorest farmers using the materials they already have. It also promises a surplus. With that, an increasing ability to purchase inputs to their farming, ending up with a top level commercial farm. This promise breaks through the stigma associated with subsistence.

We can see this complex interrelationship of subsistence and commercial strategies also appearing in the reports produced by Kulika. One farmer spoke exclusively of the food security benefits:

> The training I acquired from Kulika has helped me to learn how to use compost and led to improved yields of my crops. My expenditure on medical bills has greatly reduced due to reduced incidences of disease in my family, especially among children due to availability of quality foods like vegetables. Children look healthier...
>
> (Kulika 2009: 6)

Another began by talking about his larger harvests and healthier children but went on to say: '... as you can see my crop fields. I can see money all around' (Kulika 2009: 9).

The central strategy of the Is'Baya organization in South Africa is to offer fruit tree seedlings to householders to plant on their own residential land. These residential plots are generally used for grazing a goat or sheep and for growing a small quantity of maize for family consumption. The aim of the project is to supplement this current agriculture by providing families with abundant fruit. The project sells the trees at a subsidized price and provides advice on how to establish and care for them. They distribute varieties that will produce marketable fruit, to allow a small additional income even with a few fruit trees. At the present time, most villagers sell their surplus in their own villages. They usually go to the school or post office and sell to teachers or office workers. In some villages, there is a town nearby and villagers take a community bus into town on market day and sell some fruit at the stalls. While villagers may enter this project aiming to make an income, the most immediate effect is to greatly increase the nutritional value of food grown for household consumption. The long term plan of Is'Baya and the ARC (Agricultural Research Council) is that their farmers will expand their production to the point where it makes sense to set up cooperatives in the villages to market the fruit, taking it by truck to major urban centres. They are beginning the legal work and social organization to initiate this in the villages that show the most promise.

As Rose Du Preez says, villagers come to this package with a variety of motivations:

> And some think it would be nice to have some mangoes and guavas and so on, and that's the thing ... others immediately see the opportunity that they could make money.

She explained the way that they encouraged householders to plant a suite of varieties to ensure a continuous supply of vitamins; mangoes, citrus and guavas fruiting at different times for maximum nutritional impact. The centrality of food security and household subsistence production is promoted in the Is'Baya literature:

> The initial objective is to increase food production by each household to ensure food and nutritional security. Even modest gains in output by very large numbers of small farmers, when translated into improved diets, would have a major impact in reducing rural hunger and poverty and an immediate improvement in health.
>
> (Jones and Du Preez 2008: 12)

During Leahy's visit in 2014, he was very much aware of the fact that the leading farmers of the organization were attempting to produce a marketable crop of fruit and were having some success in doing that. However, what was also very apparent was that a large part of the fruit crop was going to their own household, being given away to relatives and neighbours or was even being stolen by local children. In addition, encouraged by Is'Baya, these farmers were also growing a lot of crops that they intended for the household food supply. They were using the land between the rows of fruit trees to grow vegetables and to extend their nutrition through that.

In Eastern Cape, Leahy stayed for several weeks in Noqhekwana village with Thembi, who is the village monitor for Is'Baya. It is her job to go round the village, writing reports on how families who are working with Is'Baya are going with their farming. Close to her house, her sister in law Nomsa is a keen member. She has a steep block that is about a half a hectare. Years of working with manure and compost have improved her soils. She is growing a great variety of food plants, which make for a rich diet. Quite a few of them have been planted with the market in mind and of course her family and relatives get much of what she grows.

Bananas are her biggest crop intended for sale and she has a lot of these on her small block. She uses blue plastic bags supplied by Is'Baya to prevent blemishes. On market days, when she has a crop of bananas, she will go into the nearby town of Port St Johns to sell some bananas at stalls. Another large area of her yard is planted out with beans. These are harvested and dried to be stored for the year. Most will be eaten by her own household. Other vegetables she is growing for her house are taro, sweet potatoes, carrots, green peppers and pumpkins. She has a large plot of weedy wild vegetables that she also picks to add to her cooking – two types of amaranth and *Bidens pilosa*. She grows sugar cane for the house and also sells little sticks of sugar cane to local children. Other fruits are avocadoes, guavas, pineapples (all for her own household) and mangoes (some for her own household and some for sale).

Low input agriculture

All three projects recommend 'low input' agriculture (Pretty 1999). If a project is intended to work on household food provision, it makes sense to avoid agricultural techniques that depend on *buying* inputs. The food you are growing for your own house will not be sold – there will be no cash generated to pay for inputs. Even if you are growing some surplus for cash, you cannot be sure that these sales will materialize. In any particular year, the market may be down or something may happen to your crop. It is also highly likely that poor villagers will end up spending the money that they earn *before* they can use it to buy inputs. This is just the economic argument. Many of the organizers of these projects were also concerned about the damage to soils, to health and to the environment from chemical fertilizers, herbicides and pesticides.

The TSURO project promotes low input agriculture as 'permaculture'. Johannes Mufakose from the TSURO centre describes the activities that they are engaged in with farmers in one ward of the district:

> And these farmers are involved in different project areas that include agroforestry and rainwater harvesting. They are also involved in small livestock management, like poultry, goats, guinea fowl, just to mention but a few.

And also, they are also involved in watershed management and water source protection. And also involved in permaculture garden design.

Mareni, a beneficiary from one of the dryer areas of the Chimanimani district, explains the way his farming practices have been helped by TSURO:

> I started putting in the terraces, because when the land is not terraced, usually the moisture runs away, taking the soil away and leaving the soil without nutrients. I put in a lot of organic stuff, manure from the cattle kraal. I had to put in a lot of compost to enrich the soil. Now I have joined the permaculture. They taught us how to make good compost. We have started planting a lot of trees, we look after chickens and turkeys, goats, cattle. Now we are getting the manure from the animals to put into the field.

In 2010, Leahy also interviewed Wilson, who explained how his farm was running according to permaculture principles:

> I do sustainable agriculture and organic farming only. I have quite a diversity of crops ranging from vegetables to fruits. These elements are related.

In 2014, Leahy went back to Wilson's place. He explained that he was using Sunhemp to control Striga weed and using crop rotation. In the first year he would put in maize and legumes, such as cow peas or peanuts. The next year he might grow sunflowers in the same field. To prepare the field he would be making sure that the ground is level and using planting stations – conservation agriculture. After harvest, he cuts the stalks and brings them back to the house to make compost. He adds manure from his chickens and goats. He turns the compost for seven weeks and then adds worms to it.

In recent years, TSURO has established farmer action learning groups for organic agriculture in each of the districts in which they are working. Both Gladys and Wilson are 'source farmers' in these groups. This organic agriculture organization set up by TSURO is cooperating with other stakeholder organizations such as ZOPPA, the organic certification organization, and AFOREST, the department of forestry and agriculture. Farmers in these groups are hoping that they will be able to market some of their produce as organic. To get this started, they are trying out various organic strategies to deal with typical problems. Other local farmers who want to save money on inputs are adopting the technologies that they pioneer. They are working on issues such as natural pest management, soil fertility and cropping with legumes. For example, Takura Pajuel, a farmer from one of these groups, has worked out a way to catch moles, which are eating his crops, using traps made from discarded plastic jars. To deter maize borers, the members of this organization are using the muore tree, chillies, ashes and tephrosia. Last season they experimented with ways to get rid of witch weed (Striga) which reduces maize production. They found that inter-planting with Sunhemp or making a compost from Sunhemp can work.

Elijah Kyamuwendo from Kulika indicated that low input agriculture has always been their preferred option. People were going hungry because of the failure of local agriculture following the civil war, so they decided to promote organic solutions. He gave an account that stressed the economic logic:

> So, the research looked at what can be done from the resources that are everywhere without bringing in new outside inputs and things where people say – 'but we can't afford that'. So we looked at the things that can be used from wherever you are, the natural resources that were at the disposal of the starving communities.

Is'Baya describes its agricultural strategy as 'conservation agriculture'. In an explanation of its project, it begins by noting the necessity to take care of the environment and goes on to specify the characteristics of conservation agriculture as follows: 'The key principles are ensuring the recycling and restoration of soil nutrients and organic matter and optimal use of rainfall through retention and better use of biomass, moisture and nutrients' (Jones and Du Preez 2008: 12). It clearly relates this strategy to the financial imperatives of food production for poor families, claiming that conservation agriculture cuts production costs (Jones and Du Preez 2008: 12). Few inputs are to be purchased because cover crops, manure, compost and management practices take the place of chemical fertilizers, herbicides and pesticides.

While Leahy was staying with the project in 2014, he saw these strategies in action. For example, every month the monitors from each village come to the project office in Port St Johns and are educated about pest problems that the beneficiaries might be having with their fruit trees. They are shown pictures of the different kinds of pests and the damage they cause. They are shown how to create various remedies that can work in their villages. For example, making up a solution with marmite to trap fruit flies in a used Coca-Cola bottle. When they go back to the villages they go round to each of the beneficiaries and explain these techniques.

The methods of assistance

Along with the substance of assistance, there are a variety of methods by which the project organizes the delivery of their assistance. These methods are equally vital in establishing a project which can work.

Individual households, rather than entrepreneurial collectives

All three organizations target individual households working on their own land. Rose Du Preez explained why Is'Baya abandoned the group project model:

> Okay, we looked at the communal sites, not even at just ours but all other projects working on communal sites … they just weren't working! We

planted at eleven communal sites, of which not one is functional today. Government or funders come in and say, 'Okay! We've got funds! Who wants to plant trees?' So people see money, they say 'We want to!' So they plant trees and then today you work, and I work, and you don't work and so tomorrow I'm cross with you, so I don't work and then no-one works and the goats get in because no one closed the gate.

Accordingly, Is'Baya moved to providing fruit trees to be planted on people's own land. Yet they depended on some group processes. A beneficiary who wanted to start the project in their village would have to recruit twenty households, form a committee and collect money for the trees. These group processes rely for success on the framework which targets individual households:

Everyone, when it comes to the actual trees, they're my trees, and they're your trees. So I want it to work because if the village falls apart, okay.

An example explains how individualistic motivation works to improve outcomes:

One man takes me to his garden and he says, 'This tree, I'll leave here for always to teach people' (there's this little citrus tree), he says, 'I was digging this big hole and I got so tired so I dug a little hole. Is'Baya won't see! They won't notice!' And then he said, 'And then I saw my other trees growing big. And these trees, I planted the next year in a big hole'. And then he saw. 'Is'Baya can't see, but *I* can see! [laughs]. I cheated myself! [laughs] Because that tree cost me ten rand!'

TSURO and Kulika likewise work with individual households to improve farming on their own land. Exceptions show the same principles. The Machete community garden was divided into individual household plots, with produce going to the household. The inputs donated by TSURO were poly pipe to bring water and fencing mesh for the whole plot. Neither of these required beneficiaries to pool money to maintain them. So there is no attempt to pool produce for sale and there is no need to pool profits to maintain equipment.

No money paid for work to improve your own land

None of these projects pay villagers to work on improvements to their own land. The example of the man who dug a small hole for his tree shows how this works. The beneficiary is working on his own land and finds that his failure to dig a large hole is his own problem.

An example from TSURO indicates that community working parties can also operate without payment. A village committee specified contour bunds as the kind of assistance they wanted from TSURO. Having accepted the project, TSURO took some villagers to look at contour bunds in use elsewhere. The local committee chose one farmer to be the first to receive a bund in their cropping field and all pitched in with labour to construct it, without payment. Later, the same process was repeated on the fields of other farmers, but without the necessity for further instruction from TSURO. There is a common belief that projects in Africa will not work unless beneficiaries are paid (see Vignette D: Working for Food – Working for Money). All three of these projects ignore this common wisdom in order to ensure that villagers are actually committed to the projects. They begin their work with the few who are willing to volunteer their labour and recruit as the fruits of this work become apparent.

All invited

The two dominant models for project design include members of a community selectively. There is a limit to who can be involved because commercial infrastructure costs a lot of money. Instead, food security outreach projects work with subsistence and can invite everyone. Along with this goes a second key element – these projects only respond to an initiative and felt need coming from the community; a need demonstrated by willingness to volunteer work.

Johannes Mufakose, one of the management team from TSURO, explained the initiation of the Machete irrigated community garden:

> Out of the need that the area is dry. Out of that the group actually visited TSURO and presented their proposals to TSURO. TSURO will assess those village based plans and see how they can intervene and support the group.

From the whole community which they service (the whole of the Chimanimani district), TSURO invites local people to form themselves into community groups and to nominate projects, which may get funding if TSURO thinks that the project makes sense.

Kulika makes a similar attempt to invite all members of a community to make improvements to their productivity. Albert described their package of suggestions like this:

> It's a comprehensive basket. Where people are allowed to choose what to actually take and what they can take in bits. Actually start with a contour, stabilize it. Put in a vegetable. Then as you put in the vegetable, we say that the chickens need a run. Because the chickens will destroy the vegetables. So it is a step-by-step build zone.

This approach has something for every class level in the community. It works with the very poor where they are at and gradually improves their situation. They will be able to pay for some inputs like fencing wire and cement to line a pond – after they have begun to sell some surplus production. Kulika does not rush in and fund these as an initial grant. The *whole* community can be invited because Kulika is not paying for expensive inputs.

Is'Baya is the same in making an effort to invite all members of a defined community (a rural village) to participate in their fruit project – rather than creating a project that can only be the vehicle of improvement for some households. What Is'Baya is offering is fruit trees provided at a subsidized cost, along with training in looking after them:

> We put criteria in. We said, we can't plant just one tree, we must plant in a year, a minimum of ten [per household] and we need in a village, a minimum of twenty households. And that we also need a village to elect out of those households who want to do it; to elect a committee. Because we can't talk to twenty households. So you form a committee.

The offer is made to all families in the village but the criteria for inclusion is demonstrated participation. News of the efficacy of this system spread, leading to further recruitment:

> So the villages started growing and every year we would get more villages. Someone would come and sit in the meeting and then say 'Okay, actually I'm not from this village. I came from that village over there, you must come to my village.'

Few material inputs

These projects avoid expensive inputs. This allows the project to roll out their invitation to anyone in the locality who expresses interest and shows commitment. The emphasis is on training and consultation. When industrial inputs are provided, they are things like poly pipe, cement or fencing mesh. Start up packages such as open pollinated seeds, small livestock or fruit trees, are sometimes donated, or subsidized. These are to be maintained and propagated further by beneficiaries, without the necessity for further cash inputs.

Mareni explained that on his farm, TSURO had assisted with educational input:

> ...the permaculture people took me for some exchange visits to see what others are doing. We get the knowledge of how to make compost, how to grow herbs, how to grow some vegetables.

His farm now demonstrated a variety of small livestock, use of terracing with rock walls, a pond, numerous fruit trees, a variety of grain crops. As an example of similar strategies from Kulika, Elijah responded to a question about chicken wire with a complex account. On the one hand, farmers who had a bit of money would be urged to buy chicken wire to fence in their poultry. Yet, for the poor they were advising the use of reeds. Living fencing was promoted to keep goats. Bundles of napier grass could be tied together to construct a fence. A pit was promoted to enclose pigs.

The bottom line is that subsistence production for food security cannot depend on the vagaries of the cash economy. So machinery which needs to be serviced by paid mechanics and operated with supplies of diesel is not a sensible donation. Nor are start up packages consisting of fertilizers and hybrid seeds – which have to be purchased again for the next crop.

Bureaucratic democracy

As in the previous chapter, I use this term to refer to a project design which establishes some democratic control of the project funds through a transparent set of regulated processes. All three organizations maintain a professionally staffed centre, which reaches out to the villages. They set up defined authority structures, involving local people in specified roles. This is 'bureaucratic' in relation to the defined, transparent and formalized structures of authority and 'democratic' in relation to the participatory mechanisms being set up. The democratic aspect of this outreach organization is necessary to discover the felt needs of a community and ensure success.

For Is'Baya, villagers show commitment by organizing a committee to liaise with the central organization. Roles are specified:

> ... a treasurer, a chairperson, a secretary, and what we call a liaison person. The liaison person was our contact. They had to have a cell phone. When they pay for their trees, the treasurer collects the money. We give them books ... books like this, and they must keep a record of it. Every household who paid their money.

An example of similar processes for TSURO is the selection of villagers as community facilitators. The first step is a village meeting of all adults. They select seven people to represent their village, including a chairperson. The committee collects a fee from the villagers to gain membership of TSURO – $10 for their whole group. Then this committee attends a ward meeting with the members of other village committees, representing up to fifteen villages. The ward meeting nominates three people who have O level (matriculation) and are known to work well with their communities as candidates for extension work with TSURO. Three wards all do this, making nine candidates in all. Each ward then sends its elected ward chairperson to a joint meeting with the other chairs from the three wards and with the TSURO management team. This joint committee selects three candidates in total. Kulika uses similar methods to call community meetings and find out what it is that communities need, before beginning their interventions.

An example of this participatory structure in action at the local level are the learning groups for organic agriculture organized by TSURO. In 2014, Leahy visited a number of farms owned by local organizers for these groups. Wilson explained that there are twenty local farmers in his group. They meet once a week and come up with a programme. They go to different places depending on what they are doing. They rotate their meetings so that they visit every farm of the people in their group. Gladys is the chairperson for her local group. Her husband used to be the source farmer of this group. When he died about two years ago she took over the role. When Leahy went there with officers from TSURO, they met with fifteen members, of whom ten were women. There are thirteen other members in their group who had to attend a funeral. TSURO brought bread, eggs, tea, peanut butter, jam and margarine so that after the visitors had toured the garden they all sat down to eat and talk about the group. This small gift of hospitality signalled the fact that Leahy was there as the guest of TSURO and represents the link between the central organization and this local community. A roll was taken and the secretary of the group took minutes for the meeting.

Another meeting of TSURO took place when Leahy was in the Chikukwa villages. This was a coordination meeting that brought together source farmers like Wilson and Gladys who are organizing local groups. There were about ten men and twenty women present. Three members of the management team from CELUCT came along. Each of the source farmers present had been chosen by their own small neighbourhood and they explained why they had been selected. For example, the woman who was the source farmer for Chitekete village said that the problem their group was most concerned about was how to make sure they had a 'relish' for dinner. In other words, fresh vegetables. She said that there had been thirty of her fellow villagers present when she was selected to represent them. Mrs Mandega explained her role as the source farmer for her neighbours:

> We started in 2011. I have livestock including cattle. I have sunflowers and grains. I have a garden down near the river. I live by farming in the field, in the garden. I use manure from my animals. Sam [one of the staff from the centre] came and talked to me about all this. He explained that if I do this I can save money using animal manure and Open Pollinated Varieties. We started here with eight members. We did workshops with AFOREST and learned about natural pest management. We joined the organic growers organization. We are not promised handouts but knowledge and how to use available resources rather than spending a lot of money. I have done a lot of experiments. We are identifying our problems and finding ways to deal with those problems. We are also doing seed saving. We meet twice a week. We learn as a group and then each farmer goes and implements it on their own land. Our group was twenty-six people. Some of our members have now started their own groups. By splitting our group we have extended to other places and people come here to see what we are doing.

A permanent presence – long term commitment to the beneficiaries

In Africa, a common strategy is to operate a project for a maximum of five years, with the intention that all projects should become self sustaining (Ferguson 1990; Leach and Scoones 2006; Marais and Botes 2007). This process almost always leads to projects failing after the professional staff leave. By contrast, all three of the food security outreach organizations nominate a set of clients and commit the organization for the long term.

Rose Du Preez from Is'Baya discussed the way large government bodies staffed by professionals expected to create and leave projects within a three year time frame:

> They want to go in for two or three years and then they withdraw. I mean we've found that in Eastern Cape. And after two, three years they say, 'Okay, now we withdraw. We've given the people the technical knowledge so that they can carry on.' But it's not sustainable. They say, 'You've been there for ten years! Move onto another place.' And I say, 'Okay, show me one of your three year projects that's still working', and then they get quiet and they leave you alone [laughs].

Is'Baya initially worked with fifteen villages in the Eastern Cape and this then expanded to fifty-two villages as other communities heard of their work and requested interventions. At this point Is'Baya refused to accept any more member villages. Instead it is concentrating on deepening its interventions in the villages where it is already working.

For the TSURO organization, the client base is defined as people of the Chimanimani district and more directly as villages, which become 'members' of the organization by paying a membership fee. Ulli Westermann explained the importance of continuity:

> You have to be integrated in the community if you want to achieve anything. And you have to know the people. It's very difficult for outsiders to quickly jump in, do a quick two or three year programme and then move on and phase out.

TSURO recruits long term professional staff and has a permanent central headquarters.

Kulika also has permanent headquarters from which it manages its operations. Like TSURO, it recruits trained professionals to be the staff:

> We select people who have back-up ground in environment, agricultural extension, agriculture, agriculture teachers. Then we bring them into our programme and we train them as tutors.

So, a permanent organization manages outreach as well as liaison with international funding charities. This organization recruits a permanent professional staff, as well as some local extension workers. The organization engages beneficiaries as clients. As beneficiaries become effective in dealing with a problem there is less need for the outreach organization to be heavily involved. Nevertheless the NGO is available for support and will engage in new projects with the same clients.

The food security outreach model as 'a winning formula'

One of the organizations considered in this chapter has made some systematic attempts to provide evidence for the efficacy of its work. In 2010, TSURO conducted a study of twenty-five beneficiary households (TSURO 2011). They were randomly selected – five each from five different wards in which the project operates. Most of these households had been involved with TSURO for more than eight years. More than twenty reported various kinds of food insufficiency before they joined TSURO. Their involvement with TSURO had helped them to grow more cereals (twenty-five respondents), root crops (fifteen), animal protein (twenty), vegetable protein (twenty-four), more vegetables (twenty-three) and more fruit (twenty). They also reported that they had been able to make some cash income to buy more food (twenty respondents). These beneficiaries were also asked to say what kinds of assistance they had received. Eighteen mentioned instructions about more effective ways to farm, twenty had received assistance with materials to help construction and nineteen had received assistance by being able to buy some supplies for their farm at a cheaper price. The technologies that had been introduced to more than twenty respondents were composting, growing vegetables at home and in the cropping fields, growing small livestock, woodlots and woodland preservation, stopping fires, mulching, and controlling larger livestock. This is a more systematic presentation of what we learned from interviews with beneficiaries and project officers. It replicates what has been quoted from these sources in this chapter.

It may seem audacious to claim the food security outreach model as 'a winning formula' for rural food security projects in Southern Africa. In terms of the kinds of evidence normally thought necessary to evaluate food security projects, we are missing some key elements. What we do not have is a before and after study in which medical indicators of nutrition were measured for a random group of beneficiaries, a group large enough to do statistical analysis. The fact is that the demand for evidence like this ends up by favouring certain kinds of project design and marginalizing others. In university disciplines which deal professionally with 'food security', what is favoured are projects which come into an area where nutrition is demonstrably inadequate – and shown to be so by arm measurements and blood analysis. These projects then provide supplements, especially to infants, for a period of one year or more. After the intervention they come back and carry out the same measurements again, demonstrating their efficacy. This is called 'evidence based' project design, but the effect is to prioritize projects that can only have short term effects.

It is difficult to provide this kind of data for agricultural projects. Usually there has been no random sample of nutritional status before the start of the project and there is no money to carry out a sample at a later date. This book has been written by social scientists but it represents an interdisciplinary approach. What we have done is to create a chain of evidence, linking together observations made in different fields of knowledge. To begin with, we know beyond the shadow of a doubt that the people in the area served by these projects are undernourished. This is because malnutrition is ubiquitous in this part of Africa and has been confirmed by numerous medical studies. There is also evidence that *the particular people* that these projects serve were undernourished before the intervention of the project. This comes from the oral histories provided by interviewees.

This chapter has presented some of the evidence for the increase in food production for household use that has followed these projects. This is a study based in qualitative research, carried out over a number of years – interviews, focus groups, participant observation. Confidence is derived from what social scientists call the 'saturation' of data. This means that a random set of investigations keeps coming up with exactly the same outcome. In this study, the increase in food production for the beneficiaries is confirmed first by numerous interviews with farmers who have explained their farming strategies and taken the authors to look at the plants and animals that they have been growing since the intervention of the project. That these are for household use has been made clear in interviews and confirmed through daily participation in the lives of people in the villages. In the course of this we have been introduced to children of all ages and witnessed their healthy condition first hand. Photographic evidence can confirm this and also give evidence of the state of the household gardens and cropping fields owned by beneficiaries. These can be compared with the gardens and fields of those who are not involved in these projects. The longevity of these projects is readily demonstrated by looking at the age of the fruit trees that have been planted as well as by interviewing farmers and project officers. In some cases there are documents from the early years of the project and photos of the area before the intervention.

Let us give an example. When Leahy was staying in Eastern Cape in 2014, he spent three weeks living in Khluleka and Noqhekwana. As he was walking around each of these villages with the monitor it was easy to see which households were working with Is'Baya. They were the households with a number of fruit trees and a good vegetable garden. You could look at a hillside and pick out the gardens of those involved in the project. Leahy had the same experience when driving to village meetings all around Eastern Cape with the project field officer. Leahy and the project officer would stop the car in the village while they waited for the meeting to take place. Leahy would stand on the road looking around and had no trouble identifying the households that were working with the project.

The other science that contributes evidence of the success of these projects is the medical science of nutrition. Numerous studies confirm such well known facts as the protein content of chicken meat, the nutritional necessity of protein, the vitamin C content of the fruit varieties grown by the beneficiaries from these projects and so on. As they say, none of this is rocket science.

By linking the biological science to the ethnographic research, we can be confident in saying that projects that *last* in Africa and which help households to produce a good variety of food, which they *then eat at home*, improve the food security of African villages. These goals, which seem simple enough, are not achieved by the vast majority of rural projects operating in Africa. There is a division of labour between different fields of academic knowledge that are most commonly concerned with rural poverty in the developing world. Some academics use techniques for evaluating evidence from medical science and talk about food security. Some use economic modelling, look at monetary outcomes and talk about rural development. It is no wonder that favoured project designs do one of two things. They either go in to give nutrient supplements or attempt to help people to make some money. As this book has made painfully obvious, commercial projects generally do not work. Even those few commercial projects that do work contribute little to nutritional outcomes for the vast majority of the poor. Nutritional supplements will certainly work in the short term. But in the long term, the problem is much too widespread to be alleviated by one year projects conducted at great expense. Giving nutritional supplements in one village will never make any impact on the village next door. By contrast, new methods of household food production and an emphasis on feeding the farmer first can become established in the culture. The more these methods work with the beneficiaries, the more likely they are to be widely adopted. Assistance that depends on technologies that are easy to understand and do not depend on cash inputs are cost effective and have more long lasting impact.

Let us finish this chapter by summarizing the characteristics of the food security outreach model:

In terms of the content of the assistance:

- The priority is food security via household subsistence.
- Households are also encouraged to make some cash income from a surplus.
- The agricultural strategy is low input farming.

So all three of these projects make food security through household production their priority. At the same time, beneficiaries are encouraged to believe that the methods being suggested will in fact produce a surplus for sale, over and above what the family needs for its own food security. There is no doubt that some beneficiaries realize this cash income while almost all benefit greatly from the increase in household food provision. The key agricultural strategy is mixed farming with a minimal use of purchased inputs. The aim is to produce all nutritional needs and for the different parts of the farming enterprise to support each other. The stress on low cost organic solutions has the effect of enabling food security to be attained without the dangers of running short of cash to provide inputs.

In terms of the method of assistance:

- Individual households are the target.
- No money is paid to beneficiaries to improve their own land.
- All potential beneficiaries are invited.
- Effective selection is by demonstrated commitment.
- Few material inputs – the most important assistance is educational.
- Bureaucratic democracy links beneficiaries and the organization.
- The donor organization maintains an ongoing relationship with its clients.

The method of assistance is just as crucial for the success of these projects. Crucially, these projects do not attempt to join households together to realize a common profit and to depend on this to maintain their collective enterprise. Instead they are directed first at improving the productivity of individual households on their own land. As we have seen this does not rule out various kinds of community organization to facilitate this household production. These organizations resist competitive pressure from projects which pay beneficiaries for work. In the food security outreach projects, people are never paid to work on their own land or on the community land. Projects may start very small because they begin with people who are willing to volunteer their own work to improve their own production. They grow as the success of the approach being promoted becomes evident. Because food security outreach projects do not attempt to set up commercial farming operations, the cost of donations of materials to individual households remains very minimal. It becomes possible for the project to be offered to all the households in a village. There is no exclusion, no community jealousy and the project does not proceed by picking winners. On the other hand, successful beneficiaries may be rewarded by having their households chosen to represent best practice and get a small payment for farmer to farmer visits to their site. Transparency and a degree of control by the beneficiaries are achieved through various kinds of representation and democratic organization. The logic is that interventions can only work if local people believe that they meet a felt need. Finally, none of these organizations works through a model in which an intervention is carried out for several years and then project staff pull out. Instead, the project team has an ongoing relationship with a set of clients. Interventions build on previous interactions. At a certain point in time, the food security outreach project will stop expanding and will restrict itself to a particular set of clients that can be handled effectively. Ideally, it inspires people from other districts or countries to receive training and set up their own similar organization.

This model is a winning formula for food security projects in rural Southern and South-Eastern Africa. We know for certain that the dominant designs for projects in this region do not work. They have proved their inadequacy over at least sixty years. Their dominance comes out of the kind of thinking which has been considered in other chapters. What we have done in this chapter is look at some of the few projects which break the mould. All three of these projects have been going for more than ten years and their success and continuity can be observed here and now by going to the villages where they have been working the longest.

Note

Some parts of this chapter have been published in an earlier version as 'Best practice for rural food security projects in Southern Africa?' *Development in Practice*, *24*(8), 933–947. DOI: 10.1080/09614524.2014.969196.

Vignette H
Composting toilets in Africa

Terry Leahy

Explaining the problem

How it used to be

A study by Fairhead and Leach (1996) looks at traditional patterns of land use in Africa. In pre-modern Africa, villages never stayed in the one place for more than a few decades. The soils of the cropping fields would become exhausted. Villagers would shift to somewhere nearby with better soil fertility. Areas surrounding villages grew the most dense woodland vegetation in an environment that was generally dry and sparsely vegetated. This woodland belt was the area where villagers went to defecate and urinate and where their small livestock deposited manure. This village woodland was accumulating soil fertility, while the cropping fields further out were being depleted. When a village moved it would reoccupy the location of an earlier village. The woodland belt fertilized by a previous occupation would be cleared to grow crops. This cycle had been repeated in twenty year rotations.

How it is now

Staying at the Kai NGO centre in Zambia in 2010, I was living next to a village much like the ones Leach and Fairhead describe. The residential area was a collection of mud rondavel houses. Surrounding this was a ring of woodland, about 500 metres deep. Beyond that, the cropping fields were laid out. Soil fertility was a huge problem. The cropping fields of villagers had clearly been exhausted. Another problem was diarrhoea, killing off some infants, contributing to childhood stunting and laying adults low for days at a time. The Kai centre believed these epidemics came about because villagers were defecating in their woodland. Flies would then spread diseases. The preferred solution was pit toilets. An NGO had offered to help. Villagers were paid to dig the pits and install a concrete squat plate over each hole. These toilet pits were in clear view between the village houses. However, there was no money left to pay villagers to complete the toilets. To finish the job it was necessary to weave a screen round each toilet and construct a thatch roof. Years later this had not been done. It was hard to understand why villagers had not done this work themselves – despite the absence of funding. Surely they knew about the problems of diarrhoea and understood how it was transmitted?

Shyness and toilets

In one of my classes a student explained what I had seen in Zambia. He was talking about composting toilets for schools in Malawi and the problems in getting the students to make use of them. The main issue was that Africans regarded it as very embarrassing to be *seen* walking off to the toilet. If you were observed, your friends would tease you. Going to defecate in the woodland surrounding a village is the perfect cover. You could just be going off to collect sticks or walk out to the fields. A set of pit toilets established in the middle of a village would never be used. It was no surprise that villagers had failed to finish the toilets near the Kai centre, since they knew they would never use them.

Implications

The most accessible source of nutrients for food crops is what Jenkins has called 'human manure' (2005) – something that traditional African agriculture took advantage of through a system of shifting cultivation. Yet these traditional methods of recycling nutrients are no longer viable. It is no longer possible to move villages every twenty years. In most of rural Africa the traditional system has not been replaced with a viable alternative and ill health, not to mention malnutrition, are the consequences. The cultural logic of current practices is ignored in well meaning interventions. There is no local enthusiasm for systems being established from above and no bottom up solution taking off in the villages. The interventions that are typically implemented do not enable the nutrient recycling that traditional practices maintained. The following discussion lays out some of the options.

Pit toilets

Pit toilets are a good cultural fit in rural Africa. No one has to handle the manure. If the toilet is screened by a belt of bushes or trees, it can be private. Pit toilets can smell but this can be controlled with a chimney coming up from under the squat plate – a 'very improved' or 'Blair' pit toilet. Pit toilets are the preferred solution for governments and NGOs. So why are they still rare?

The reason is that they cost governments or NGOs quite a lot of money. The pit is one metre wide and up to five metres deep. A hole that deep has to be lined with strong walls. Then there is the toilet building, with its hinged door and waterproof roof. In the Eastern Cape villages of South Africa, pit toilets are far from universal. The government is constructing some with walls of concrete bricks, an enterprise well beyond the financial and technological capacities of most villagers. Pit toilets were also constructed with help from an NGO as part of the Chikukwa project in Zimbabwe (see Chapter 7). As they filled up (after about fifteen years) some villagers were constructing replacements. At one house I visited the family had dug a large hole in their banana patch and were lining it with a wall of stones and cement. This required great commitment. So pit toilets are generally unlikely without very substantial funding. This is unlikely for most of rural Africa.

Another problem with pit toilets is that the pathogens in excrement can live on in the pit and migrate into the ground water, contaminating streams, gardens and fields. So you do not want ground water coming into the bottom of the toilet pit and carrying pathogens elsewhere. To determine whether this is a risk, you must conduct an expert study, making this technology a very top down solution. The most serious problem is that pit toilets bury the nutrients in human manure below the root zone for food crops. This is a lost opportunity for village agriculture. Most families do not own cattle. Legumes are good for nitrogen but you also need phosphorus. Composted human manure is a very valuable source of phosphorus as well as other plant nutrients (Gunther 2002).

Composting toilets

A good compost heap will destroy the pathogens in excrement. These are bacteria, viruses and the eggs of intestinal worms. It is the heat and bacterial activity of composting which destroys pathogens. Six months of composting can destroy all relevant pathogens (Jenkins 2005). An effective compost heap will have a good ratio between carbon (from plants) and nitrogen (in manure). Half a bucket of plant material to a cup of manure is good. The second requirement is water. A compost heap should be damp but not wet. In the rainy season it must be covered. Jenkins recommends collecting urine as well as faeces for the best compost mix. The size of the compost bin must be at least a cubic metre to get good decomposition.

The Jenkins 'Humanure' system

The Jenkins 'Humanure' system (2005) is the simplest of three composting systems. A small wooden frame houses a plastic container (about twenty litres) and the toilet seat is on the top (see Figure H.1). A lid closes it so flies cannot get in. A bin contains a plant based cover material (a mulch), which you sprinkle on after you have used the toilet. This cover material blocks odour and begins the process of composting. After the container is about three-quarters full you take it to a compost heap and dump it, covering up with yet more mulch. You wash out the container and pour the water from that onto the compost heap. There are two composting heaps, at least one cubic metre each (see Figure H.2). You use one heap for approximately a year and then move onto the empty one. After another year all pathogens have been destroyed in the first heap and the compost is ready to use. Between the two composting heaps is a bin to store the mulch. This could be sawdust, leaves or grass straw.

THE HUMANURE SYSTEM
PART ONE

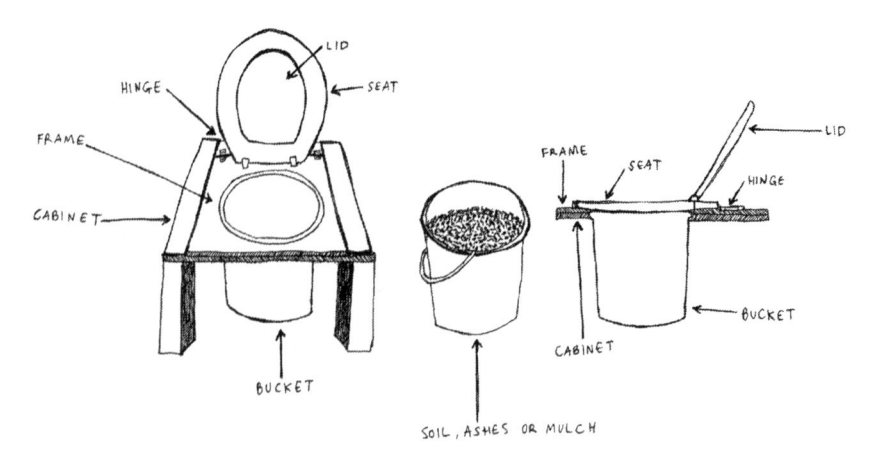

Figure H.1 The Jenkins 'Humanure' system – part one (from photos in Jenkins 2005).
Source: Illustration by Miriam Joan Montgomery.

THE HUMANURE SYSTEM
PART TWO – COMPOST BINS

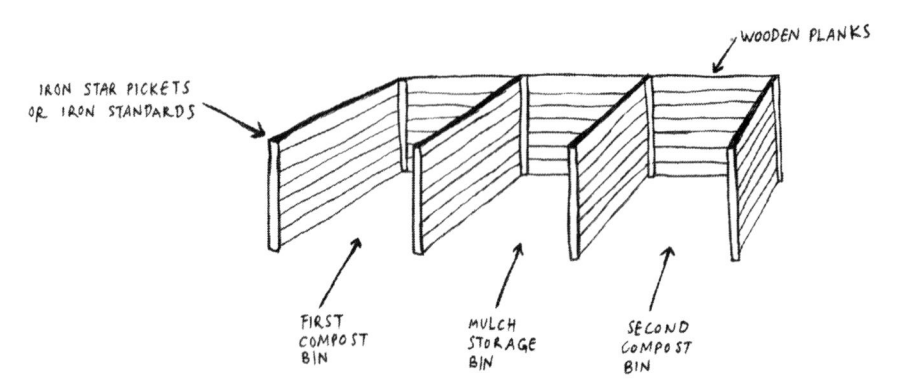

Figure H.2 The Jenkins 'Humanure' system – part two, compost bins (from photos in Jenkins 2005).
Source: Illustration by Miriam Joan Montgomery.

Vignette H: composting toilets in Africa

This system is cheap and there is very little fuss. As of 2018 these toilets are in use in a number of African countries. There is no doubt that the system works and is easy to operate. Yet I have some concerns about cultural impediments to getting it established widely. The main issue could be taking the plastic container to the compost heap and cleaning it out. That might well be regarded as disgusting or even dangerous. However, you would not have to dig out the compost until it had been rotting for a year and looked and smelled just like ordinary soil. You would have to screen the toilet and compost heap with trees and shrubs to ensure privacy.

The Malawi school system

This leads us to the next composting toilet system, which I will call the Malawi school system, in acknowledgement of a photo I saw in 2009 at the Permaculture Convergence in Malawi (see Figure H.3 and Figure H.4). There are two storeys. The compost heap is on the ground floor. The squat plate is on the first floor. A little staircase provides access. After you have used the toilet you sprinkle in a trowel full of mulch to dampen smells and to start a composting process. The manure and mulch gradually moves down a sloping ramp to a black metal door at the back. The door faces the sun and absorbs heat, aiding the composting process. After six months the toilet is swapped to the one next to it. A piece of

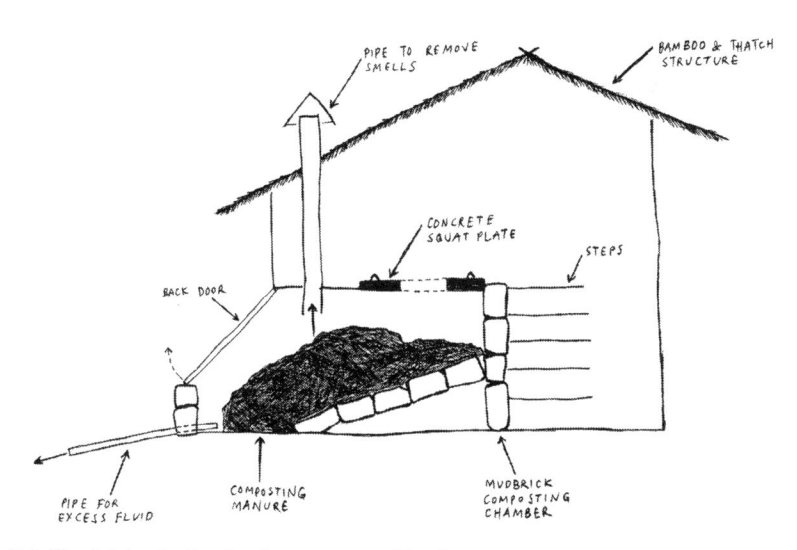

Figure H.3 The Malawi school toilet system – side view.
Source: Illustration by Miriam Joan Montgomery.

THE MALAWI SCHOOL TOILET - FROM ABOVE

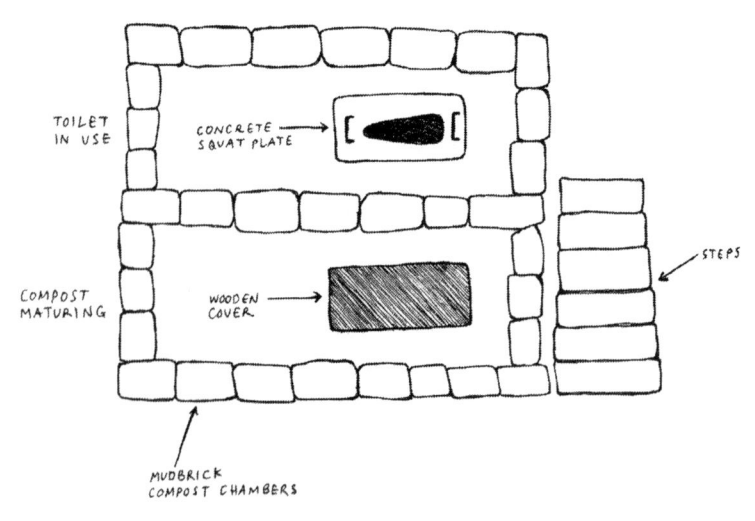

Figure H.4 The Malawi school toilet system – from above.
Source: Illustration by Miriam Joan Montgomery.

wood covers the hole in the first toilet and the squat plate is moved across. The compost heap below the first toilet sits for six months, after which it can be dug out to use on the fields or orchards.

This kind of toilet certainly works. It can be constructed using mud bricks, with bamboo and straw for timber and walls. A concrete squat plate is the only expensive item. It might be considered demeaning to shovel out the compost after the six months was up. There is also a lot of work in constructing this toilet, and you would need expert advice on hand.

The arborloo system

The 'arborloo' was designed by Peter Morgan (2007 – see Figure H.5) – so called because a tree (*arbor*) is planted on the site after the toilet has moved on. The hole is 1.5 metres deep and about 0.8 metres wide. A ring of bricks is laid around the edge and packed on the sides with dirt. The ring prevents water from draining into the pit. On top of this is the squat plate; a concrete disk about one metre wide, with a hole in the middle. Bricks and black plastic make the mould for the squat plate and fencing wire reinforces the concrete. A plastic bucket, squashed into a pear shape, creates the shape for the hole in the middle. To complete the structure, a movable toilet room provides privacy, with a roof to keep out rain. When you are not using the toilet, cover the hole with a board to keep out flies.

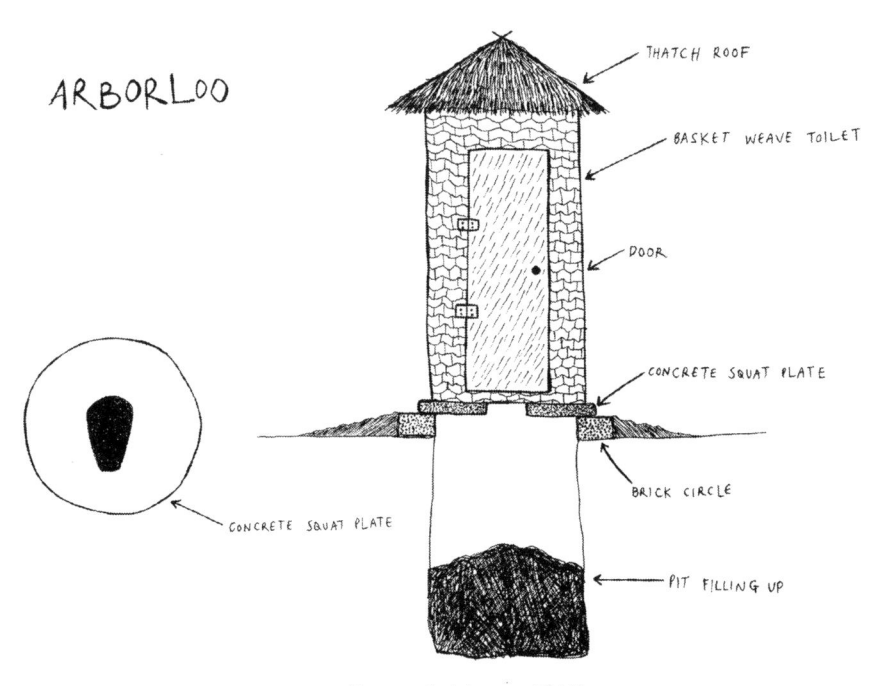

Figure H.5 The arborloo (from a diagram in Morgan 2007).
Source: Illustration by Miriam Joan Montgomery.

After using the toilet throw in some plant matter (mulch), about half a bucket. This makes the compost. Use the arborloo for between six and twelve months until the hole is almost full. Then move the toilet structure away. Fill up the used hole with soil. Later on, plant a tree seedling. The roots will grow into the rich compost. Dig another hole and begin again, using the same bricks, squat plate and toilet room. With this design, there is no need to handle the manure. The toilet should be screened by shrubs to achieve privacy. If there is no room for more trees as you move the toilet around the yard, the compost can be dug up and used after six months.

Tippy taps

In all cases toilets should have a 'tippy tap', a station for washing your hands (Brazier and Saw 2015). A large plastic juice bottle with a handle is ideal (see Figure H.6). There is a small hole in the top so water can be poured out. The bottle hangs by a string tied around the handle. Another string from the neck leads down to a stout stick. As you push down on the stick the neck tips down and the water pours onto your hands. There is also a tray for soap for washing your hands.

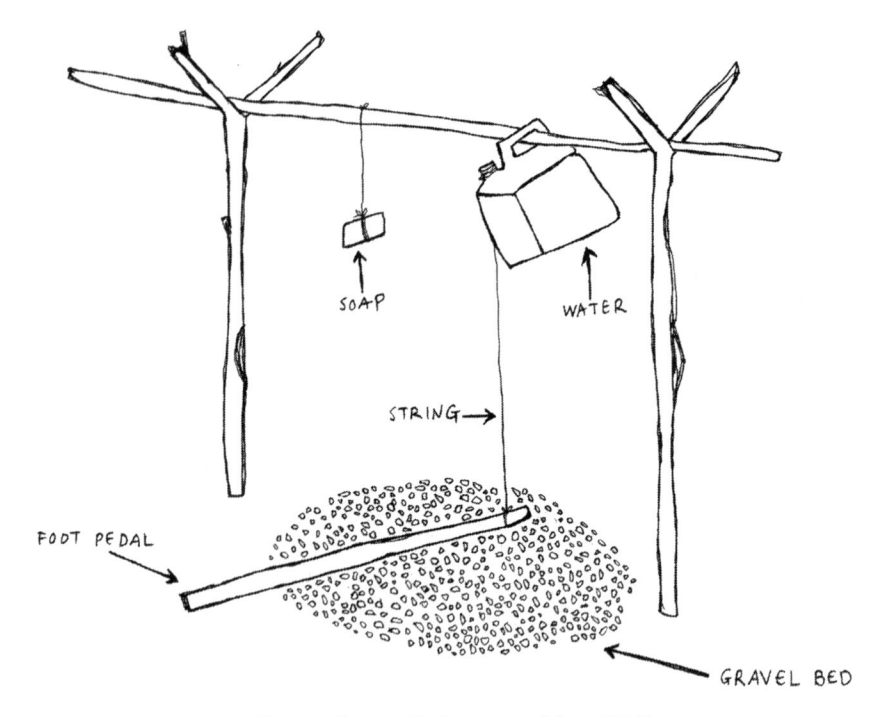

Figure H.6 The tippy tap (from a diagram in Brazier and Saw 2015).
Source: Illustration by Miriam Joan Montgomery.

9 The political economy of food security strategies

Terry Leahy

Three strategies for interventions

In a Marxist and anthropological analysis, the smallholders of the region of Africa who are the focus of this book would be referred to as 'peasant' agriculturalists. While the term 'peasant' can often be used abusively, anthropologists give it a different, more technical meaning, referring to people who play a particular part in a social system. The smallholder farmers of Africa would be defined by anthropologists as 'peasants' because some of their livelihood is gained through subsistence farming and they are also integrated into the commodity and labour markets of the national and global economy (Bryceson 2000b). In the classic analysis of the trajectory of peasant agriculture under capitalism, Marx predicted the disappearance of the peasantry, as their holdings were taken over for capitalist agriculture run by big firms (Goodman and Redclift 1981). It has not worked out exactly like this in the rich countries. Family farms still predominate in agriculture, though subsistence production has largely vanished. These commercial family farms are dominated by large input and distribution companies (Goodman and Redclift 1991; Watts and Goodman 1997). In the developing countries there is a patchwork of different economic forms in agriculture, well summarized by Hart as the 'simultaneous persistence, refashioning, and re-emergence of supposedly "pre-capitalist" forms – household production, sharecropping and so forth' in the context of 'divergent trajectories of capitalist development' (1997: 60, 57).

In the region considered in this book, that trajectory has been the combining of subsistence agriculture, largely performed by women, with circular migration of rural male workers into capitalist wage work – as Potts calls it, 'worker-peasants and farmer-housewives' (2000). Theoretically, this pattern was presented in the 1970s by Meillassoux as an 'articulation' of subsistence and capitalist modes of production:

> ...reproduction of the rural domestic community preserved the pre-capitalist society and facilitated its articulation to capital. Capitalist enterprises operated on a low-cost basis, recruiting male labour, paying low wages and returning workers to their rural homes at the end of the labour contract period.
>
> (Bryceson 2000b: 16; 2000c)

Bryceson (2000c) traces the way in which this arrangement was actively constituted by the colonial state. For example, colonial governments barred African women from taking up residence in cities and prevented land in native reserves from being sold or used as collateral for loans (see also Ferguson 1990; Potts 2000).

Within the conceptual framework of political economy we have two ways of describing such an arrangement. Following Gunder Frank we could see capitalism as a 'system on a world scale' (de Janvry 1990: 1). Within that description we would treat subsistence production as a 'specific *form of reproduction of labour-power* within a capitalist process of production' (Goodman and Redclift 1981: 88; Watts 1983: 21). In other words, we would see subsistence production as analogous to housework, as conceived within many Marxists accounts. Housework is performed, without pay, by members of the proletariat. All that unpaid housework fits the worker for their employment and enables their bosses to extract surplus value from their work. Using this framework we could very well regard subsistence production as *a kind of housework*, sometimes performed by men as well as women. Alternatively we could follow Meillassoux and see the smallholder subsistence mode of production as 'articulated' *with* the capitalist mode of production (Bryceson 2000b; see also Gibson-Graham 2006b). In that account we would be treating subsistence agriculture today as *a different system* of production, linked to capitalism now, but having its own logic and history.

Given this discussion, there are three possible kinds of interventions that might assist food security and three kinds of political approach connected to these:

1 To raise the wages of the poor in their mining, industrial or agricultural employment so that they have no need to grow their own food. The poor of rural Africa will migrate to their place of work, ending the current articulation of subsistence with wage employment. The land on which these poor smallholders now engage in subsistence agriculture will be taken over by commodity agriculture, supplying food to the cities. We can think of this as the trade union strategy. In the trade union analysis, smallholder subsistence agriculture is seen as an exploitation that allows employers to pay less than a living wage to 'worker peasants'.

2 To persuade the poor to become successful commodity producers – farmers in the European sense (Goodman and Redclift 1991). They will run family farms integrated into the market economy. They will be able to afford to buy all the food they need, without producing it on their own farms. A shift to petty commodity production instead of proletarianization. This has clearly been the strategy promoted by the IMF, the World Bank and African governments in the postcolonial period (Sitko 2008; see Chapter 1). Theoretically, this approach is tied in to neo-liberal theories of development. It sees subsistence agriculture as a barrier to efficient agricultural production and the law of comparative advantage (Bryceson 2000b).

3   To boost the success of the subsistence economy by producing more use value with less labour input. In most recent approaches to this, a diverse, poly-cultural low input agriculture is being promoted. This could allow smallholder families to produce all the food they need – without depending on a cash income through the sale of their agricultural production. They will not need to purchase fertilizers and hybrid seeds or to supply oxen or tractors for ploughing. The effect will be to allow the diverse livelihood strategies of peasant families to be more effective. The context is that wage work has become very unreliable and governments are not effectively supporting poor families in times of hardship (Bryceson 2000c; Sitko 2008).

This third strategy fits very well with the articulation theory of Meillassoux. More recently, Gibson-Graham (2006b) and Olin Wright (2010) valorize non-capitalist productive enterprises as an opportunity for leftist intervention. The subsistence mode of production is to be *disarticulated* from capitalism, at least to some extent. As Bryceson notes, this strategy has been promoted by some recent development economists as 'sustainable development' with a side benefit of poverty alleviation (Bryceson 2000b: 28). Focusing on the micro level, they have avoided the controversy that might come from an open promotion of subsistence agriculture. In this book, this strategy, named as 'feeding the farmers first', has been promoted in reverse order, as poverty alleviation, with a side benefit of sustainability.

This book has been written to address the context in which none of these three strategies has proved particularly successful. The trade union strategy, while not totally fruitless, has been thwarted by problems in boosting the real incomes of worker-peasants. Low wages have not been improved by the impact of mechanization and consequent unemployment in industry, mining and agriculture. They have not been improved by neo-liberal strategies that have pulled subsidies from commercial farming in many African countries (Walker 2007).

As this book has made abundantly clear, the rural commercialization strategy has been an almost total failure in this part of Africa. The reasons for this have been explored in this book. To begin with, on the *very* smallholdings available to the poor in this region of Africa it actually does not make economic sense to *replace* subsistence cropping for staples with cash cropping. The difference between the retail price of staples purchased for food and the producer price for cash crops from the same plot makes it uneconomic to produce anything but a small surplus for sale (see Chapter 2). To add to this are problems with transport, human capital, economies of scale and quality control (see Chapter 4). We have traced these problems in detail, looking at the types of project that are typically rolled out to embody the commercialization agenda. As we have seen, group entrepreneurial projects are a complete failure in this part of the world (see Chapters 3, 4, 7, 8). Emerging farmer projects may work in some cases but do not do much for the poor. Attempts to direct these emerging farmer projects to the poor make them even less likely to succeed as projects (see Chapters 2, 3, 4, 6).

212 *The political economy of food security*

So far the third form of intervention has rarely been tried. In some of the situations where it has been tried it has not been a success. For example, funded government programmes to promote conservation agriculture have not had much impact in the villages. Notwithstanding these failures, this book has argued that it is this third solution which is the most feasible of the three. We have maintained that interventions should aim at increasing the production of household food supply through subsistence agriculture – feeding the farmers first. Accordingly, a key concern of this book has been the barriers to the adoption of the third strategy. We have approached this question in a number of ways. One has been to look at the ways in which typical project designs are not tailored to this goal but instead pursue ineffective commercial strategies (Chapters 2, 4, 6). A second approach has been to look at the cultural barriers at the local level. Why is it that local people are unlikely to see low input solutions to household food security as a solution to their problems (Chapter 3)? A third approach has been to consider the ideological barriers to subsistence solutions where the professional middle class are concerned. How do members of this middle class, employed to assist the poor in the villages, see their role? How does their background, the surrounding cultural environment and the pressure of their jobs contribute to an emphasis on entrepreneurial success as the route out of poverty (Chapter 5)? Finally, we have demonstrated that projects that do work on subsistence productivity can be effective and we have considered the project designs that have made that possible (Chapters 7 and 8).

Village perspectives and solutions

Considering the three strategies of intervention described here, there is no doubt that the villagers of this region are most committed to some version of the first strategy and the understandings that go with that. Subsistence agriculture is a sign that modernity has not yet been achieved. It may be necessary but it is not regarded as ideal. What would be preferred would be an increase in the income going to wage labour. What is seen as morally necessary as a first step is an increase in income which would be sufficient to fund a 'modern' practice of subsistence agriculture for cereals and the purchase of non-carbohydrate foods in sufficient quantities. Beyond that, income should be sufficient to fund school fees and uniforms, a house made of bricks and corrugated iron, a few cattle to fund retirement. The full trade union strategy of *replacing* subsistence agriculture is not entertained. Subsistence agriculture is regarded as a current necessity, but the aspiration is to frame subsistence agriculture in a way that links it to modernity and the package of values associated with modernity. At the same time, villagers certainly hope that their children will escape rural life and subsistence agriculture.

The effect of this understanding is a 'fatal strategy' where food provision is concerned. The current global economy and the political landscape associated with that makes it unlikely that these aspirations for higher wage incomes will be met. These aspirations stand in the way of a more effective practice of subsistence agriculture that could detach food provision from the inadequacy and unreliability of paid employment.

There is a need to take these cultural factors into account in any attempt to help rural Africans to a more effective subsistence and food security through that. This is not a problem that can be solved by the usual practices of agricultural extension. Visits by scientifically trained outsiders, along with incentives to help farmers, are clearly insufficient. This book has explained why such measures are not working. What is required is a much more thorough cultural change. Such a change would revise the understanding of the role of subsistence agriculture in Africa. Sustainable subsistence alternatives would be presented as the latest scientific advance. Those promoting these ideas would be a constant presence, representatives from the villages would work in liaison with experts, attention would be focused on particular sites for decades.

We have seen that it is actually quite possible to summarize a project design that can work to improve food security in this region of Africa. We have considered this in detail in the previous two chapters. It is worth re-stating the broad outlines of this approach to conclude the book.

In terms of the content of the assistance:

- The priority is food security via subsistence – feeding the farmers first.
- Households are also encouraged to make some cash income from a surplus.
- The agricultural strategy is low input farming.

In terms of the method of assistance:

- Individual households are the target.
- No money is paid to beneficiaries to improve their own land.
- All potential beneficiaries are invited.
- Effective selection is by demonstrated commitment.
- Few material inputs – the most important assistance is educational.
- Bureaucratic democracy links beneficiaries and the organization.
- The donor organization maintains an ongoing relationship with its clients.

As we have explained, none of this is particularly difficult to implement. This strategy is cheap compared to the money being spent every day on doomed attempts to kick-start entrepreneurial development. An improvement in household food security through low input agriculture requires NGO or government initiatives to get started. However, this strategy for food security could readily spread beyond these origin points. There is nothing in these recommendations which is beyond the financial capacity that already exists in the villages. The scandalous failure of aid in sub-Saharan Africa is not because everything has been tried. It is not because aid can never work. It is because we have yet to see any major impetus behind strategies that could actually make a difference.

References

Agona, A. and Muyinza, J.N.H. (2013). *An overview of maize in Uganda.* Retrieved 24 October 2013 from www.egfar.org/.../A-2-008-001-A18_Maize_in_Uganda.pdf.

Aliber, M. (2001). *Study of the incidence and nature of chronic poverty and development policy in South Africa: An overview.* University of Western Cape, South Africa: Programme for Land and Agrarian Studies, School of Government.

Arslan, A., McCarthy, N., Lipper, L., Asfaw, S. and Cattaneo, A. (2013). *Adoption and intensity of adoption of conservation farming practices in Zambia.* Working Paper 71. Lusaka, Zambia: Indaba Agricultural Policy Research Institute.

Bachmann, L., Cruzada, E. and Wright, S. (2009). *Food security and farmer empowerment: A study of the impacts of sustainable agriculture in the Philippines.* Los Banos, Philippines: MASIPAG.

Bachou, H. (2002). The nutrition situation in Uganda. *Nutrition, 18* (4), 356–358.

Balirwa, E.K. (1992). *Maize research and production in Uganda.* Retrieved 24 October 2013 from http://pdf.usaid.gov/pdf_docs/PNABT623.pdf.

Barkworth, C. and Harland, C. (2009). *Zambia: Situational analysis of women and children 2008.* Lusaka, Zambia: The United Nations Children's Fund.

Baudrillard, J. (1983). *In the shadow of the silent majorities: Or the end of the social and other essays* (P. Foss, P. Patton and J. Johnson, trans.). New York: Semiotext(e).

Baudrillard, J. (1990). *Fatal strategies: Crystal revenge* (P. Beitchman and W.G.J. Niesluchowski, trans.). New York: Semiotext(e)/Pluto.

Binns, T., Dixon, A. and Nel, E. (2012). *Africa: Diversity and development.* Milton Park, Abingdon, Oxon: Routledge. Kindle Edition.

Biovision Foundation for Ecological Development (2010). *Infonet-biovision: Fodder production.* Retrieved 20 October 2013 from www.infonet-biovision.org/default/ct/666/fodder.

Biovision Foundation for Ecological Development (2012). *Infonet-biovision: Fish farming.* Retrieved 20 October 2013 from www.infonet-biovision.org/default/ct/277/livestockSpecies.

Biovision Foundation for Ecological Development (2013). *Infonet-biovision: Agroforestry.* Retrieved 26 October 2013 from www.infonet-biovision.org/default/ovvImg/-1/agroforestry.

Bond, P. (2009). Dossier: South Africa's 'developmental state'. *Distraction, Mediations Journal of the Marxist Literary Group.* Retrieved 5 January 2010 from www.mediationsjournal.org/articles/developmental-state-distraction.

Borras, S.M. (2003). Questioning market-led agrarian reform: Experiences from Brazil, Colombia and South Africa. *Journal of Agrarian Change, 3* (3), 367–394.

Brazier, A. and Saw, E. (2015). *Learning about nutrition: A facilitator's guide for food security and livelihoods field agents*. Myanmar: LEARN (Leveraging Essential Nutrition Actions to Reduce Malnutrition).

Bryceson, D. (2000a). Rural Africa at the crossroads: Livelihood practices and policies. *Natural Resource Perspectives, 52*. London: Overseas Development Institute.

Bryceson, D. (2000b). Peasant theories and smallholder policies: Past and present. In D. Bryceson, C. Kay and J. Mooij (eds), *Disappearing peasantries? Rural labour in Africa, Asia and Latin America* (pp. 1–36). London: ITDG Publishing.

Bryceson, D. (2000c). African peasants' centrality and marginality: Rural labour transformations. In D. Bryceson, C. Kay and J. Mooij (eds), *Disappearing peasantries? Rural labour in Africa, Asia and Latin America* (pp. 37–63). London: ITDG Publishing.

Buckles, D. and Triomphe, B. (1999). Adoption of Mucuna in farming systems of Northern Honduras. *Agroforestry Systems, 47*, 67–91.

Bunch, R. (1997). *Two ears of corn: A guide to people-centered agricultural improvement*. Oklahoma: World Neighbours.

Byaruhanga, Y.B. and Opedum, P.M. (2007). *The impact of culture on food security in Uganda*. Retrieved 3 June from www.siu.no/magazine/layout/set/print/content/view/full/11443.

Cabañero-Verzosa, C. (2005). *Counting on communication: The Uganda nutrition and early childhood development project*. Working Paper 59. Washington: The World Bank.

Carmody, P. (2002). Between globalisation and (post) apartheid: The political economy of restructuring in South Africa. *Journal of Southern African Studies, 28*(2), 255–275.

Chambers, R. (1983). *Rural development: Putting the last first*. Harlow: Prentice Hall.

Chambers, R. (2005). *Ideas for development*. London: Earthscan, Institute of Development Studies.

Chang, H.J. (2002). *Kicking away the ladder: Development strategy in historical perspective*. London: Anthem.

Chang, H.J. (2006). Re-thinking development economics: An introduction. In H. Chang (ed.), *Re-thinking development economics* (pp. 1–19). London: Anthem Press.

Chapoto, A., Chisanga, B., Kuteya, A. and Kabwe, S. (2015). *Bumper harvests a curse or a blessing for Zambia: Lessons from the 2014/15 maize marketing season*. Working Paper 93. Lusaka, Zambia: Indaba Agricultural Policy Research Institute (IAPRI).

Chapoto, A., Chisanga, B. and Kabisa, M. (2017). *Zambia agricultural status report*. Lusaka, Zambia: Indaba Agricultural Policy Research Institute (IAPRI).

Chibudu, C., Chiota, G., Kandiros, E., Mavedzenge, B., Mombeshora, B., Mudhara, M., Murimbararimba, F., Nasasara, A. and Scoones, I. (2001). Soils, livelihoods and agricultural change: The management of soil-fertility in the communal lands of Zimbabwe. In I. Scoones (ed.), *Dynamics and diversity: Soil fertility and farming livelihoods in Africa* (pp. 116–163). London: Earthscan.

Chilton, M. and Rose, D. (2009). A rights based approach to food insecurity in the United States. *American Journal of Public Health, 7*(99), 1203–1211.

Chipeta, S., Christopolos, I. and Katz, E. (2008). *Common framework on market-oriented agricultural advisory services*. Lindau, Switzerland: Neuchatel Group, Swiss Centre for Agricultural Extension and Rural Development (AGRIDEA).

Climate-data.org. (2014). *Climate: Sironko*. Retrieved 25 October 2014 from http://en.climate-data.org/location/52985/.

Congressi, P. and Kennedy, P.J.F. (2009). *The growing demand for land: Risks and opportunities for smallholder farmers*. Discussion paper prepared for the Round Table organized during the Thirty-second session of IFAD's Governing Council, 18.

Connell, R. (2007). *Southern theory: The global dynamics of knowledge in social science*. Cambridge: Polity.

Connors, L. and Mitchell, W. (2013). *Framing modern monetary theory*. Working Paper 06–13. Newcastle, Australia: Centre of Full Employment and Equity.

Corbeels, M., de Graaf, J., Ndah, T.H., Penot, E., Boudron, F., Naudin, K., Andrieu, N., Chriat, G., Schuler, J., Nyagumbo, I., Rusinamhodzi, L., Traore, K., Mzoba, H.D. and Adolwa, I.S. (2014). Understanding the impact and adoption of Conservation Agriculture in Africa: A multi-scale analysis. *Agriculture, Ecosystems and Environment, 187*, 155–170.

Cousins, B. (2007). Agrarian reform and the 'two economies': Transforming South Africa's countryside. In L. Ntebeza and R. Hall (eds), *The land question in South Africa: The challenge of transformation and redistribution* (pp. 222–245). Cape Town: Human Sciences Research Council.

Culbertson, E. and Kalyebara, M. (2005). *Participatory approach to food security, Uganda*. Retrieved 3 June 2010 from http://fex.ennonline.net/25/uganda.aspx.

Danida. (2005). *A joint evaluation: Uganda's plan for the modernisation of agriculture*. Oxford: Ministry of Foreign Affairs.

Davies, R. (2012). 'Alarming' rise in rural unemployment. *Mail and Guardian*, 12 September.

De Janvry, A. (1990). *The agrarian question and reformism in Latin America*. Baltimore: John Hopkins University Press.

De Janvry, A. and Sadoulet, E. (2011). Subsistence farming as a safety net for food-price shocks. *Development in Practice, 21* (4–5), 472–480.

De Onis, M., Blossner, M. and Borgh, E. (2011). Prevalence and trends of stunting among pre-school children, 1990–2020. *Public Health Nutrition, 15* (1), 142–148.

Deane, G. (2012). *Water hyacinth woes*. Retrieved 21 October 2013 from www.eattheweeds.com/water-hyacinth-stir-fry-2/.

Defoer, T. and Scoones, I. (2001). Participatory approaches to integrated soil management. In I. Scoones (ed.), *Dynamics and diversity: Soil fertility and farming livelihoods in Africa* (pp. 164–175). London: Earthscan.

Del Ninno, C., Dorosh, P.A. and Subbarao, K. (2007). Food aid, domestic policy and food security: Contrasting experiences from South Asia and sub-Saharan Africa. *Food Policy, 32*, 413–435.

Department of Agriculture. (2002). *Integrated food security strategy*. Pretoria; Department of Agriculture.

Department of Agriculture. (2005). *Annual report 2004/05*. Pretoria: Department of Agriculture.

Devereux, S. (2001). Transfers and safety nets. In S. Devereux and S. Maxwell (eds), *Food security in sub Saharan Africa* (pp. 267–293). Bourton-on-Dunsmore, UK: ITDG Publishing.

Dorosh, P.A., Dradri, S. and Haggblade, S. (2009). Regional trade, government policy and food security: Recent evidence from Zambia. *Food Policy, 34*, 350–366.

Dovie, D.B.K., Witkowski, E.T.F. and Shackleton, C.M. (2004). The fuelwood crisis in southern Africa: Relating fuelwood use to livelihoods in a rural village. *GeoJournal, 60* (2), 123–133.

Drinkwater, M. (1989). Technical development and peasant impoverishment: Land use policy in Zimbabwe's midlands province. *Journal of Southern African Studies, 15* (2), 287–305.

Ehrenreich, B. and Ehrenreich, J. (1979). The professional-managerial class. In P. Walker (ed.), *Between labor and capital* (pp. 5–45). Boston: South End Press.

Ekesa, B.N., Walingo, M.K. and Abukutsa-Onyango, M.O. (2009). Accessibility to and consumption of indigenous vegetables and fruits by rural households in Matungu division, Western Kenya. *African Journal of Food Agriculture Nutrition and Development, 9* (8), 12–24.

English, J., Tiffen, M. and Mortimore, M. (1994). Land resource management in Machakos district, Kenya 1930–1990. *World Bank Environment Paper 5.* Washington, DC: World Bank and Overseas Development Institute.

Englund, H. (2008). Extreme poverty and existential obligations: Beyond morality in the anthropology of Africa? *Social Analysis, 52* (3), 33–50.

Facio, A. (1995). From basic needs to basic rights. *Gender and Development, 3* (2),16–22.

Fairhead, J. and Leach, M. (1996). *Misreading the African Landscape: Society and ecology in a forest-savanna mosaic.* Cambridge: Cambridge University Press.

FAO. (2003a). *The anti-hunger programme: A twin track approach to hunger reduction: Priorities for national and international action.* Rome: FAO.

FAO. (2003b). *Trade reforms and regional food security: Conceptualizing the linkages.* Rome: FAO.

FAO. (2010). *Uganda nutrition profile 2010.* Retrieved 12 April 2011 from ftp://ftp.fao.org/ag/agn/nutrition/ncp/uga.pdf.

FAO. (2012). *Crop calendar Uganda (eastern savannah and eastern highlands).* Retrieved 24 October 2013 from www.fao.org/agriculture/seed/cropcalendar/welcome.do.

FAO. (2015). *Regional overview of food insecurity, Africa: African food security prospects brighter than ever.* Accra: FAO.

FAO. (2018). *Conservation Agriculture.* Retrieved 22 January 2018 from www.fao.org/ag/ca/.

FARA. (2006). *Framework for African agricultural productivity.* Accra: Forum for Agricultural Research in Africa.

Ferguson, J. (1990). *The anti-politics machine: 'Development', depoliticization, and bureaucratic power in Lesotho.* Cambridge: Cambridge University Press.

Fermont, A. and Benson, T. (2011). *Estimating yield of food crops grown by smallholder farmers: A review in the Uganda context.* IFPRI discussion papers 1097. Washington, DC: International Food Policy Research Institute.

Fine, B. (2007). South Africa: Looking for a developmental state. *Alternatives International.* Retrieved 5 January 2010 from www.alterinter.og/article1195.html.

Firth, D.J. (2003). *Cover crops for sub-tropical orchards.* Agfact, *H6.3.10.* Sydney: NSW Agriculture.

Fischler, M. and Wortmann, C.S. (1999). Green manures for maize-bean systems in Eastern Uganda: Agronomic performance and farmers' perceptions. *Agroforestry Systems, 47,* 123–138.

Florentin, M., Penalva, M., Calegari, A. and Derpsch, R. (2011). Green manure/cover crops and crop rotation in Conservation Agriculture on small farms. *Integrated Crop Management,* 12. Rome: FAO.

Foresti, M., Ludi, E. and Griffiths, R. (2007). *Human rights and livelihood approaches for poverty reduction.* Poverty-wellbeing.net, 1–10. London: Interco-operation and Development Institute.

Foucault, M. (1988). *Technologies of the self: A seminar with Michel Foucault.* L.H. Martin, H. Gutman and P.H. Hutton (eds), Amherst: University of Massachusetts Press.

Freudenberger, D., Cawsey, M.E., Stol, J. and West, P.W. (2004). *Sustainable firewood supply in the Murray-Darling basin.* Canberra: Australian Department of Environment and Heritage, CSIRO.

Gibson-Graham, J.K. (2006a). *The end of capitalism (as we knew it): A feminist critique of political economy*. Minneapolis: University of Minnesota Press.

Gibson-Graham, J.K. (2006b). *Post-capitalist politics*. Minneapolis: University of Minnesota Press.

Giller, K.E., Witter, E., Corbeels, M. and Titonnell, P. (2009). Conservation agriculture and smallholder farming in Africa: The heretic's view. *Field Crops Research, 114* (1), 23–34.

Goeb, J. (2013). *Conservation farming adoption and impact among first year adopters in central Zambia.* Working Paper 80. Lusaka, Zambia: Indaba Agricultural Policy Research Institute (IAPRI).

Goodman, D. and Redclift, M. (1981). *From peasant to proletarian: Capitalist development and agrarian transitions*. Oxford: Basil Blackwell.

Goodman, D. and Redclift, M. (1991). *Refashioning nature: Food, ecology and culture*. London: Routledge.

Govereh, J., Shawa, J.J., Malawo, E. and Jayne, T.S. (2006). *Raising the productivity of public investments in Zambia's agricultural sector*. Working Paper 20. Food Security Research Project. Retrieved 4 January 2012 from www.aec.msu.edu.agecon/fs2/zambia/index.htm.

Gramsci, A. (1988). *A Gramsci reader: Selected writings 1916–1935.* D. Forgacs (ed.), London: Lawrence and Wishart.

Gumede, A. and Mbatha, A. (2017). The charts that show South Africa's under-employment problem. Bloomberg, 1 June. Retrieved 2 January 2018 from www.bloomberg.com.

Gunther, F. (2002). Fossil energy and food security. *Energy and Environment, 12* (4), 253–275.

Haile, M. (2005). Weather patterns, food security and humanitarian response in sub-Saharan Africa. *Philosophical Transactions of the Royal Society B (Biological Sciences), 360*, 2169.

Hall, S. (1986). The problem of ideology: Marxism without guarantees. *Journal of Communication Inquiry, 10* (2), 28–44.

Hart, G. (1997). Multiple trajectories or rural industrialisation: An agrarian critique of industrial restructuring and the new institutionalism. In D. Goodman and M. Watts (eds), *Globalising food: Agrarian questions and global restructuring* (pp. 56–78). London: Routledge.

Harvey, D. (2005). *A brief history of neo-liberalism*. Oxford: Oxford University Press.

Headley, D.D. and Jayne, T.S. (2014). Adaptation to land constraints: Is Africa different? *Food Policy, 48*, 18–33.

Heuzé, V., Tran, G. and Archimède, H. (2013). *Banana leaves and pseudostems*. Washington: INRA, CIRAD, AFZ and FAO.

Hobbs, P.R. (2007). Conservation agriculture: What is it and why is it important for future sustainable food production? *Journal of Agricultural Science, 145*, 127–137.

Hoffman, T. and Ashwell, A. (2001). *Nature divided, land degradation in South Africa*. South Africa: University of Cape Town Press.

Holt, R. (2005). *Towards sustainable LandCare practices in South Africa: Version two*. Pretoria: LandCare South Africa.

Hoogvelt, A. (2001). *Globalization and the postcolonial world: The new political economy of development*. Basingstoke: Palgrave.

International Food Policy Research Institute. (2016). *Global nutrition report: From promise to impact*. Washington, DC: IFPRI.

References

IRIN. (2010). *Uganda: Kapchorwa district farmers incurring big losses, IRIN humanitarian news and analysis*. Retrieved 3 June 2010 from www.irinnews.org/Report.aspx?ReportId=87974.

ISDA South Africa – Australian Institutional Strengthening for the Department of Agriculture. (2002). *Koringkoppies LandCare water harvesting project: A good LandCare practice model – Draft framework for the guideline on the LandCare good practice assessment*. Pretoria: National Department of Agriculture.

Japan Association for International Collaboration of Agriculture and Forestry. (2008). *The maize in Zambia and Malawi*. Tokyo: JAICAF.

Jayne, T.S., Zulu, B. and Nijhoff, J.J. (2006). Stabilizing food markets in Eastern and Southern Africa. *Food Policy, 31*, 328–341.

Jenkins, J.C. (2005). *The Humanure handbook – A guide to composting human manure, 3rd edition*. Grove City, PA: Joseph Jenkins Inc.

Jenkins, W. (2008). *Ecologies of grace: Environmental ethics and Christian theology*. Oxford: Oxford University Press.

Jones, P. and Du Preez, R. (2008). *Integrated village renewal programme: A comprehensive multi-year development programme for rural villages*. Mthatha: Is'Baya Development Trust and Nelspruit: Agricultural Research Council Institute for Tropical and Subtropical Crops.

Jones, R.B. and Sakala, W.D. (1991). An informal survey of maize agronomic practices in Kasungu and Lilongwe agricultural development divisions, Malawi. *Farming Systems Bulletin Eastern and Southern Africa, 8*.

Kamiri, J., Gathumbi, S., Cadisch, G. and Giller, K. (no date). *Mixed species improved fallows for Western Kenya*. Nairobi: World Agroforestry Centre.

Karnani, A. (2009). Romanticising the poor harms the poor. *Journal of International Development, 21*, 76–86.

Kassam, A., Friedrich, T., Shaxson, F. and Pretty, J. (2009). The spread of Conservation Agriculture: Justification, sustainability and uptake. *International Journal of Agricultural Sustainability, 4*, 292–320.

Kennedy, E. (1994). Effects of sugarcane production in Southwestern Kenya on income and nutrition. In J. von Braun and E.T. Kennedy (eds), *Agricultural commercialization, economic development, and nutrition* (pp. 252–263). International Food Policy Research Institute (IFPRI) and Johns Hopkins University Press.

Kimani, M. (2010). Women claim legal right to access land. *United Nations Africa Renewal*. Retrieved 10 July 2014 from www.un.org/africarenewal.

Kirimi, L., Sitko, N., Jayne, T.S., Karin, F., Muyanga, M., Sheahan, M., Flock, J. and Bor, G. (2011). *A farm gate-to-consumer value chain analysis of Kenya's maize marketing system*. MSU International Development Working Paper 111. Michigan State University, Michigan.

Kirungu, B.A.M., Shiundu, P., Kamwana, S., Kasiti, J., Wamalwa, E., Nderitu, S. and Mukongo, M. (2000). A legume green manure system developed for small-holder maize production in Trans Nzoia district. *Legume Research Project Newsletter, 2*, 3–4.

Konde, A., Dea, D., Jonfa, E., Folla, F., Scoones, I., Kena, K., Berhanu, T. and Tessema, W. (2001). Creating gardens: The dynamics of soil-fertility management in Wolayta, Southern Ethiopia. In I. Scoones (ed.), *Dynamics and diversity: Soil fertility and farming livelihoods in Africa* (pp. 45–77). London: Earthscan.

Koning, N. (2002). Should Africa protect its farmers to revitalise its economy? *Gatekeeper Series, International Institute for Environment and Development, Sustainable Agriculture and Rural Livelihoods Programme, 105*.

Kretzmann, J.P. and McKnight, J.L. (1997). *Building communities from inside out: A path toward finding and mobilizing a community's assets.* Chicago: ACTA Publications.

Kulika. (2009). *Kulika Uganda since 1981: Annual report 2009.* Kampala, Uganda: Kulika.

Kwesiga, F.R., Franzel, F., Place, F., Phiri, D. and Simwanza, C.P. (1999). Sesbania sesban improved fallows in eastern Zambia: Their inception, development and farmer enthusiasm. *Agroforestry Systems, 47*, 49–66.

Kwon, H. and Yi, I. (2009). Economic development and poverty reduction in Korea: Governing multifunctional institutions. *Development and Change, 40* (4), 769–792.

Lahiff, E. (2002). *Land reform in South Africa: An overview, with particular reference to protected areas.* Programme for Land and Agrarian Studies, University of the Western Cape. Retrieved 6 February 2006 from www.sasusq.net.

Lahiff, E. (2003). The politics of land reform in Southern Africa. Sustainable livelihoods in Southern Africa. *Institute of Development Studies, 19.*

Lahiff, E. (2007). 'Willing buyer, willing seller': South Africa's failed experiment in market-led agrarian reform. *Third World Quarterly, 28* (8), 1577–1597.

Lahmar, R., Bationo, B.A., Lamso, N.D., Guéro, Y. and Tittonella, P. (2012). Tailoring conservation agriculture technologies to West Africa semi-arid zones: Building on traditional local practices for soil restoration. *Field Crops Research, 132,* 158–167.

Lammers, P.J., Carlson, S.L., Zdorkowski, G.A. and Honeyman, M.S. (2009). Reducing food insecurity in developing countries through meat production: The potential of the guinea pig (*Cavia porcellus*). *Renewable Agriculture and Food Systems, 24* (2), 155–162.

Lappé, F.M., Collins, J. and Rosset, P., with Esparaza, L. (1998). *World hunger: 12 myths.* New York: Grove Press.

Leach, M. and Scoones, I. (2006). *The slow race: Making technology work for the poor.* London: Demos.

Leahy, G. and Leahy, T. (2013). The Chikukwa project. www.thechikukwaproject.com.

Leahy, T. (2009). *Permaculture strategy for the South African villages.* Brisbane, Australia: PI Productions.

Leahy, T. (2011). The gift economy. In A. Nelson and F. Timmerman (eds), *Life without money* (pp. 111–138). London: Pluto Press.

Leathers, H.D. and Foster, P. (2009). *The world food problem: Toward ending undernutrition in the Third World.* Boulder, Colorado: Lynne Rienner Publishers.

Leavy, J. and Poulton, C. (2007). *Commercializations in agriculture.* Future Agricultures Working Paper 003. Retrieved 18 December 2012 from www.future-agricultures.org.

Lebone, K. (2005). Two faces of South African farming. *Fast Facts, 1* (January).

Lodge, T. (2002). *Politics in South Africa: From Mandela to Mbeki.* Cape Town: David Philip.

Luiz, J. (2009). Institutions and economic performance: Implications for African development. *Journal of International Development, 21,* 58–75.

MAAIF. (2000). *Plan for Modernisation of Agriculture: Eradicating poverty in Uganda.* Kampala, Uganda: Ministry of Agriculture, Animal Industry and Fisheries, Ministry of Finance, Planning and Economic Development.

MAAIF. (2009a). *Implementation in Uganda of the 'Comprehensive Africa Agriculture Development Programme' through the agriculture sector development strategy and investment plan.* Kampala, Uganda: Ministry of Agriculture, Animal Industry and Fisheries.

MAAIF. (2009b). *Uganda: Long-term funding for agricultural growth, poverty reduction, and food and nutrition security.* MAAIFF, 5. Kampala: MAAIF.

Magadzi, D. (2008). Limpopo Department of Agriculture budget speech 2008/09. *South African Government Information*. Retrieved 5 September 2008 from www.info.gov.za/speeches/2008/08052816451002.htm.

Marais, L. and Botes, L. (2007). Income generation, local economic development and community development: Paying the price for lacking business skills? *Community Development Journal, 42* (3), 379–395.

Marenya, P.P. and Barrett, C.B. (2007). Household-level determinants of adoption of improved natural resources management practices among smallholder farmers in western Kenya. *Food Policy, 32*, 515–536.

MASIPAG. (2013). GM corn farmers lose lands, increase debts says new research. Retrieved 12 May 2015 from http://masipag.org/2013/09/gm-corn-farmers-lose-lands-increase-debts-says-new-research/.

Mason, N.M., Jayne, T.S. and Mofya-Mukuka, R. (2013a). *A review of Zambia's agricultural input subsidy programs: Targeting, impacts, and the way forward*. Working Paper 77. Lusaka, Zambia: Indaba Agricultural Policy Research Institute (IAPRI).

Mason, N.M., Jayne, T.S. and Mofya-Mukuka, R. (2013b). Zambia's input subsidy programs. *Agricultural Economics, 44* (6), 613–628.

Matete, N. and BakamaNume, B.B. (2010). Climate of Uganda. In B.B. BakamaNume (ed.), *A contemporary geography of Uganda*. Oxford: African Books Collective.

Mather, C. and Adelzadeh, A. (1998). *Input paper, poverty and inequality report: Macroeconomic strategies, agriculture and rural poverty in post-apartheid South Africa*. Retrieved 5 January 2006 from www.gov.za/otherdocs/1998/poverty/macroecon.pdf.

Maxwell, S. and Fernando, A. (1989). Cash crops in developing countries: The issues, the facts, the policies. *World Development, 17* (11), 1677–1708.

McCall, W. (1980). *Chicken manure*. Retrieved 26 October 2013 from www.ctahr.hawaii.edu/oc/freepubs/pdf/GHGS-02.pdf.

McCann, J. (2001). Maize and grace: History, corn, and Africa's new landscapes, 1500–1999. *Society for Comparative Study of Society and History, 0010-4175* (01), 246–272.

Milligan, S., Price, A., Sommeling, E. and Struyf, G. (2011). Connecting smallholders with dynamic markets: A market information service in Zambia. *Development in Practice, 21* (3), 357–370.

Ministry of Finance. (2008). *Planning and economic development: Annual report 2007/2008*. Retrieved 4 September 2009 from www.finance.go.ug/docs.

Mitchell, B. (2001). *Resource and environmental management*. London: Pearson Education Limited.

Mkize, N. (2008). *Insect pests of cultivated and wild olives, and some of their natural enemies, in the Eastern Cape, South Africa* (Unpublished doctoral dissertation). University of Rhodes, South Africa.

Mloza-Banda, H.R. and Nanthambwe, S.J. (2010). *Conservation Agriculture programmes and projects in Malawi: Impacts and lessons*. National Conservation Agriculture Task Force Secretariat, Lilongwe, Malawi: Land Resources Conservation Department.

Mohamoud, Y. and Canfield, H.E. (1998). Deployment of a rapid assessment and monitoring technique for soil erosion in Malawi. *Malawi Environmental Monitoring Program*. Retrieved 14 July 2013 from http://ag.arizona.edu/OALS/malawi/Reports/Full_Report2.html.

Mojela, C. (2005). *Assessing the effectiveness of Korringkoppies LandCare Project, South Africa* (Unpublished Masters Research Report). University of Newcastle, Australia.

Molefe, R. (2006). Limpopo to 'grab' 71 black farms. *City Press*, 15 January, 5.
Mollison, B. (1988). *Permaculture: A designers' manual.* Tyalgum, Australia: Tagari Publications.
Morgan, P. (2007). *Toilets that make compost.* Retrieved 24 June 2016 from www.ecosanres.org/pdf_files/ToiletsThatMakeCompost.pdf.
Morrow, R. (1993). *Earth user's guide to permaculture.* Sydney: Kangaroo Press.
Mortimore, M. (1998). *Roots in the African dust: Sustaining the sub-Saharan drylands.* Cambridge: Cambridge University Press.
Moyo, S. (2007). The land question in Southern Africa: A comparative review. In N. Lungisile and R. Hall (eds), *The land question in South Africa: The challenge of transformation and redistribution* (pp. 60–86). Cape Town: Human Sciences Research Council.
Mugwe, J., Mugendi, D., Kungu, J. and Muna, M. (2009). Maize yields response to application of organic and inorganic input under on-station and on-farm experiments in central Kenya. *Experimental Agriculture, 45*, 47–59.
Mukadasi, B. and Nabalegwa, M. (2007). Gender mainstreaming and community participation in plant resource conservation in Buzaya county, Kamuli district, Uganda. *African Journal of Ecology, 45* (1), 7–12.
Mupangwa, W., Twomlow, S. and Walker, S. (2012). Reduced tillage, mulching and rotational effects on maize (Zea mays), cowpea (Vigna unguiculata) and sorghum (Sorghum bicolor) yields under semi-arid conditions. *Field Crops Research, 132*, 139–148.
Nakileza, B. (2010). Soils and soil degradation. In B.B. BakamaNume (ed.), *A contemporary geography of Uganda.* Oxford: African Books Collective.
National Department of Agriculture. (2000). *Implementation framework for the LandCare programme.* Pretoria: Agricultural Resource Management, National Department of Agriculture.
National Department of Agriculture. (2005). *Annual report 2004/05.* Pretoria: Department of Agriculture.
Newell, P. (2008). CSR and the limits of capital. *Development and Change, 39*(6), 1063–1078.
Ngoma, H., Mulenga, B.P. and Jayne, T.S. (2014). *What explains minimal usage of minimum tillage practices in Zambia? Evidence from district-representative data.* Working Paper 82. Lusaka, Zambia: Indaba Agricultural Policy Research Institute (IAPRI).
Ngoma, H., Mason, N.M. and Sitko, N. (2015). *Does minimum tillage with planting basins or ripping raise maize yields? Meso-panel data evidence from Zambia.* Working Paper 91. Lusaka, Zambia: Indaba Agricultural Policy Research Institute (IAPRI).
Njarui, D.M.G. and Mureithi, G. (1999). *Legume Research Network project newsletter; Issue number one.* Nairobi: Kenya Agricultural Research Institute.
Njira, K.O.W., Semu, E., Mrema, J.P. and Nalivata, P.C. (2017). Biological nitrogen fixation by pigeon pea and cowpea in the 'doubled-up' and other cropping systems on the Luvisols of Central Malawi. *African Journal of Agricultural Research, 12* (15), 1341–1352.
Ntebeza, L. and Hall, T. (eds) (2007). *The land question in South Africa: The challenge of transformation and redistribution.* Cape Town: Human Sciences Research Council.
O'Laughlin, B. (2007). A bigger piece of a very small pie: Intrahousehold resource allocation and poverty reduction in Africa. *Development and Change, 38* (1), 21–44.
Oakley, P. (1991). *Projects with people: The practice of participation in rural development.* Geneva: International Labour Organization.
Otipal, M.J., Kimenju, J.W., Mutitu, E.W. and Karanja, N.K. (2003). *Legume Research Project Newsletter, 9,* 14–16.

References

Parliamentarians. (2006). The Cape Town proclamation: Parliamentarians' recommendations supporting CAADP goals in championing agricultural successes for Africa's future. Somerset West, South Africa, 18 May.

Pasternak, A. (2005). Stuart Hall and the concept of ideology: A critical assessment. *International Journal of the Humanities, 3* (2), 33–38.

Peeters, L.E.A. and Maxwell, D.G. (2011). Characteristics and strategies favouring sustained food access during Guinea's food-price crisis. *Development in Practice, 21* (4–5), 613–628.

Perrett, S.R. (2001). *Poverty and diversity of livelihood systems in post-apartheid rural South Africa: Insights into local levels in the Eastern Cape province.* Working Paper 2001–12. Pretoria: Department of Agricultural Economics, Extension and Rural Development, University of Pretoria.

Phiria, D., Franzelb, S., Mafongoyac, P., Jered, I., Katangac, R. and Phiric, S. (2004). Who is using the new technology? The associations of wealth, status and gender with the planting of improved tree fallows in Eastern Province, Zambia. *Agricultural Systems, 79,* 131–144.

Ponte, S., Roberts, S. and van Sittert, L. (2007). 'Black economic empowerment': Business and the state in South Africa. *Development and Change, 38* (5), 933–955.

Potts, D. (2000). Worker-peasants and farmer-housewives in Africa: The debate about 'committed' farmers, access to land and agricultural production. *Journal of Southern African Studies, 26* (4), 807–832.

Potts, D. (2011). We have a tiger by the tail: Continuities and discontinuities in Zimbabwean city planning and politics. *Critical African Studies, 4* (6), 15–46.

Pretty, J.N. (1995). Participatory learning for sustainable agriculture. *World Development, 23* (8), 1247–1263.

Pretty, J.N. (1999). *Regenerating agriculture: Policies and practice for sustainability and self-reliance.* London: Earthscan.

Putnam, R.D. (2000). *Bowling alone.* New York: Touchstone.

Reilly, G. (2006). Crime will go nowhere until more jobs created. *The Star.* 30 March, 15.

Rockström, J. (2000). Water resources management in smallholder farms in Eastern and Southern Africa: An overview. *Physical Chemistry of the Earth, 25* (3), 275–283.

Rural Poverty Portal. (2012). Land: Statistics. Retrieved 31 May 2012 from www.ruralpovertyportal.org/web/guest/topic/statistics/tags/land.

Rusinamhodzi, L., Corbeels, M., van Wijk, M.T., Rufino, M.C., Nyamangara, J. and Giller, K.E. (2011). A meta-analysis of long-term effects of conservation agriculture on maize grain yield under rain-fed conditions. *Agronomy and Sustainable Development, 31,* 657–673.

Scoones, I. (2001). Transforming soils: The dynamics of soil-fertility management in Africa. In I. Scoones (ed.), *Dynamics and diversity: Soil fertility and farming livelihoods in Africa* (pp. 1–44). London: Earthscan.

Scoones, I., Devereux, S. and Haddad, L. (2005). Introduction: New directions for African agriculture. *IDS Bulletin, 36* (2). Institute of Development Studies.

Sender, J. and Johnston, D. (2004). Searching for a weapon of mass production in rural Africa: Unconvincing arguments for land reform. *Journal of Agrarian Change, 4* (1/2), 142–164.

Serraj, R. and Siddique, K.H.M. (2012). Conservation agriculture in dry areas. *Field Crops Research, 132,* 1–6.

Shackleton, C.M. (1993). Fuelwood harvesting and sustainable utilisation in a communal grazing land and protected area of the eastern Transvaal lowveld. *Biological Conservation, 63,* 247–254.

Shackleton, C.M., Shackleton, S.E. and Cousins, B. (2001). The role of land-based strategies in rural livelihoods: The contribution of arable production, animal husbandry and natural resource harvesting in communal areas in South Africa. *Development Southern Africa, 18* (5), 581–604.

Shively, G.E. and Hao, J. (2012). *A review of agriculture, food security and human nutrition issues in Uganda*. Retrieved 20 October 2013 from http://purl.umn.edu/135134.

Sibanda, S. (2001). Land reform and poverty alleviation in South Africa. *SARPN Conference on Land Reform and Poverty Alleviation in Southern Africa*. Pretoria: Human Sciences Research Council.

Sitko, N.J. (2008). Maize, food insecurity, and the field of performance in southern Zambia. *Agriculture and Human Values, 25* (1), 3–11.

Sitko, N.J. (2013). My hunger has brought business: Efficiency and the de-moralizing logic of maize distribution in an era of market liberalization. *The Journal of Peasant Studies, 40* (2), 379–396.

Sosola, B., Sileshi, G., Festus, A. and Ajayi, O. (2011). *Conservation Agriculture practices in Malawi: Opportunities and challenges*. Retrieved 14 July 2013 from www.evergreen agriculture.net/content/conservation-agriculture-practices-malawi-opportunities-and challenges.

Takaidza, T., Mhizha, S., Maposa, I. and Sobhutana, B. (2011). *Baseline survey report Chimanimani district*. Chimanimani, Zimbabwe: The TSURO Trust.

Tarawali, G., Manyong, V.M., Carsky, R.J., Vissoh, P.V., Osei-Bonsu, P. and Galiba, M. (1999). Adoption of improved fallows in West Africa: Lessons from mucuna and stylo case studies. *Agroforestry Systems, 47*, 93–122.

Terreblanche, S. (2002). *A history of inequality in South Africa 1652–2002*. Pietermaritzburg: University of Natal Press.

Timmer, P.C. (2005). *Agriculture and pro-poor growth: An Asian perspective*. Working Paper 63, July.

Toulmin, C. and Scoones, I. (2001). Ways forward? Technical choices, intervention strategies and policy options. In I. Scoones (ed.), *Dynamics and diversity: Soil fertility and farming livelihoods in Africa* (pp. 175–208). London: Earthscan.

Tschirley, D., Zulu, B. and Shaffer, J. (2004). Cotton in Zambia: An assessment of its organization, performance, current policy initiatives and challenges for the future. *Food Security Research Project Working Paper 10*. Retrieved 4 January 2012 from www.aec.msu.edu.agecon/fs2/zambia/index.htm.

Tschirley, D.L. and Kabwe, S. (2007). Cotton in Zambia: 2007 assessment of its organization, performance, current policy initiatives, and challenges for the future. *Food Security Research Project Working Paper 26*. Lusaka, Zambia. Retrieved 19 December 2012 from www.aec.msu.edu/agecon/fs2/zambia/index.htm.

TSURO. (2011). *TSURO Trust survey report*. Unpublished paper compiled by M. Samoko and T. Samushonga. Chimanimani, Zimbabwe: TSURO.

UNICEF. (2017). *Levels and trends in child nutrition*. Washington, DC: UNICEF, WHO, World Bank.

Vail, L. (1977). Ecology and history: The example of Zambia. *Journal of Southern African Studies, 3* (2), 129–155.

Valbuena, D., Erenstein, O., Tui, S.H., Abdoulayed, T., Claessens, L., Duncan, A.J., Gérarda, B., Rufinoh, M.C., Teufeli, N., Van Rooyen, A. and Van Wijk, M. (2012). Conservation Agriculture in mixed crop–livestock systems: Scoping crop residue trade-offs in Sub-Saharan Africa and South Asia. *Field Crops Research, 132*, 175–184.

Von Braun, J., Hotchkiss, D. and Immink, M. (1989). *Nontraditional export crops in Guatemala*. Research Report 73, Washington, DC: International Food Policy Research Institute.

Walker, C. (2007). Redistributive land reform: For what and for whom? In L. Ntebeza and R. Hall (eds), *The land question in South Africa: The challenge of transformation and redistribution* (pp. 132–151). Cape Town: Human Sciences Research Council.

Watkinson, E. and Makgetla, N. (2002). *South Africa's food security crisis*. Pretoria: National Labour and Economic Development Institute.

Watts, M. (1983). *Silent violence: Food, famine and peasantry in Northern Nigeria*. Berkeley: University of California Press.

Watts, M. and Goodman, D. (1997). Agrarian questions: Global appetite, local metabolism: Nature, culture and industry in fin de siècle agro-food systems. In D. Goodman and M. Watts (eds), *Globalising food: Agrarian questions and global restructuring* (pp. 1–34). London: Routledge.

Webersik, C. and Wilson, C. (2008). Achieving environmental sustainability and growth in Africa: The role of science, technology and innovation. *Sustainable Development, 17*, 400–413.

Westermann, E. (2008). *The three circles of knowledge: How to build constructive community relations by understanding conflicts in rural African communities*. Chimanimani, Zimbabwe: CELUCT, Tien Wah Press.

Williams, G. (1996). Setting the agenda: A critique of the World Bank's restructuring programme for South Africa. *Journal of Southern African Studies, 22* (1): 139–167.

Wilson, K.B. (1989). Trees in fields in Southern Zimbabwe. *Journal of Southern African Studies, 15*(2), 369–383.

Wolter, D. (2008). Tanzania: The challenge of moving from subsistence to profit. OECD Development Centre. Retrieved 18 December 2012 from www.oecd.org.

World Agroforestry Centre. (2010). *Creating an Evergreen Agriculture in Africa*. Nairobi: World Agroforestry Centre.

World Bank. (2013). *Uganda*. Retrieved 23 October 2013 from http://data.worldbank.org/country/uganda.

Wright, E.O. (2010). *Envisioning real utopias*. New York: Verso.

Wright, S. (2008). Practising hope: Learning from social movement strategies in the Philippines. In R. Pain and S.J. Smith (eds), *'Fear': Critical geopolitics and everyday life* (pp. 223–233). Farnham: Ashgate Publishing Ltd.

Index

Page numbers in **bold** denote figures, those in *italics* denote tables.

accumulation by dispossession 113
Africa, mainstream economics' view 5–6
Africa: Diversity and Development (Binns et al) 44
African Union 130
agricultural economy, effects of growth 47
agricultural officers, experiences of entrepreneurialism 112–17
agriculture, economic forms 209
Alinyo, F. 129
alley cropping 24
ANC 120
animal fats 78–9
anthropological perspective 209
aquaculture 151–2
arborloo system 206–7, **207**
Asia: economic growth 9; mainstream economics' view 6–7

Bachmann, L. 1
Baudrillard, J. 57
Binns, T. 37, 43, 44
Black Economic Empowerment (BEE) 116, 119
Bond, P. 120
book: aim 20; key ideas 45–53; overview 1; recommendations 213; summary and conclusions 211–12
bottom up projects 44
Bryceson, D. 120, 132, 209–11
Buckles, D. 22
Building Constructive Community Relationships 172–3
Bukwo district *see* Uganda study
bunds 31
bureaucratic democracy, successful projects 194–5

burning crop residues 162
business projects 99–100

capitalism 209–10
carbohydrate 77–8
cash cropping: as cause of food insecurity 18; cotton 50–1; Kenya study 13–15; problems of 40–2; vs. staple cropping 15–16
cash economy participation: Zambia 69; *see also* food provisioning
cash income, and food security 40
cash shortage, Zambia 60–3
cassava 64
catchment approach 141
cattle: effect of conservation agriculture 29–30; Zambia 68
cattle projects, Malawi 89–91
CELUCT project 102–3, 161; Building Constructive Community Relationships 172–3; Permaculture Club Committee 170–1; values 172; *see also* Chikukwa project
Chambers, R. 33
charitable giving, possible benefits 13
Charles, experiences of entrepreneurialism 119
Chibharo, J. 157, 166, 167, 173, 176
chicken project, leading and emerging farmer projects 95
chickens: Uganda 148; Zambia 67
Chikukwa Ecological Land Use Community Trust *see* CELUCT project
Chikukwa project: bureaucratic democracy 170–1; clubs 168; community water tanks 162; conflict transformation 171–3; conflict workshop 163–4; context and

overview 157–8; counter-cultural technologies 171–3; crops 162–3; decision making 168–9; development and success of 159–60; embeddedness 164–5, 182; focus on food security 166–7; food sufficiency by ward *159*; funding 161, 175–6; gifts 175–7; history 160–1; human capital 165; hybridity 176; joint projects 170; location 157; new landscape 162–3; ownership 157; participatory initiation 168–70; permaculture design 167–8; success factors 164–77, 182; summary and conclusions 177–8; training provision 169; understanding of permaculture 163; working methods 162; working with indigenous world-view 173–5; *see also* CELUCT project
Chikukwa, Z. 173–4
children, effects of malnutrition 3, *3*
Chiloshana, P. 165, 166
Chimbarawa, S. 179
China 9, 17
Chipeta, S. 46–7
Chitekete village 160
Chituwu, C. 160, 165, 169
circular migration 45
citizenship, requisites for 46
class analysis: implications for project design 127–8; importance of 126–7; summary and conclusions 128
colonial legacy: fruit growing 67; gardens 72; land ownership 45–6; political economy 210; Zambia 65
commercial agriculture, diverse livelihoods 44
commercial farming: argument for 49; and productivity 39–40
commercialization 36; arguments for 46; benefits of 47; success factors 131
communal title 16
communities, entrepreneurial projects 106
community economies 121
community group entrepreneurial projects: corruption 84; distrust 84–5; dominance 82, 92–3; financial skills 85–6; focus group discussions 91; Komonani projects 86–7; Lilydale 86–8; Lilydale community vegetable garden 87–8; limited opportunities for income 83–4; Malawi 88–91; Mmatau project 83–4, 85; overview 81–2; problems 83–6; social connections 84; theft 84–5; vandalism 85; Voordonker project 85–6; what goes wrong 82–3

community group projects, Uganda 133–5
community water tanks 162
competition, between developing countries 9
composting 22; permaculture design 149
composting toilets 203–6; *see also* toilets
Comprehensive African Agricultural Development Programme (CAADP) 46
Comprehensive African Agriculture Development Programme 130
conflict, entrepreneurialism 109
conflict transformation 171–3
conflict workshop, Chikukwa project 163–4
conglomerates, South Africa 120
conservation agriculture 27–31, 190; cover crop seeds 29; effect on cattle 29–30; extra work 28–9; herbicides and weeding 28–9; mulch shortage 30; pests 30; problems 28–31; use of lime 30; Zambia 71
cooperatives 110
copper, Zambia 63
cotton, as cash crop 50–1
counter-cultural technologies, Chikukwa project 171–3
cover crop seeds 29
crop rotation, legumes 23–4
crop yields 150
cropping, land need 54
crops: Chikukwa project 162–3; choice of 71; diversity 144; gendered segregation of 142–3; most advantageous 6
cultivation methods, Zambia 65
cultural capital 124
culture, working with 173–5
customary title 16
cycles of debt 2

David, experiences of entrepreneurialism 112–13
De Janvry, A. 73
debt: cycles of 2; effect of subsidies and price controls 12; and land title 16–17; and loss of land 19; smallholders 1
deforestation 4
demonstration projects 81
dependence, encouraging 136
development, implications/expectations 34
development through enterprise 105
Devereux, S. 142
diabetes, dietary guidelines 179–81
Diana, experiences of entrepreneurialism 114–15
diarrhoea 201–2

Diaz, G. 1
diet 48; and health 179–81
diverse livelihoods 35, 41; commercial agriculture 44
diversification 120–1
Du Preez, R. 187, 190–1, 196

economic contexts, of malnutrition 17–18
economic dependence, breaking 2
economic development, potential of subsistence agriculture 122
economic expansion, source of 4
economic growth, as solution 9–10
economic makeover 120
education: coordinating with food production 39; impact of food insecurity 133; involving schools 104; middle class aspirations 118; rural poor 124; TSURO project 193; Zambia 69
efficiency 52
egg project, Malawi 88–9
Egypt, food subsidies 11–12
embeddedness 164–5, 182
emerging farmer projects 95–7
emerging farmers 125–6; John 125–6; Mary 126
employment: availability 41; as supplement to farming 60–3
empowerment 2
entrepreneurialism: agricultural officers' experiences 112–17; as barrier to success 112; as common sense 111–12; communities 106; context and overview 105–6; defining success 112; as distorted view 111; entrepreneurial state 108; failure/success 121–2; ideological change 122; ideological constraint 108; as ideology 106–7; infrastructure 109; internal conflict 109; Koringkoppies project 109; and middle class 117–18; middle class experiences 118–19; policy alternatives 120–2; political pressure 110; project design 110; reasons for failure 111; research background 107–8; research location 107; success measurement 109
Ethiopia studies 40–1
exports, limitations on 9–10
external resources, dependence on 136

Fairhead, J. 201
fallowing, improved fallows 23–4
Fambidzanai Training Centre, Harare 160
FAO 4–5, 147
FARA 46, 130

farm gate price, vs. retail price 49–50
Farmer Support Programmes 110
farmers, market oriented vs. subsistence 6
farming scale 51–2
fatal strategy 57–8, 73, 212–13
fats 77; animal fats 78–9
Feeding the farmers first 73, 184–8; origins and overview 1–2
Ferguson, J. 68
fertilizers: ability to buy 60–3; alternative fertilizers 39; subsidies on 16; use 4
food crop/cash crop dichotomy 18
food forests 104
food imports, significance of 18–19
food insecurity: and gender dynamics 137–8; harvest cycle 138–9; and land tenure 139–40; roots of 137–40; seasonal 75–9; social context 57; *see also* Zambia case study; Uganda 133
food prices 5; effects of technology 131; lowering 11–12; retail price vs. farm gate price 49; undercutting 19
food production: conflicting needs 19; local consumption 19; per capita 5–6
food provisioning 63–9; alternative form 70–2; and gender 69–70; maize 64–5; summary 68
food redistribution 12–16
food security: approaches to 132; and cash income 40; crop diversity 144; dealing with gender issues 140; definitions 4–5; explanation of problem 5–8; and land tenure 140–1; leftist approaches 17–20; mainstream economics' view 5ff; and participation 141; political economy 209–13; rural poverty and health 130; strategies 140–4; and subsistence farming 36; three intervention strategies 209–12
food security outreach model: characteristics 199; successful projects 197–200
food spending, ways to reduce 13
food subsidies 11–12
food supply increase 16–17
Foster, P. 5ff
Framework for African Agricultural Productivity (FAAP) 46
Frank, G. 210
freehold title 16
fruit, Zambia 66–7
fruit trees 51; land need 55
funding, priorities 47

Gardenia scenario 19–20

gender, and food provisioning 69–70
gender divisions: and expectations 34; and strategy targeting 121; working for food or money 103
gender dynamics: dealing with issues of 140; and food insecurity 137–8
gendered segregation, of crops 142–3
Gibson-Graham, J.K. 121, 132, 177
gifts, Chikukwa project 175–7
Giller, K.E. 28–31
Global Nutrition Report 2016 3
globalization, success of 9
goats: Malawi 99–100; Zambia 74
Goodman, D. 209
government subsidies, lowering food prices 11–12
grain availability, effect of meat consumption 12–13
Gramsci, A. 107, 111
growth and storage 38
Growth, Employment and Redistribution (GEAR) 120
Guatemala, maize study 15
Guinea 73

Hall, S. 107, 111
Hall, T. 52
Hart, G. 209
harvest cycle 138–9
health: impact of food insecurity 133; rural poor 124; rural poverty and food security 130
heart disease, dietary guidelines 179–81
herbicides, and weeding 28–9
HIV/AIDS: talking circles 161, 172; Uganda 133
Holmgren, D. 158
Holt, R. 82, 108
honey project 44
household food security, means of 2
households, mix of strategies 35
housing, Zambia 69
human capital, Chikukwa project 165
human manure 202
hunger, overview 3–4
hybrid seeds 60–1, 62–3

ideology: changing 122; as constraint 108; perspectives on 106–7
improved fallows 23–4
inclusive family projects 98–101; business projects 99–100; Lilydale 99; Malawi 99–100; Selwane fencing project 99; South Africa 98

inclusivity, successful projects 192–3
income, and type of farming 6–7
income diversion 70
income redistribution 10; international 13
incomes, raising 9–11
India, mainstream economics' view 7
intercropping 17, 22, 24–5, 38–9
International Monetary Fund (IMF) 12; development policy 36
international permaculture convergence (IPC) 157
international trade 9–10
interventions, lack of effect 4
Iowa farmers 51–2
Is'Baya project 183; abandonment of group project mode 190–1; bureaucratic democracy 194; conservation agriculture 190; inclusivity 193; long-term commitment 196; Nomsa 188; nutrition as focus 187–8; strategy 187; targeting households 190–1
ISDA 109

Jenkins, J.C. 203
Joan, experiences of entrepreneurialism 119
John: emerging farmers 125–6; experiences of entrepreneurialism 118–19

Kabwe, S. 50–1
Kapchorwa district *see* Uganda study
Kaproron 136
Karnani, A. 105
Kenya: subsistence farming 13–15; value chains 49–50
key ideas 45–53
Khayakhulu 95–6
Kirimi, L. 49–50
Kirungu, B.A.M. 25, 29
Komonani projects 86–7
Komspruit collective 95
Konde, A. 43
Koringkoppies project 109
Kulika project 183; Albert 192; Elijah 193; focus of 186; inclusivity 192; long-term commitment 196; low input agriculture 190; material inputs 193; targeting households 191
Kyamuwendo, E. 186, 190

labour requirements 37, 38–9
land insufficiency 36–7, 38
land leasing, leading and emerging farmer projects 95–6

land loss, risk of 19
land need 54–6
land ownership 45–6; and usage 146–7; and women 137–8
land redistribution 121; South Africa 96–7
land reform 10–11; leftist approaches 20; Philippines 1
land shortage, Zambia 59–60
land tenure 139–41
land title, and debt 16–17
Landcare programme 81ff 108
landholdings, size of 6
Leach, M. 201
leading and emerging farmer projects: chicken project 95; dilemma 94; emerging farmer projects 95–7; impact 98; Khayakhulu 95–6; Komspruit collective 95; land leasing 95–6; land redistribution 96–7; overview 93–4; spill over effects 141; Uganda 135–6; *see also* Uganda study
leading farmers 70–1; use of term 94
leafy mulches 22
Leathers, H.D. 5ff
leftist approaches, to food security 17–20
Legume Research Network 25
legumes: alley cropping 24; crop rotation 23–4; intercropping 24–5; legume parkland 24; as mulch/ dug in 23; nitrogen fixing 23
Lilydale: community group entrepreneurial projects 86–8; inclusive family projects 99
lime, use of 30
limited "state capacity 120
livelihoods: diverse 35; mix of strategies 35
livestock: herding 162; land need 54–5; Zambia 67–8, 74
loans, for fertilizer 43
location, effects of 7
long-term commitment, successful projects 195–6
low input agriculture: Kulika project 190; successful projects 188–90
low input technologies 21–32; combining 27–31; conservation agriculture 27–31; context and overview 21–2; controversy 21–2; herbicides and weeding 28–9; intercropping 38–9; legumes and mulching 22–6; low till cultivation 26–7; mulching 38–9; summary and conclusions 32; water harvesting 31
low till cultivation 26–7

mainstream economics: explanation of problem 5–8; failing the poor 17; policy suggestions 9–17; recommendations of 17; view of food security 5ff; welfare state measures 10–11
maize 64–5
Makerenje, J. 172
Makgetla, N. 47
Malawi: community group entrepreneurial projects 88–91; inclusive family projects 99–100
Malawi school toilet system 205–6, **205, 206**
malnutrition 197–8; definitions 4–5; economic contexts of 17–18; increase in 4; overview 3–4; South Africa 48; Uganda 146; Zambia 58–9
managed business projects 80–1
manure: human 202; use of 22
Marianne, experiences of entrepreneurialism 113–14
market fluctuations 35; effects of 35
market oriented, vs. subsistence farming 6
markets, reliability 130–1
Marxist perspective 106–7, 111, 209
Mary, emerging farmers 126
masculinity 70
MASIPAG 1–2; strategy 2
Matsekete, E. 170–1
Matsekete, G. 163
Maxwell, S. 73
Mbale/ Moroto region 146, 147
McCann, J. 64
meat consumption, effect on grain availability 12–13
micro-loans 43
middle class, entrepreneurialism 117–19
mineral resources, economic expansion 4
minimum wages 10
mixed livelihoods strategy *see* multiple livelihoods strategy
Mmatau project 83–4, 85
modernization 34; Zambia 69
Mollison, B. 158
morality 57; Zambia 65
Morgan, P. 207
Mortimore, M. 38, 40
motivation, individualistic 191
Mtisi, J. 168
Mufakose, J. 192
Mukadasi, B. 142
Mukaronda, P. 173–4
Mulambo, A. 160
mulching 23, 25–6, 38–9

multiple livelihoods strategy 120–1, 124–6, 128
Muruthei, G. 25

Nabalegwa, M. 142
National Advisory Agricultural Services 135
native reserves 45
needs, conflicting 19
neoliberalism 12, 105; errors of 43; promotion of 46
New Partnership for Africa's Development (NEPAD) 46
Newell, P. 120
Nigeria 7
nitrogen fixing 23
Njarui, D.M.G. 25
Noqhekwana village study 48
Ntebeza, L. 52
Nuchidza Dzakasimba (Strong Bees) 160–1, 168
nutrient mining 22
nutrition: animal fats 78–9; carbohydrate 77–8; fats 77; protein 78–9; vitamin A 75–6; vitamin C 75, 77
nutrition gardens 71–2

oils and fats 72
orchard, land need 55
organic farming 2
OXFAM 57

participation 33–4; and food security 141
participatory initiation, Chikukwa project 168–70
Participatory Rural Appraisal (PRA) 33
peasants 209
Peeters, L.E.A. 73
per capita food production 5–6
permaculture 104; defining 158; TSURO project 188–9
permaculture design 146–56; aquaculture 151–2; around house 147–9; background scenario 146; Chikukwa project 167–8; composting 149; cropping area 150–2; location 146; manure fertilizer requirements 151; maps and diagrams 152–6; orchard and kitchen garden 149–50; organization of holding 147–52; pond 151; residential area diagram **154**; residential area map **153**; soil fertility 151; summary and conclusions 152; understanding 163; whole farm diagram **156**; whole farm map **155**; woodlot and wilderness 152; working with indigenous world-view 173–5
persistence of subsistence farming 47–9
pest control 189
pests, conservation agriculture 30
philanthropy, Zambia 73
Philippines, land reform 1
pit toilets 202–3
Piti, J. 174–5
Plan for Modernisation of Agriculture 129–31, 137, 140
policy suggestions: food redistribution 12–16; food supply increase 16–17; lowering food prices 11–12; mainstream economics 9–17; raising incomes 9–11; *see also* entrepreneurialism
political economy: capitalism 209–10; commodity production 210; economic forms of agriculture 209; food security 209–13; raising wages 210; recommendations 213; subsistence economy 211; three intervention strategies 209–12; village perspectives and solutions 212–13
political will, South Africa 120
population density, Zambia 60
Potts, D. 42, 166, 209
poverty: impact on food security and health 130; as result of subsistence farming 36; South Africa 105–6; Uganda 146
poverty rates, defining 6
poverty reduction: export-led approach 9–10; minimum wages 10; problems of cash crop solution 40–2; welfare state measures 10–11
Pretty, J.N. 141
price controls 43–4
price setting 10
productivity, and commercial farming 39–40
project design: entrepreneurialism 110; implications of class 127–8
project failure: community group entrepreneurial projects *see* separate heading; context and overview 80–1; demonstration projects 81; inclusive family projects 98–101; leading and emerging farmer projects 94–7; managed business projects 80–1; summary and conclusions 101; top-down service delivery 80–1
prostitution 133
protein 78–9; Zambia 67–8, 72, 74

reduced tillage 26–7
reforestation 162
Regional Overview of Food Security 2015 3–4
religion, working with 173–5
retail price, vs. farm gate price 49
Revitalisation of Small Irrigation Schemes (RESIS) 115–16
rights-based approach 132
rights to cereal harvest 143
Rural Development: Putting the Last First (Chambers) 33, 43
rural poor 124–5
rural tenure arrangements 45–6

Sadoulet, E. 73
scale of farming 51–2
schools, involving 104
Scoones, I. 39, 42, 43, 44
seasonal food insecurity 75–9
Selwane fencing project 99
sex trade 133
Shackleton, C.M. 55, 132
Shumba, M. 168–9
single crops, risks of 35
Sithole, P. 160, 163, 165, 172, 175
smallholders, debt 1
soap operas 117–18
social capital 92–3, 110
social class: emerging farmers 125–6; how it works 124; implications for project design 127–8; importance of analysis 126–7; rural poor 124–5; summary and conclusions 128
social context: of food insecurity 57; *see also* Zambia case study
social mobility 117
social security, South Africa 120
social technologies 171–3
soil fertility: fall in 60; means of 39; permaculture design 151
soil quality 4
source farmers 189, 195
South Africa 10; aims of development work 105; conglomerates 120; economic makeover 120; fruit trees project 51; inclusive family projects 98; land redistribution 96–7; Landcare programme 81ff; persistence of subsistence farming 47–9; political will 120; poverty 105–6; social mobility 117; social security 120; welfare 47, 48; *see also* entrepreneurialism; Is'Baya project

South Asia 9
South Korea 9
Southern Theory 158
spill over effects 141
staple cropping, vs. cash cropping 15–16
state intervention 43–4
state owned food production 13
Stephen, experiences of entrepreneurialism 115–16
storage 38, 39
strategies, targeting 121
Strong Bees 160–1, 168, 169
strong welfare state strategy 20
subsidies 43–4; on fertilizers 16; lowering food prices 11–12; Zambia 62–3
subsistence farming: as best practice 121–2; vs. commercial 35–6; constraints 36–9; constraints not real 38–9; as destined to fail 7–8; economic argument 49; economic necessity 45–6; Kenya study 13–15; vs. market oriented 6; mindset change 104; persistence of 47–9; as rational choice 7; use of term 2
success through hard work mythology 118
successful projects: bureaucratic democracy 194–5; context and overview 182–3; Feeding the farmers first 184–8; food security as priority 184; food security outreach model 182–3, 197–200; inclusivity 192–3; long-term commitment 195–6; low input agriculture 188–90; material inputs 193–4; methods of assistance 190–6; no payments for improving own land 191–2; nutrition 198–9; pest control 189; source farmers 195; substance vs. methods of assistance 184; summary and conclusions 197–200; targeting households 190–1; *see also* Is'Baya project; Kulika project; TSURO project
sustainability 2
sustainable livelihoods framework 132
synthetic fertilizers, use of 22

talking circles 161, 172
tariffs 20
taxation, to reduce food spending 13
technologies: counter-cultural 171–3; of the self 171; social 171–3
television 117–18
terminology: emerging farmers 125–6; problem of 124; rural poor 124–5
Terreblanche, S. 118

The World food Problem: Toward Ending Malnutrition in the Third World (Leathers and Foster) 5ff
Tiger economies 16, 17
tillage, reduced 26–7
Timmer, P.C. 9
tippy taps 207–8, **208**
toilets 149, 201–8; arborloo system 206–7, **207**; embarrassment 202; implications 202; Jenkins 'Humanure' system 203–5, **204**; Malawi school system 205–6, **205**, **206**; pit toilets 202–3; problem 201–2; risk of contamination 203; tippy taps 207–8, **208**
top-down service delivery 80–1
Toulmin, C. 39
transport, and participation in international trade 10
Triomphe, B. 22
Tschirley D.L. 50–1
TSURO project 183; bureaucratic democracy 194–5; educational input 193; evaluation 197; farmer action learning groups 189; Gladys 184–6, 195; inclusivity 192; learning groups 194–5; long-term commitment 196; Mareni 189, 193; Mrs Mandega 195; no payments for improving own land 191–2; permaculture 188–9; skill development 184–5; source farmers 189; stakeholders 189; targeting households 191; Wilson 189, 194–5
TSURO Trust 159

Uganda: Development Strategy and Investment Plan 129; economy 129; HIV/AIDS 133; permaculture design 146–56; Plan for Modernisation of Agriculture 129–31, 137, 140; *see also* Kulika project
Uganda study 129; approach to food security 132; community group projects 133–5; context and overview 129–30; crop diversity 144; current projects 133–6; dealing with gender issues 140; encouraging dependence 136; food insecurity 133; food security strategies 140–4; gender dynamics 137–8; gendered segregation of crops 142–3; harvest cycle 138–9; land tenure 139–41; lead farmer projects 135–6; locations 129, 131–2; methods 132; participation 141; roots of food insecurity 137–40; summary and conclusions 144; women's rights to cereal harvest 143
Ugandan Plan for Modernisation of Agriculture 46
UK academic paradigm: alternative fertilizers 39; author's view of 45; commercial farming and productivity 39–40; constraints not real 38–9; constraints of subsistence 36–9; context and overview 33; diverse livelihoods 35, 41; growth and storage 38, 39; labour requirements 37, 38–9; lack of answers 42; land insufficiency 36–7, 38; as leftist critique 43–5; low input technologies 38–9; participation 33–4; problems of cash crop solution 40–2; subsistence vs. commercial farming 35–6; sufficient yield, requirements 37–8
unemployment 41, 105; South Africa 48, 53
USA Department of Agriculture studies 26

value chains 49–50
vegetables: land need 54; Zambia 66
vignettes: diet and health 179–81; land need 54–6; low input technologies 21–32; permaculture design 146–56; seasonal food insecurity 75–9; social class 124–8; toilets 201–8; working for food or money 102–4
vitamin A 72, 75–6
vitamin C 75, 77
Voordonker project 85–6

wages 46
Walker, C. 120
Washington consensus 9; UK paradigm as critique of 43
water harvesting 31, 167
Watkinson, E. 47
Webersik, C. 46
weeding, and herbicides 28–9
welfare state measures: land reform 10–11; poverty reduction 10–11; South Africa 47, 48
Westermann, E. 160, 161, 165, 169, 172
Westermann, U. 160, 161, 165
Williams, G. 110
Wilson, C. 46
Wilson, J. 158, 160
women: land ownership 137–8; malnutrition 3; rights to cereal harvest 143; role in food production 18, 28–9, 137; *see also* gender headings

women's clubs 72
women's crops, promotion of 142–3
woodlot: land need 55–6; permaculture design 152
working for food or money: CELUCT project 102–3; gender divisions 103; mindset change 103–4; motivation 103; overview 102; realistic ideas 103
World Agroforestry 23, 30–1
World Bank 12; development policy 36
World Hunger 12 Myths (Lappé et al) 17–20
world view, working with 173–5
Wright, S. 2

yields 4; family farms vs. businesses 7; improving 8

Zambia 12; copper 63; cotton study 50–1
Zambia case study: cash and fertilizer shortage 60–3; cash economy participation 69; cattle 68; chickens 67; choice of crops 71; colonial legacy 65; conservation agriculture 71; context and overview 57; cultivation methods 65; education 69; employment for supplementary income 60–3; fatal strategy 73; food insecurity in villages 58–9; food provisioning 63–9; food provisioning, alternative 70–2; gender and food provisioning 69–70; goats 74; housing 69; income diversion 70; increasing production 73; land shortage 59–60; leading farmers 70–1; livestock 67–8, 74; location 58; maize 64–5; mindset change 73; modernization 69; morality 65; nutrition gardens 71–2; oils and fats 72; outsider perspectives 73; philanthropy 73; population density 60; protein 67–8, 72, 74; subsidies 62–3; vegetables and fruit 66–7; women's clubs 72
zero tillage 71
Zimbabwe: CELUCT project 102–3; economic collapse 166; *see also* Chikukwa project; TSURO project